Interruptions in Early Modern English Drama

ARDEN STUDIES IN EARLY MODERN DRAMA

Series editors:
Lisa Hopkins, Sheffield Hallam University, UK
Douglas Bruster, University of Texas at Austin, USA

Published titles

Early Modern Theatre and the Figure of Disability
by Genevieve Love
ISBN: 978-1-350-01720-7

Imagining Cleopatra
by Yasmin Arshad
ISBN: 978-1-350-05896-5

Staging Britain's Past
by Kim Gilchrist
ISBN: 978-1-3501-6334-8

Forthcoming titles:

Materializing the East in Early Modern English Drama
Edited by Aisha Hussain and Murat Öğütcü
ISBN: 978-1-3503-0045-3

Money and Magic in Early Modern Drama
Edited by David Hawkes
ISBN: 978-1-3502-4704-8

Interruptions in Early Modern English Drama

Michael M. Wagoner

THE ARDEN SHAKESPEARE
LONDON • NEW YORK • OXFORD • NEW DELHI • SYDNEY

THE ARDEN SHAKESPEARE
Bloomsbury Publishing Plc
50 Bedford Square, London, WC1B 3DP, UK
1385 Broadway, New York, NY 10018, USA
29 Earlsfort Terrace, Dublin 2, Ireland

BLOOMSBURY, THE ARDEN SHAKESPEARE and the Arden Shakespeare logo are trademarks of Bloomsbury Publishing Plc

First published in Great Britain 2023
This paperback edition published 2024

Copyright © Michael M. Wagoner, 2023

Michael M. Wagoner has asserted his right under the Copyright, Designs and Patents Act, 1988, to be identified as the author of this work.

For legal purposes the Acknowledgements on p. ix constitute an extension of this copyright page.

Cover image © Photo by Birmingham Museums Trust, licensed under CC0

All rights reserved. No part of this publication may be reproduced or transmitted in any form or by any means, electronic or mechanical, including photocopying, recording, or any information storage or retrieval system, without prior permission in writing from the publishers.

Bloomsbury Publishing Plc does not have any control over, or responsibility for, any third-party websites referred to or in this book. All internet addresses given in this book were correct at the time of going to press. The author and publisher regret any inconvenience caused if addresses have changed or sites have ceased to exist, but can accept no responsibility for any such changes.

A catalogue record for this book is available from the British Library.

A catalogue record for this book is available from the Library of Congress.

ISBN: HB: 978-1-3502-3831-2
PB: 978-1-3502-3834-3
ePDF: 978-1-3502-3833-6
eBook: 978-1-3502-3832-9

Series: Arden Studies in Early Modern Drama

Typeset by Deanta Global Publishing Services, Chennai, India

To find out more about our authors and books visit www.bloomsbury.com and sign up for our newsletters.

For Sara

CONTENTS

Illustrations viii
Acknowledgements ix

Introduction 1

Section I Microinterruptions 23

1 Dialogue 25

2 Self 57

3 Action 89

Section II Macrointerruptions 119

4 Dramaturgy 121

5 Convention 158

Continuation 201

Notes 207
Bibliography 259
Index 278

ILLUSTRATIONS

Figures

1.1 William Shakespeare, *Hamlet*, in *Mr. William Shakespeares Comedies, Histories, & Tragedies* 29
1.2 William Shakespeare, *Hamlet*, in *The Works of Mr. William Shakespear* 30
2.1 Volturcius's speech, Ben Jonson, *Catiline*, in *The Workes of Benjamin Jonson* 63
2.2 Celia's speech, Ben Jonson, *Volpone* 66
2.3 Celia's speech continued, Ben Jonson, *Volpone* 67
3.1 The direction for the women's song, John Fletcher, *The Woman's Prize* 110
3.2 The direction for the woman's song, John Fletcher. *The Woman's Prize* 110
3.3 The woman's song with lyrics, John Fletcher, *The Woman's Prize* 112
3.4 The men's response to the song, John Fletcher, *The Woman's Prize* 113
5.1 Truewit's final speech, Ben Jonson, *Epicoene*, in *The Workes of Benjamin Jonson* 183

Tables

1.1 A Comparison of the Microinterruptions in *Volpone*, *The Tempest*, and *The Humorous Lieutenant* 34
5.1 Plays with MTF Cross-dressing (1584–1636) 163

ACKNOWLEDGEMENTS

As this project reflects many stages of my life, there are many people to thank.

To my peers who gave hours of feedback and support. At USNA: Gabriel Bloomfield, Audrey Wu Clark, Mike Flynn, Joan Shifflet, Jane Wessel, and Shirley Lau Wong. At FSU: Taylor Clement, Jamie Gillhespy, and Rachel Stuart Duke. At Mary Baldwin: my MFA Company Roving Shakespeare, especially Rachel Ratkowski, Stephanie Tschetter, Bobby Byers, AJ Sclafani, Brian Maxwell, Liz Lodato, Deb Streusand, and Angelina LaBarre. And to colleagues more widely: to Kerry Kisa for turning me toward Shakespeare; to my conference buddies, Jess Hamlet and Amy Bolis; to Claire M.L. Bourne and José Pérez-Díez, who provided advance copies of their work; to Simone Chess, who communicated about ideas in Chapter 5; and to the participants in the seminar 'Shakespeare's Forms' at SAA 2019 and those in 'Finding Fletcher' at SAA 2017.

To my professors, who guided my intellectual life and thinking. At FSU: Stan Gontarski, Kris Salata, Celia Caputi, Helen Burke, David Gants, and A.E.B. Coldiron. At Mary Baldwin: Matt Davies, Mary Hill Cole, Doreen Bechtol, and Jeremy Lopez. To those even more anterior: Lesley Wheeler and Holly Pickett.

To my students, who have challenged my assumptions and made me clarify my arguments: to the midshipmen I currently teach at USNA and to all those at FSU and MBU. I am especially grateful for the experience of directing at FSU, in creating some beautiful productions, which often developed into insights in this book. So too, to my FSU undergraduate research assistants: Elliot Foster, Shannon Lechon, Maxwell Adolph, and Logan Bell, whose work and feedback oftentimes has found its way into this document.

A special thanks to Amy Kimball from the Sheridan Libraries at Johns Hopkins University, Paul Espinosa from the Peabody Library, and Amber Kohl at the University of Maryland, College Park, who facilitated my acquisition of several important images.

To the feedback from the anonymous reviewers and to the team at Bloomsbury for taking on this book, especially Douglas Bruster and Lisa Hopkins.

Above all, a few people deserve special acknowledgement. Firstly, to Gary Taylor, who has generously guided me and corrected many errors throughout. His encouragement and feedback have been indispensable, as well as his willingness to listen. Next, to Terri Bourus, who has shown me what true collaboration is both on the stage and on the page. Before FSU, I had the amazing opportunity to work with Paul Menzer and Ralph Alan Cohen at Mary Baldwin. Each offered guidance, even if sometimes at odds, over intellectual and professional projects; their support and encouragement is the foundation of this book.

Personally, I must thank my parents for their tireless support and encouragement, especially as they pushed me to be a reader and lover of books. To my sisters, who have always given love, support, and laughter. To my daughter Lucy, the kindest interruption, who provides hours of frustration and entertainment, and to the most recent rupture: my son Rowland. But, above all, I must thank my wife Sara: her support was fundamental. Without her, I could never have made it through the drafts and ideas and frustrations and successes of this work. She permeates my thinking, in every good way imaginable.

Introduction

In *Romeo and Juliet*, Mercutio attempts to continue his Queen Mab speech, when Romeo suddenly silences his friend:

> MERCUTIO: This is the hag, when maids lie on their backs,
> That presses them and learns them first to bear,
> Making them women of good carriage.
> This is she—
> ROMEO: Peace, peace, Mercutio, peace,
> Thou talk'st of nothing.
> (*RJ* 1.4.92-95)

Despite Mercutio's frantic desire to continue the diatribe, his friend cuts him off, calms him down, and changes the course of the conversation. Romeo alters the exchange and exerts conversational power over his friend.

When King Lear is faced with the united front of his daughters, he exclaims:

> LEAR: I will have such revenges on you both
> That all the world shall—I will do such things—
> What they are yet I know not, but they shall be
> The terrors of the earth!
> (*KL* 2.2.474-77)

His emotional outburst cannot finish or explain what the 'world' will do. His mind redirects his thoughts from the world's reactions to the punishments that he intends to inflict. He begins with one thought before redirecting towards another, never letting the daughters or audience know how he expects the world to react. This speech gives the audience a sense of his mind actively working as it attempts to take in the perceived ingratitude of his daughters.

At the end of *Love's Labours Lost*, the pageant of the Nine Worthies spins out of control into a riotous attempted combat between Don Armado and Costard over Jaquenetta. But before the fight can start, a character unexpectedly enters:

> *Enter a messenger*, Monsieur MARCADÉ.
>
> MARCADÉ: God save you, madam.
> PRINCESS: Welcome, Marcadé,
>   But that thou interruptest our merriment.
> MARCADÉ: I am sorry, madam, for the news I bring
>   Is heavy in my tongue. The King your father—
> PRINCESS: Dead, for my life!
> MARCADÉ: Even so; my tale is told.
>   (*LLL* 5.2.710-715)

This event – an entrance with a brief message – transforms the entire play, and despite the warning of the title, it is supremely unexpected. As the Princess herself declares, Mercadé 'interrupt[s]' the 'merriment'. In fact, his entrance and the Princess's own line, as she interrupts his message, underscore the overall move. Suddenly, the preceding actions and romantic comedy become tonally tragicomic as the political reality of the outside world invades the isolated court of Navarre. The Princess, now Queen, and the King do not end up together, or as Berowne says, 'Jack hath not Jill' (*LLL* 5.2.863). The playful alteration of generic expectation takes an audience by surprise and redirects the expectations of the final scene, driving the play towards different and new conclusions.

Romeo's silencing of Mercutio, Lear's incomplete speech, and Mercadé's entrance may seem to be various moments within Shakespeare's plays. However, all three are interruptions. Romeo interrupts Mercutio, Lear interrupts himself, and Mercadé's entrance interrupts the course of the romantic comedy. As such, all three moments possess a similar form that, once articulated, allows for scholars and practitioners to understand how these moments, crafted by playwrights, shape characters and plays.

Though many have used interruptions as an idea to facilitate interpretation, they do so without articulating what the form is.[1] This book investigates the significance of interruptions as a form within drama of the late sixteenth and early seventeenth century in England, an important era for the development of Western drama. Drama itself, from the emergence of the singular actor from the chorus (a moment of rupturing expectation), is predicated upon interruption.[2] As this study encompasses questions of printed texts, performed texts, author's texts, and reader's texts, it defies the idea that interruptions are part of a 'givenness of form'.[3] Interruptions are instead a form as Caroline Levine defines this concept, 'an ordering, patterning, or shaping'.[4] Their participation or production among these facets of textuality necessitate that we understand it as a 'revisable interpretive structure',[5] which necessitates the operation of a 'recovered literary formalism'.[6] So too, we may consider interruptions in light of their affordances as Levine suggests, asking 'instead what potentialities lie latent—though not always obvious—in aesthetic and social arrangements'.[7] This formal feature of texts, the interruption, is a persistent but ever-changing phenomenon. It is a form that 'acquires its proper form only as it converges in the process of analysis',[8] a process that this book undertakes. So too, interruptions as a form in plays are particularly theatrical because they exist within dramatic scripts, written by an author, but also depend upon live performance.[9] The interruption as form may begin as drama, but lives in a theatrical space. These forms then reveal the theatrical dynamics between characters as well as between performance and audience; however, their dramatic basis also reveals aspects of authorial style.

An Anatomy of Interruptions

What is the form of an interruption? An interruption has three parts: premise, rupture, and continuation. Interruptions begin with a premise or a statement. The premise indicates that it will come to a completion, which creates expectation. Even if that expectation is for a grammatically complete sentence, audiences anticipate that the premise (in either action or words) will conclude. The second part is the rupture, when a conversant speaks out of turn or an action occurs that halts the premise from reaching its expected completion. While not the only part of the form, the rupture is the crucial moment that defines an interruption. Without it, we would have a completed premise, an idea begun and finished. Therefore, the rupture is almost synonymous with the interruption itself; however, to fully consider the importance of the form, we must consider the other pieces. The final part is the continuation. After a rupture occurs, the premise has been altered and cannot continue as the original expectation dictated. The continuation could meld the premise with the rupture and create a synthetic new expectation; the continuation could allow the rupture's language or event to dominate, completely taking over the premise; or the continuation could ignore the rupture and follow the premise's initial path. These three options demonstrate the outcomes of an interruption, and while I present them as discrete, they exist on a spectrum from no change to complete change. No interruption can continue in a way that completely discounts the rupture or completely ignores the premise. Even if a speaker ruptures and continues in a way divergent from the premise, an audience member or reader will interpret and evaluate the continuation through a consideration of the premise. So too, if the premise reasserts itself, it does so with the understanding that the rupture has occurred, and the failure or lack of alteration becomes embedded within the continued consideration of the premise now as continuation.

If we relook at the initial examples: in *Romeo and Juliet*, Mercutio's speech about Mab is the premise, and his speech indicates that it will continue to describe what she is. Romeo's command of 'Peace' is the rupture that breaks into Mercutio's premise. The continuation is the rest of Romeo's line that recolours Mercutio's speech: 'Thou talk'st of nothing', which Mercutio agrees with: 'True, I talk of dreams' before continuing his ideas in a new vein (*RJ* 1.4. 96). In *Lear*, King Lear's premise is his description of the world's reaction to his revenges. His rupture is an internal one in which he does not know how to complete the idea, so his continuation is to revert to the earlier idea of the revenges themselves. Finally, in *Love's Labours Lost*, the scene (5.2) is hurtling towards the romantic ending with all four pairs of lovers happily together, which is the premise. Mercadé's entrance is the rupture in which he arrives with unexpected news, the news of the King's death, which disrupts the festivities. The continuation is the ending of the play in which none of the lovers end up together.[10] While Mercadé's entrance is a rupture that dominates the continuation, Mercutio's continuation melds together his speech with Romeo's interjection, and Lear's confused outcry leaves the continuation unclear as it shows his own lack of clarity in the moment.

Because interruptions are based upon speaking rights or privileges, the form encodes a complicated struggle for power.

To make a premise asserts a sense of authority. To rupture is to challenge that authority. Even if the rupture agrees with the premise (as in backchannel utterances),[11] it either moves power towards the rupturing speaker or connects the rupturing speaker to the power of the premise, coalescing power within that premise. The continuation then becomes the demonstration of the outcome of the power struggle that the rupture initiates. Whether the premise is only slightly or completely altered signals the shift or reification of the power relationship demonstrated by the interruption. Again, our examples are briefly illustrative. Mercutio in melding the rupture to the continuation regains the power of the scene by further elaborating on Mab. Lear's emotional outburst shows his instability of power that is slipping. And, finally, in Mercade's entrance, the Princess gains the power as she becomes Queen and, in doing so, asserts a political future over her romantic one.

Interruptions seem negative, aligned with disruption and, therefore, with disorder and chaos. This derives from the Latin etymology of the word, where the root *rumpere* means to break, violate, or destroy.[12] Even with this root, however, the negative connotations reside only if we think that discontinuity is inherently negative. We see this tension in the earliest theories of drama, espoused by Aristotle. In the *Poetics*, Aristotle offers that plots must be 'unified and whole' and of a 'length that can be readily held in memory',[13] leading towards the idea of drama needing unity of time, place, and action. However, even within this desire to see the plot as a unified whole, Aristotle's own descriptions of reversals and recognitions that produce tragedies hinge upon interruptions.[14] The action of breaking in serves the scope of the dramatic action, creating unity through a structure that seems to destroy that unity. Therefore, we may distinguish between disruptions that embrace the *rumpere* root, emphasizing the rupture over continuation, as opposed to interruptions, which break into (*inter-* means between), thereby creating a distinctive form. Interruptions are not only the form that possesses the rupture but also that which the rupture comes between, namely the premise and continuation. So too, playwrights in the late sixteenth/early seventeenth century did not inherently view a lack of unity as bad. While some, such as George Puttenham and Philip Sidney, strongly advocated for such unity,[15] others like Shakespeare and John Fletcher seem less concerned with a unified whole.[16] Ultimately, to examine the forms of interruption within drama, we must consider it not as a negative structure that breaks down but as a form that is itself aesthetically neutral to be deployed disparately by disparate artists.

Discussions of literary texts and interruptions meld together three general types of interruptions: creational (interruptions relating to the crafting or production of the text), external (those connected to reception of the text), and internal (those found within the language of the text itself). Creational interruptions are when the creator of a piece is either literally or figuratively interrupted, thereby altering the transmission of a work as its eventual presentation indicates.[17] These interruptions represent the interruption of the creative process that the artist/author undergoes and also can be viewed as both internal and external. While these interruptions are often beyond the text proper and relate to forces external to it, they usually leave their imprint in the text. In the commercial theatre of the late sixteenth/early seventeenth century, significant creational interruptions derive from censorship.[18] Two examples briefly demonstrate the importance of creational interruptions. The original ending of *Every Man Out of His Humour* by Ben Jonson (1599) showed Macilente encountering Queen Elizabeth I and suddenly reversing his character. The printed versions of the text attest to the controversy over this ending, requiring the printing of a second version that removed the impersonation of the Queen.[19] The 1616 Folio of Jonson's Works printed two more endings roughly coinciding with the two presented in the Quarto (the theatrical and the censored one), but they are both altered, attesting to two new possibilities for ending the play. These four differing iterations of endings demonstrate the creational interruptions involved within Jonson's revisions and re-craftings mostly due to outside censorial voices. The text's ending is both complete and not complete as presented in any printed text of the period or of today. To choose one ending is to ignore what Jonson changed, responding to both his own tastes and the external demands of larger societal forces. The critical voices over his originally intended ending ruptured both the creation of the text and its presentation in its earliest printed forms, leaving only a composite for later generations.

We may also view the *New Oxford Shakespeare: Modern Critical Edition* of *The History of Cardenio* as an example of the polychronic nature of creationally interrupted texts. The complete play is lost and exists only in snippets of adapted text; therefore, to present it as a text requires a sense of interruption and openness akin to choosing Jonson's ending. However, here the problem is one of dearth not plenitude.[20] In this edition of the lost play, Gary Taylor 'has removed from the 1727 text [of *Double Falsehood*] everything demonstrably or probably written, or overwritten, by Theobald, Davenant, or Cibber'.[21] To do so means that the reader is presented with fragments of text as 'Blank lines or spaces call attention to [their] removal of material'.[22] This presentation creates an attempt to recover the text written only by Fletcher and Shakespeare, but in doing so presents a text that is interruption after interruption: the first one occurs on line 8:

> DUKE: I've worn the garland of my honours long
> And would not leave it withered to thy brow
> But flourishing and green; worthy the man
> [
> RODERICK: [
> DUKE: [
> While fond [Fernando] thy irregular brother,[23]

Using blank space and open brackets, the *New Oxford* version of Cardenio creates a fragmented text to rectify the ensuing years of transmission that adaptation had overwritten or interrupted. Here, the text has been creationally interrupted first by adapters and then by scholars, leaving a collection of fragments presented to readers who then must create their own idea of the textual whole.

External interruptions, those pertaining to the reception of texts by audiences and readers, are a second general type. These interruptions are when something outside of the text ruptures the text/event. In performance, these are moments in which an audience member engages in a way that is not planned by the author or producers.[24] One early modern example may be the 'Confusion and Errors' that attended upon the early performance of *The Comedy of Errors* as recounted in the *Gesta Grayorum*.[25] Sarah Neville, editor of the play in the *New Oxford*, states, 'When the play was performed for the Gray's Inn Christmas revels of 1594, the event became so disorderly that the performance was abandoned'.[26] If her reading of the *Gesta* is accurate, the riotous incompletion of the performance would be a clear example of an external interruption. The drunken revelry of the law students precluded the performance from continuation.

Even without the incompletion of the performance—of the rupture dominating the continuation—the disruptive behaviour that the account describes clearly indicates continued external interruptions and points towards their ability to destroy a premise.[27] Such is the power of external interruptions. Early modern theatre may have invited these types of interruptions through audience contact moments;[28] however, the paucity of audience responses from the period make this investigation more difficult. Furthermore, as Richard Preiss articulates, the variety of evidences provides no clear narrative.[29] If Hamlet's advice to the players is any indication, then clowns in the period might have encouraged such interruptions or inserted such interruptions themselves into the text.[30] The unexpected nature of these events, while making them more akin to what we might consider 'true' interruptive experiences, means that these are not crafted by the author/producers into the text/work/event themselves. Studying these interruptions then necessitates the existence of recorded audience responses or the ability to study current audience reflections. While some responses from the period exist and while Shakespeare remains a highly produced playwright, the lack of complete records and the inability to see non-Shakespearean texts performed preclude better research on the possibility of interruptive audiences.[31] Additionally, external interruptions are not limited to the stage. Readers, like live audiences, employ external interruptions by adding annotations and marginalia to printed texts. While not called interruptions (though they function as such), these texts demonstrate the usage of printed texts and important responses by readers.[32] So too, as Arlynda Boyer argues, actor's scripts provide external interruptions that actually bridge potential gaps between author and reader.[33] Therefore, studying these interventions allows scholars to consider the impact that reading and producing these texts have historically had.

The final general type is internal interruptions, or those that an author crafts as part of a text. Authors create these interruptions and intend them to be representational and mimetic. As these are situated within a constructed text, audiences and readers may be able to expect them. A rereading of a text, a rewatching of a performance, or the rehearsal process all preclude the unexpected nature of a rupture. Even so, as crafted forms they are authorially engendered affective structures. As internal interruptions are forms that one can identify within dramatic texts, this book focuses exclusively on this type of interruption. We can further subdivide this general type into two broad categories based upon their specificity and localization: microinterruptions and macrointerruptions.

Microinterruptions are specific and localized moments articulated within dialogue. They are when a speech or a specific action ruptures a specific premise (speech or action). For example, at beginning of *Hamlet*, Bernardo tells Horatio about his experience of the Ghost last night:

> Last night of all,
> When yond same star that's westward from the pole
> Had made his course t'illume that part of heaven
> Where now it burns, Marcellus and myself,
> The bell then beating one—
>
> (*Ham* Q2 1.1.34-38)

Bernardo's grammatical syntax clearly illustrates that he has not completed his thought, despite both the second Quarto text (1604) and the First Folio text (1623) using a full stop at the end of the speech. The decision to use a dash is a typical editorial emendation that helps modern readers notice the interruption.[34] What follows is the stage direction, '*Enter Ghost*', which prompts Marcellus to respond, 'Peace, break thee off, look where it comes again' (1.1.39). This moment is an internal microinterruption of a speech by an action. The Ghost's entrance ruptures Bernardo's premise in which he was attempting to describe what happened last night and leads to a continuation in which the three men try to get information out of the silent spectral figure. While the repercussions in continuation from a microinterruption may be long-lasting, the interruption itself can be identified as a specific moment within the work, as with the example from *Hamlet*. These interruptions may colour overall reception through iteration, but they always aesthetically colour a specific instance. It is *an* event, or a definable moment. These are the moments that journalists and sociologists attempt to count.[35] However, in a literary text, these moments can be easier to spot because of grammar, punctuation, or other textual conventions such as stage directions. Microinterruptions are the ubiquitous ones that we encounter all the time. This book further distinguishes them by consideration of what ruptures the premise: dialogue, self, or action.

Dialogue interruptions are when another speaker interjects into a speech by using words. Importantly, they rely upon the presence of another person/character. Within drama, this structure is built upon cues. An actor can ruin a dialogic interruption by not picking up on his/her cue quickly enough to give the sense of the interruption. A lag in cue time could give the audience the sense that the first character is lapsing into aposiopesis, thereby transforming the type of interruptive moment and transforming the meaning and effect of the moment as well. As these interruptions are between people, they are also built upon relationships, which imply hierarchical structures of power. These structures further dictate the use and effect of these interruptions as issues of rank, status, gender, race, and so on further inform them. Any and all alterity becomes significant to how the dialogic interruption is both presented in text and received by an audience. In many ways, it is this aspect that Derrida envisions in suggesting that 'to enter into a relation with the other, it is necessary that interruption be possible; it is necessary that the relation be a relation of interruption'.[36]

Dialogue interruptions, while hard to account for accurately in real-world situations, are usually indicated through either grammar or punctuation, and sometimes through both. Grammar is the most obvious indicator, meaning an interruption occurs when a grammatical structure is incomplete, as demonstrated earlier in Bernardo's speech. The lack of completion followed by another speaker tends to mean a dialogic interruption has occurred. Even so, modern readers of early modern texts might miss several interruptions because of their unfamiliarity with early modern punctuation or pointing. While we commonly use the em dash (—) to represent the trailing off end of a line that has been interrupted, the usage of this piece of punctuation was only beginning to become standard at the beginning of the seventeenth century.[37] Some lines in early modern texts end with a full stop/period even if the grammar clearly indicates that the second speaker interrupts the first. This lack of clarity means that while dashes are a good indicator, as I will discuss in relation to both Jonson and Fletcher, they cannot be the only one. Furthermore, performance adds yet another variable to dialogic interruptions in that an actor/director can transform a moment that is grammatically whole and not punctuated with a dash or other interruptive pointer into an interruption through inflection or speed of cue. Such interpretation allows for performance to create its own experience of dialogic interruptions that live alongside those indicated within any printed text, augmenting the dramatic text with a theatrical one. Self-interruptions occur, as the term indicates, when a character interrupts themself. Most examinations of interruption from the standpoint of specific rhetorical figures fit into this type of interruption. 'The figure of interruption', according to George Puttenham, is aposiopesis, which is a type of self-interruption when one breaks off one's speech usually because of emotion.[38] Parenthesis (another common rhetorical figure in which additional information is added) is often (though not always) a form of self-interruption. In performance, these rhetorical figures feel unexpected, and in fact that delivery of expectation may help clarify interruptive parenthesis versus non-interruptive parenthesis. However, as a moment within a work, we cannot ignore that this interruption is a structural form. Often the parenthetical rupture does not much alter the continuation, but as aposiopesis the continuation transforms into silence and exclamations of the inability to continue, allowing for another speaker to engage. This passing off of speaking rights renders the speaker himself as interrupter and not the other conversant. Finally, we may consider that repetitively self-interrupting begins to create a specific characterization. If one were only ever self-interruptive, one could not communicate at all.[39] Self-interruptions, while adding a sense of being in the moment, also must be tempered by the necessity of communication itself.

A somewhat different subset of microinterruptions is action interruptions. As opposed to purely dialogue interruptions, these contain an element of action in either premise, rupture, or continuation. Entrances and exits are two of the most common actions that interrupt or are interrupted, just as the Ghost interrupts Barnardo.[40] Action interruptions are significant to drama because they move towards the performance, making them a uniquely theatrical type of interruption. While narrative forms can describe interruptive actions, the encapsulation of the action within the narrative language itself differentiates the effect of the action as action. In drama, the action may be implied through dialogue, indicated by stage direction, or interpolated into a performance choice in a completely extra-textual manner.[41] Just as a performer can make dialogue interruptive in performance, despite the grammar or punctuation, interpolated actions can always be inserted in ways that interrupt. These performance choices offer moments of effect and meaning creation for the audience as transformed by the producers of the performance (meaning actors/directors/dramaturges/etc.).

As opposed to the microinterruptions, macrointerruptions are large scale and less localized. They are interruptions of plot or convention, and they significantly rely on external awareness of the internal structures. While they may be connected to a specific microinterruption, they are broader in scope and consequence, texturing the overall reception of a play, not just a moment. Generally, macrointerruptions affect an audience's expectation of events, and the rupture alters the audience's premised expectation of a situation, plot, or character. Macrointerruptions can be broken down into two types based not upon what ruptures as in microinterruptions, but upon what the premise is: dramaturgy and convention. As these types relate to less precise moments and hinge upon audience expectation, they are harder to designate; however, they still possess the same form (audiences expect something to occur, something else occurs, and the event moves on). A macrointerruption to one audience member may have been expected by another, depending on varying levels of awareness and perception. Even so, authors use these forms with an eye towards audience expectations that the printed texts record.

The first are those that affect the plot or dramaturgy of a given work: such as when characters arrive when they should not or when information is suddenly revealed. An example of a dramaturgical macrointerruption is the end of *The Comedy of Errors*, when the Abbess reveals herself also to be Emilia. Her dialogue does not interrupt the other speakers; rather, she responds to Dromio's language of being bound and reveals her true identity (5.1.339-45). This revelation interrupts the already-climactic ending where the audience has finally seen the twins together on stage. Her revelation ruptures the moment as she and Egeon become the focus until the Duke brings back in the Antipholi. The effect of a macrointerruption is on the audience's expectation and perception; therefore, foreknowledge of a work or cultural knowledge of a work disrupts and interferes with this specific form. This effect means that theorizing macrointerruptions requires hypothesizing a primary moment of reception. As students of Western literature in the twenty-first century know what Oedipus or Hamlet are going to do, whether they have ever read or seen the plays, Sophocles's and Shakespeare's macrointerruptions are not as potent as they perhaps once were. However, adaptation as well as performance allow for the macrointerruptions to be reinvigorated.[42] We still watch Shakespeare to see how a company approaches a text. Our interruptions then become meta-macrointerruptions as the audience watches not for the interruptions that the author crafted into the text but for the interruptions of their own critical reading/previous experience as challenged by the producers (meaning directors, actors, etc.).[43]

Conventional macrointerruptions are those connected to aspects of a text that the audience understands prior to that text, meaning they affect an audience's expectation of a work based on previous experiences of similar literary artifacts. For example, in 1608, audiences seemingly expected that pastorals had 'country hired shepherds' drinking 'whitsun ales' and engaging in 'morris-dances'.[44] John Fletcher's *The Faithful Shepherdess* interrupted these conventional expectations by presenting an ironic twist on the pastoral genre, leading to the play's failure.[45] Therefore, these interruptions rely on audience reception, and indicate a playwright's engagement with his audience. Interrupting conventions is a place for playwrights to develop their relationship to the plays and writers before them. However, once such conventions are interrupted, they can become expected and rendered uninterruptive. When Fletcher's *The Faithful Shepherdess* was performed in 1634, it succeeded as a straightforward paean to chastity and the pastoral genre.[46] Therefore, in roughly thirty years the play transformed from a 'bitter . . . nihilistic send-up'[47] to something thoroughly expected in the dominant culture. Knowledge of the genre then both offers and possibly prohibits some effect of these interruptions. Even if the ultimate path of the continuation is predicted through generic expectations, performance and the intricacies that the playwright takes to get there, both instantiate methods for revivifying the expected interruption.

While I have endeavored in this section to anatomize interruptions into specific and distinct forms, my discussions of types have also demonstrated the interdependence and complicated intersection among them. For example, a creational interruption may become or be seen as an internal interruption as is the case with the ending of *Every Man Out*. Furthermore, a microinterruption may lead or be a part of a moment of dramatic irony that may signal a macrointerruption. Distinguishing among these types gives the critic a vocabulary for engaging the forms within the text, and their intermixture provides further venues for consideration of how the forms work.

To examine the structure of interruptions in the large body of drama from 1580 to 1642 would require more space than is available, and, therefore, texts and authors must emerge as strong and influential constructors of this specific form. In narrowing down my examination, I am not precluding other authors or texts from being examined in this manner. In fact, I would hope that this examination will be useful in driving others to consider the many playwrights that I must ignore and the many play texts that I must forego. While the importance of this historical moment to the development of English language drama cannot be underestimated, myriad playwrights—from Samuel Beckett to Harold Pinter to Caryl Churchill to Suzan-Lori Parks—offer and most likely merit examination of their own development of this quotidian form. I leave those explorations to later work.

In the text that follows, I develop an argument about the three principal playwrights that this work will examine; however, the notion of playwriting in the early modern period is extremely difficult to excise from the generally and specifically collaborative nature of theatre.[48] To illustrate my point, we need only turn to the most recent edition of John Fletcher's works, which is found in the aptly titled *The Dramatic Works in the Beaumont and Fletcher Canon*, edited by Fredson Bowers and others. The dual name of Beaumont and Fletcher stands in an author function to cover plays that are authored by either man, both men, both men with others, either man with others, and neither man.[49] The collection contains the writing of Francis Beaumont and John Fletcher, but here 'Beaumont and Fletcher' also means Nathan Field and Philip Massinger and John Ford and William Shakespeare and maybe even Ben Jonson. So too, we may look to Kathleen McLuskie's usage of Fletcher for the author of all 'plays by Fletcher and his collaborators' in order 'to avoid the minefield of the authorship of the Beaumont and Fletcher canon'.[50] The hypothetical Fletcher that McLuskie offers like the Beaumont and Fletcher that Bowers uses is only a persona—a mask that covers the identity of several actors or human beings. The slippage between a physical human and a character is important as we move about through the body of work where collaboration often occurred and public personas were crafted. Such usages elide the actual physical labour undertaken by specific people.

Therefore, the persons reflected in this text will be best articulated through the most recent and up-to-date attribution work, an attempt to peer behind the masks and 'locate a working distinctiveness for the orchestrator of voices, influences, sources, and contexts' in these plays.[51] While Cyrus Hoy's work on the 'Beaumont and Fletcher' plays (here I use that loose personic signifier) is still foundational,[52] the work of Martin Wiggins and Catherine Richardson in their catalogue *British Drama 1533-1642* has offered new arguments about the dates of several plays,[53] which necessitates new examination of these old attributions. This book focuses on plays that can be most confidently identified as solo-authored by Shakespeare, by Fletcher, and more easily by Jonson, but this is not to say that the interruptions that I note do not derive from another writer, let alone from the theatre or the printing house. Myriad people were involved in transmitting these texts, and we must represent their work validly without allowing the multiplicity to derail the discussions of the text as it is or authors as they were. At some point Shakespeare, Fletcher, and Jonson wrote these plays and, in doing so, employed interruptive techniques that can be examined.

No study of the period currently can escape the behemoth that is Shakespeare. He has dominated and continues to dominate the critical discussion of drama from the period and looms large over the drama of our own time. This valuation demands attention when one attempts to examine an important and significant aspect of all drama, especially within this historical period. Aside from that somewhat obvious fact, as any Shakespearean might tell you (and would tell you), Shakespeare has several important moments of interruption, from the dialogue and masque of *The Tempest* to the titular moment of *Love's Labours Lost*. Shakespeare employs microinterruptions and macrointerruptions in ways that challenged his audience and helped develop his particular dramaturgy, all of which are aspects that will be discussed more fully in the subsequent chapters.

Ben Jonson is often seen as the second most important dramatist of the period, especially in critical studies.[54] His legacy, beginning with the 1616 *Works*, leaves an output that has specifically been crafted by the author. However, what many do not know is that out of all playwrights with extant texts from 1580 to 1647, Jonson is one of the most prolific users of the specific word 'interrupt' and its variations.[55] While James Shirley dominates with forty-seven usages, Jonson follows behind him with twenty-five and is significantly ahead of John Ford with seventeen (another Caroline writer). As the two Caroline authors are working later than

Shakespeare, Jonson, and Fletcher (who are all late Elizabethan/Jacobean authors), Shirley and Ford's work represents the next step or development in the term and would need to be considered in a subsequent examination. Jonson's specific interest, however, in this word merits particular attention not only to when he uses this term but also to his usage of the form the word represents. From his boys in *Cynthia's Revels* to fearful Volturcius in *Catiline*, his works engage and use the term interruption in an overt and specific methodology of dramaturgy that contrasts with Shakespeare as the chapters will explore.

John Fletcher, a name now largely forgotten and often ignored even among literary critics of the period, was the theatrical heir of Shakespeare, writing exclusively for the King's Men after Shakespeare's retirement. Despite Fletcher's neglect and devaluation, he was the dominant playwright of the seventeenth century. After the Restoration, he had almost double the number of plays performed than Shakespeare, many without alteration.[56] Therefore, as the literary inheritor and potentially chosen protégé of the playwright widely regarded as the greatest of all time, we as critics of the period must resurrect the dilapidated situation of his canon and examine what he offered. Significantly, his works contain a plenitude of microinterruptions that only further reflect his interest in manipulating audience expectations through macrointerruptions. In this way, he seems to have noticed and developed an interest in this structure from his precursor Shakespeare and his contemporary Jonson. Despite working alongside both men, he developed a dramaturgy completely his own, an immensely popular dramaturgy that has been rarely examined for its contributions to English theatricality and drama.

While critics often discuss Fletcher and Shakespeare in light of their collaborations, and contrast Shakespeare and Jonson as literary rivals, and sometimes mention Jonson and Fletcher because of their mutual respect, these three dramatists and their canons have not been placed into conversation until now. The Restoration considered these three as the most memorable of the period, but now Shakespeare predominates with Jonson a far second and Fletcher nearly in the waste bin. To resituate Fletcher and Jonson alongside their collaborator and contemporary helps us see how three interconnected dramatists approached the same form in significantly differing ways. The works of these playwrights offer a significant range of approaches to interruptions in drama from the period and illuminate both the textures of their personal dramatic styles and the potential for this form in their theatre.

A Path into Interruptions

This book focuses on internal interruptions, one of the three major types. I use the subdivision of microinterruptions and macrointerruptions to constitute the two halves, beginning with micro and ending with macro. I move from the most obvious and agreed-upon interruptions (dialogic microinterruptions) to the most subjective and broadly defined (conventional macrointerruptions). Each chapter deals with the three authors differently, sometimes placing them in a chronological relationship and sometimes considering further subdivisions of the types of interruptions. While I often focus on one exemplary text per author in each chapter, this is not always the case, nor does it mean that that play is the only one to fit the aspect being discussed. While each chapter uses and builds upon each other, they also constitute distinct units. Therefore, my own structuring of these four types in this order is only one of many ways that the chapters may be read or constructed.

Chapter 1 examines dialogue microinterruptions by first examining their typographic representation in the punctuation of the dash. I locate the dash within the printed texts of the three playwrights, noting that it was a relatively new piece of punctuation in the early modern period. Through a brief examination of a passage in *Hamlet*, I illustrate the problems in presenting a text with dashes and in defining interruptions. I then establish the most microinterruptive texts in each playwright's canon: *Volpone*, *The Tempest*, and *The Humorous Lieutenant*, and consider each play's most interruptive sequence. In *Volpone*, Jonson fixates the power of the interruption in Mosca's counting, despite the several attempts to rupture his premise. Jonson presents a subversive rendering of the power struggle that interruptions represent by illustrating the power of the servant within a seemingly unpowerful place. In Shakespeare's *The Tempest*, Antonio and Sebastian mercilessly interrupt and mock Gonzalo as he attempts to console the King. What this highly interruptive schema presents is perhaps a rendering of interruptions as a negative power grab by villainizing those who participate. Shakespeare colours the idea of rupture as detrimental through the repeated incursions. Fletcher offers a unique approach in *The Humorous Lieutenant* where the traditional power struggles of Jonson and Shakespeare are transferred into a communal coalescing. While the soldiers of Fletcher's play mock and deride, their interruptive moments lead towards a sense of community that while competitive is ultimately compassionate. This community becomes most obvious through a second scene in which Fletcher presents a group of women who use interruptions to competitively work together. From subversive struggles to traditional roles to community, these three playwrights and these three works illustrate the range that dialogic microinterruptions encode even as they point towards balances of power. Furthermore, they demonstrate a way in which Shakespeare responds to Jonson and Fletcher responds to both of his predecessors.

Chapter 2 examines the moments when a character interrupts themself, either breaking off entirely, as in aposiopesis, or to correct their approach. These moments become harder to identify as almost any change in syntax could potentially be a self-interruption. I once more use *Hamlet* as an example of the possibilities within these interruptions. These moments reveal aspects of character creation through hints of interiority as well, which an audience fills. I explore the dynamic between character and audience through the idea of inner-working and inter-working, where inner-working describes the connections that are interior to a character and inter-working expresses the connections between character and audience (both on- and off-stage). These related dynamics help explore the power struggles at play in deploying self-interruptions. I divide self-interruptions into subtypes: emotional, manipulative, and comedic. I give examples from each playwright of emotional self-interruptions, showing development and divergence in approach. Shakespeare dominates the section on manipulative self-interruption with the character of Iago whose use of the self-interruption as a specifically manipulative medium is unrivalled. I end this chapter with a brief examination of Mistress Quickly and how self-interruptive strategies can also be comedic. The interjection of comedy highlights the constructed nature of the interruption in self-usage and further connects this seemingly micro structure into its macro effect on the off-stage audience.

Chapter 3 considers interruptions where non-linguistic occurrences (entrances, exits, music, fighting) interrupt a scene's dialogue. While such moments align with dialogic and self-interruptions, they move the dramatic text towards a theatrical realization. Furthermore, their existence in stage directions means that they are often altered by the incursion of editorial quibbling. After exploring the paratextual nature of the stage direction, arguing that their status is interruptive by nature—inserting the theatre into the dialogue and vice versa—I move onto three ways in which each author uses such moments within their plays. I begin the chapter by considering Jonson's use of scene breaks as another way in which the dramatic and the theatrical meet within action interruptions. Jonson famously used French scenes in his printed texts, which demarcate a new scene anytime a character enters. These breaks interrupt the theatrical flow of the text that would otherwise be continuous. This emendation is authorial and emphasizes Jonson's relationship to his audience and his readership. Through an examination of *The Alchemist*, I develop a reading of this complicated interrelationship between a readerly dramatic text and a hypothetical theatrical text, illustrating Jonson's crafting of two contrasting experiences. I then move to Shakespeare's employment of ghosts and their entrances to argue how he engenders surprise at such entries but then often deflates their power. So too, I consider that his use of ghosts demonstrates a rupture of narrative form with the theatrical. As a unique example, Banquo's ghost in *Macbeth* both defies Shakespeare's other deployments by creating a larger rupture with his audience, which caused much editorial angst, especially in the nineteenth century, and further illustrates the underlying problems of stage directions as both text and action. Finally, I consider how Fletcher, like Shakespeare's ghosts, also ruptures the dramatic text through his use of songs. Music (with or without lyrics) is something that is beyond the dramatic text and is only available via the theatrical event. Specifically, I examine the placement of the song in Fletcher's *The Woman's Prize, or The Tamer Tamed*, noting that editorial intervention and lack of understanding of Fletcher's engagement with interruptions have caused editors to needlessly alter the placement of the song from its earliest instantiations in the Lambarde Manuscript to its reprinting in the Second Folio of 1679 (where it first appears with lyrics). Fletcher's use of music as a theatrical aspect of drama reflects his engagement with ruptures as well as his exploration of gendered power. Through exploring these action interruptions (scenes, ghosts, and songs), I aim not only to further show these authors' relationships to interruptions but also to highlight how editors can work against the texts that they are editing.

Chapter 4 moves into the realm of macrointerruptions by considering interruptions of dramaturgy. Macrointerruptive structures are different from microinterruptive ones because they rely upon an outside audience to create the rupture. An audience has to have an expectation of a play's story in order for it to be ruptured. In this chapter, I explore how the playwrights crafted interruptions within theatrical narrative structures to manipulate their audiences. I begin with Jonson's *Every Man Out of His Humour*, considering how his 'theoretical manifesto'[57] playfully ruptures and controls audience expectations throughout its complicated dramaturgy. The play defies typical understandings of drama through its use of the Grex as chorus and through several sudden reversals. These aspects present Jonson's conception of dramaturgy and desire for authorial control. I then move to Shakespeare's experiment in dramaturgy in *The Winter's Tale* where he adapts a prose narrative and almost writes a surprise ending. Despite his tendency for dramatic irony, Shakespeare creates an unexpected conclusion in Hermione's survival. In this construction, he interrupts his own typical dramaturgy within the construction of a new dramaturgy, but ultimately reverts towards his more typical approach. I end with Fletcher's ruptured exposition in *The Chances*, which is a play that is only ever studied as an adaptation of Cervantes. Doing so, however, ignores the methodology that Fletcher uses in imbuing the play with interrupted exposition as it hurtles forward. This in media res opening creates a rupturous dramaturgy that explores an audience's need for exposition and explication.

The final chapter examines another type of macrointerruptions, those that affect conventions. These interruptions demonstrate a playwright's relationship to his audience by exploring the extent to which he is willing to defy the accepted notions of what constitutes a theatrical experience. To explore these specifically, I focus on how disguise in connection to the all-male stage intersect in the convention of male-to-female (MTF) cross-dressing. As a rarer convention than the similar female-to-male cross-dressing, MTF cross-dressing offers a unique convention that comments upon the theatrical energy of the early modern stage itself. In this chapter, I examine how Shakespeare, Jonson, and then Fletcher each pursue this convention with differing results for the audience. In the Induction to *The Taming of the Shrew*, Shakespeare uses MTF cross-dressing with the audience's awareness of the disguise, creating the expectation for a reveal. However, the extant text never delivers that reveal and leaves the character subsumed within the convention. Jonson follows Shakespeare with his coup de théâtre in *Epicene*, where the audience learns in the final moment that the female character Epicene is actually a boy in disguise, using the convention of the all-male stage to rupture our expectations. I reconsider the structure of this scene as well as the scholarship over it to discuss how Jonson purposefully ruptures expectations while also controlling their reception, leading towards a reappraisal of characters after the moment. Finally, Fletcher's *The Loyal Subject* presents another unexpected cross-dressing scenario, but unlike Jonson, Fletcher blurs the lines between gender expectations. Fletcher embraces the theatricality of the convention so thoroughly that the discovery of Alinda's supposedly true gender highlights the performativity of all gender and the playfulness of all theatre. Therefore, the playwrights develop expectation by responding to each other within the reception of convention, always further rupturing expectations, leading towards newer conventions.

I end the book with a short continuation that explores one final moment of interruptions both on stage and in print: the Praeludium to Jonson's *Cynthia's Revels*. This scene offers a combination of the various types within this study, underscoring the power dynamics not only among characters but also between text and reader/audience that interruptive forms engage. After any interruption, the conversants, participants, characters, or people must move on, must continue, must go forward. This introduction has only begun to consider the form in play by laying out the centrally important aspects that will govern the subsequent analyses. Each following chapter will use the terminology from the anatomy, adding specifics and complicating what at first seems straightforward. Marjorie Garber, in her examination of interruptions, concludes, 'So the life of mankind is an attempt, a plot, to restore what has been interrupted. Or rather, to acknowledge that the myth of interruption is life itself.'[58] But instead of a restoration, dwelling on the rupture, why not examine the interruption for what it is, allow the continuation to carry us on towards what will inevitably be another interruption?

SECTION I

Microinterruptions

1

Dialogue

The dash is the punctuation mark of interruption. While it can indicate 'nuances of semantic significance', the variance in historical texts, especially seventeenth-century plays, means that dashes rarely 'resolve structural uncertainties' and more likely indicate further ones for editors to argue over.[1] The dash, like all punctuation, exists in relation to the text, whose 'paradoxical performances produce excessive meaning'.[2] While the history of the dash 'has yet to be written',[3] what follows is only a piece as it relates to the form of interruption.[4] The dash comprises a horizontal line, usually aligned in the approximate centre of adjacent letters, that can be the length of an en (–) or an em (—) or longer (——) or can be made of several horizontal lines (---). The dash indicates that language existed or would exist but has now been omitted. Whether that was an expurgated oath, a name, or the character's next word, the dash supplies the place of the language that ought to be there, but now must be inferred. Its presence demands attention to absence. As a signifier, it visually represents the rupture of an interruption; it displays the movement from one premise to a different and separate premise. Claire M. L. Bourne notes how dashes 'create visual breaks in the printed dialogue'.[5] The linearity of its shape leads a reader from one thought to another, providing a 'structure of relation' or 'reading lens',[6] either between one character and another character or between character and self. Through these gestures of connectivity,[7] we might then see how this punctuation mark can help us theorize interruptions. The punctuation mark here is one that gestures towards and bridges the gap between the theatrical moment and the written text.[8] Importantly, the dash makes the microinterruption visible.

While modern editions use this mark to represent interruption,[9] the dash was an emergent piece of punctuation in the seventeenth century, with inconsistent and variable usage. Some texts, authors, and printers use the dash to indicate that an interruption has occurred; others use a comma, a semicolon, or even a full stop.[10] Shakespeare's *The Tempest*, which critics have often acknowledged as a significantly interruptive play,[11] contains only one dash in its earliest text from 1623. Even though Shakespeare's texts do not contain many dashes, other dramatic documents in the period use them to make their microinterruptions clear and obvious to a reader. Jonson not only was 'one of the first English authors to employ the dash,' but he did so 'conspicuously'.[12] Jonson's texts are replete with dashes, and given his oversight of most of his published works, these texts possess a claim towards authorial usage.[13] Jonson's texts, therefore, call specific attention to their interruptions through their employment of this emergent punctuation. Similar to Jonson is Fletcher, whose texts, preserved in the Beaumont and Fletcher First Folio of 1647 (B&F F1), have high usages of dashes and, therefore, indicate an investment in making interruption clear.

The dash both points to the microinterruption and demonstrates its relational nature. The connective line of the dash joins together two parts, combining a premise with a specific rupture in the form of more language or a stage direction. The dash as punctuation not only demonstrates the rupture that it represents, a presence signaling an absence, but it also joins and unifies two pieces of text, conjoining them into a unit, a unit that is an interruption. To examine microinterruptions within drama is to examine the relational activities between and among differing characters. This relationship characterizes by insinuating a relative differential of authority and power between the two characters. As Brian Gibbons succinctly asserts, 'interruption is the expression of power.'[14] The relational dynamics of these interruptions encode power through interpellation, meaning through the process in which individuals are made subjects.[15] Interruptions are interpellative practices because they use ruptured discourse to encode ideological positions of subject/object and relative power. However, the ruptures of interruptions allow for breaks that signal uncertainties within these larger power structures. This is all to say that microinterruptions and their complex notions of power dynamics reflect the problems of ideological subject formation and, therefore, represent sites of complex iterations of identities. The decision to interrupt or the reaction to being interrupted becomes predicated upon the perceived relationship to the other that is rupturing one's premise. Therefore, analysing such moments reveals the relationship among characters, specifically the fluctuating power dynamics. Furthermore, through comparative analyses of similar moments, one can begin to perceive the differing approaches of various playwrights in representing power relationships.

This examination of microinterruptions focuses on three texts: Jonson's *Volpone*, Shakespeare's *The Tempest*, and Fletcher's *The Humorous Lieutenant*.[16] All three plays are each author's most interruptive and, therefore, articulate a sense of each playwright's usage of the form. Each play also contains an intensely interruptive scene that intends to ridicule certain characters. *Volpone*'s *Act Five*, Scene Three depicts Mosca attempting to count his supposed inheritance despite the clamorous interruptions of Voltore, Corbaccio, Corvino, and Lady Would-Be. In *The Tempest Act Two*, Scene One, Antonio and Sebastian mock Gonzalo's and Adrian's attempts to console the grieving Alonso. Finally, in *The Humorous Lieutenant Act Four*, Scene Six, Leontius harangues the love-addled Lieutenant. Beyond the fact that all three scenes share a high usage of interruptions within dialogue, they also present a scene in which the interrupters are outside of another conversation, creating a duplication of conversation. These scenes possess a bifurcated structure, where the ruptures reach across a separation of the action. In other words, the interrupter tries to enter a conversation in which he is not a principal conversant, and the ruptures bridge that divide. In *Volpone*, the first layer is Mosca's inventory of his inheritance, and the second is the attempt by the would-be heirs to understand what has just happened. They are not part of his inventory but attempt to make themselves a part of it. In *Tempest*, the first is Gonzalo's assuaging Alonso, and the second is Antonio and Sebastian's commentary. In *Lieutenant*, the first is the Lieutenant attempting to express his love for the King, and the second is Leontius's mockery of the Lieutenant's language. This structure within the microinterruptive dialogue intensifies a sense of antagonism among the characters and highlights the interruptions' potential for disjunction. The ruptures try to overtake the premises, and when they do, they derail the premise of the entire scene (Mosca's inventory, Gonzalo's consolation, and the Lieutenant's love declaration), creating a chaotic divergence from that original action. However, the playwrights do not approach this structure with the same concluding affect. The deployment of the microinterruptions and specifically their continuations demonstrate Jonson's ridicule of assumed power structures, Shakespeare's vilification of ruptures, and Fletcher's celebration of community.

The Problem with Pointing

Before turning to the specific texts, I will first demonstrate the problems and potentialities for the analysis of interruption and its relationship to published texts, using a key moment from *Hamlet*. When Polonius re-enters to announce the arrival of the players to Elsinore, his exchange with the Prince demonstrates the complicated history of editing and punctuation in seventeenth-century plays and the power that punctuation exerts over characterization. The variant presentations of the passage's punctuation alter the power dynamic between Polonius and Hamlet, offering stronger and weaker versions of both characters. The Folio is the first of the early texts to introduce dashes to this passage.[17] Figure 1.1 shows the passage as it appears in the 1623 First Folio. It begins with an exchange in which Polonius makes a statement concluded by a full stop, which is followed by Hamlet's line, which ends with a dash. Therefore, Polonius has syntactically and rhetorically completed his thought without any character, namely Hamlet, impeding his ability to do so. This statement is then followed by Hamlet's line, which Polonius ruptures, transgressing niceties and immediately establishing a power dynamic between the characters. Polonius's desire to finish his announcement ruptures Hamlet's tangent about Roman actors. Because Hamlet is Polonius's superior, the interruption is potentially rude. This interruption then signals information about the encounter between the two men and adds to Polonius's character. Either he is willing to wrest speaking rights from Hamlet or is oblivious to Hamlet's lack of participation in the premised conversation. All editions since the Folio have used a dash here, cementing this relationship in this moment.

> *Ham.* I will Prophesie. Hee comes to tell me of the
> Players. Mark it, you say right Sir: for a Monday mor-
> ning 'twas so indeed.
> *Pol.* My Lord, I haue Newes to tell you.
> *Ham.* My Lord, I haue Newes to tell you.
> When *Rossius* an Actor in Rome——
> *Pol.* The Actors are come hither my Lord.
> *Ham.* Buzze, buzze.
> *Pol.* Vpon mine Honor.
> *Ham.* Then can each Actor on his Asse——
> *Polon.* The best Actors in the world, either for Trage-
> die, Comedie, Historie, Pastorall: Pastoricall-Comicall-
> Historicall-Pastorall: Tragicall-Historicall: Tragicall-
> Comicall-Historicall-Pastorall: Scene indiuible, or Po-
> em vnlimited. *Seneca* cannot be too heauy, nor *Plautus*
> too light, for the law of Writ, and the Liberty. These are
> the onely men.

FIGURE 1.1 *William Shakespeare,* Hamlet, *in* Mr. William Shakespeares Comedies, Histories, & Tragedies *(London, Isaac Jaggard and Edward Blount, 1623), sig. oo4r. The John Work Garrett Library, Sheridan Libraries, Johns Hopkins University.*

Following the first interruption, the Folio prints the third and fourth speeches as complete with full stops, and all subsequent editions agree with this choice; however, the fifth and sixth speeches of this passage provide significant disagreement, which creates different variations on the power dynamic between Polonius and Hamlet. The punctuation helps to answer the question of which character controls the exchange, and the alternative texts give differing responses. The first speech is Polonius's 'Upon mine honour' in response to Hamlet's buzzing. In F1, Polonius's line is a full stopped statement. His line then is an objection to Hamlet's onomatopoeia. It is an oath he says because Hamlet does not take him seriously. If the speech ends in a full stop, Polonius completes his thought, even if it is one of exasperation. However, beginning with Nicolas Rowe in 1709, some editions have ended Polonius's

> Hamlet, *Prince of* Denmark. 2403
>
> *Ham.* I will Prophesie, he comes to tell me of the Players. Mark it, you say right, Sir ; for on *Monday* Morning 'twas so indeed.
> *Pol.* My Lord, I have News to tell you.
> *Ham.* My Lord, I have News to tell you,
> When *Roscius* was an Actor in *Rome* ———
> *Pol.* The Actors are come hither, my Lord.
> *Ham.* Buzze, buzze.
> *Pol.* Upon mine Honour ———
> *Ham.* Then came each Actor on his Ass ———
> *Pol.* The best Actors in the World, either for Tragedy, Comedy, History, Pastoral, Pastorical-Comical-Historical-Pastoral, Tragical-Historical, Tragical-Comical-Historical-Pastoral, Scene undividable, or Poem unlimited. *Seneca* cannot be too heavy, nor *Plautus* too light, for the law of Wit, and the Liberty. These are the only Men.

FIGURE 1.2 *William Shakespeare*. Hamlet, *in* The Works of Mr. William Shakespear, *ed. Rowe (London, Jacob Tonson, 1709), Volume 5, sig. Y6r, p. 2403. George Peabody Library, The Sheridan Libraries, Johns Hopkins University.*

line with a dash,[18] signalling interruption (see Figure 1.2). In this reading, Polonius is about to deliver further information about the arrival of the actors beginning with a mild oath but is prevented from doing so, as Hamlet ruptures the upcoming speech with a quip. Here, Hamlet asserts a prerogative to control the conversation by not allowing Polonius to continue his information. Instead of Polonius completing a mild oath of exasperation over Hamlet's inattention, Hamlet is in charge. With this interruption, we then might see how the power shifts back and forth between the two characters from Polonius's initial interruption to Hamlet's reassertion of his primacy in the conversation. While this is a quick passage, the dynamic fluctuations of power are significant between the characters.

Hamlet's rupture and continuation lead to the final speech and its contested punctuation, where both F1 and Rowe provide a dash, while modern editors such as John Jowett in the *New Oxford Shakespeare* do not. The reading of F1 with full stop for Polonius's line and dash for Hamlet best makes sense through its unique wording where Hamlet says, 'Then *can* each Actor on his Asse—' (emphasis mine). The Folio's verb 'can' provides a clearer logic for its adoption of the dash as it opens up the possibilities of what the actors 'can' do: a possibility that is not completed when Polonius interrupts. Polonius then precludes Hamlet from describing what the actors can do upon their respective asses. As in the first interruption, Polonius asserts power in the situation through his determination to deliver information and ignore Hamlet's tangential utterances. Rowe is the first edition after F1 to go back to the Q2 reading 'came', which loses the interruptive clarity. In fact, the *New Oxford Shakespeare* (edited from the Q2 text, so using 'came') adopts a full stop there, insinuating that if the actors come 'upon' Polonius's 'honour' then they came upon their asses as Polonius has no honour. It appears as follows:

> POLONIUS: My lord, I have news to tell you.
> HAMLET: My lord, I have news to tell you: when Roscius was an actor in Rome–
> POLONIUS: The actors are come hither, my lord.
> HAMLET: Buzz, buzz.
> POLONIUS: Upon mine honour–
> HAMLET: Then came each actor on his ass.
> POLONIUS: The best actors in the world . . .[19]

Hamlet's line then is the rupture and continuation that uses a barb to end the exchange. In this reading, Hamlet has the final word in crafting a critique of Polonius, using his interruptions and his ability to complete his thoughts to wield his conversational power.

This short passage from *Hamlet* illustrates the complex issues at stake within punctuation, interruptions, and the power relationships between characters. The first exchange between the characters is clear in its interruptive scheme. Polonius asserts a premise and completes the idea in it. Hamlet begins his own premise, but before he can complete it, Polonius ruptures Hamlet's premise to return to his original premise, and he then completes the second thought in the premise. The second exchange is less clear, which leads to problems with the punctuation. Hamlet's response to Polonius's completion of his second thought is not an interruption, nor does it clearly add to the conversation. His onomatopoeia has no clear interpretation, which makes the next exchange also unclear in its initial premise. Either Polonius responds to Hamlet's sounds with a mild oath brought to completion, which evokes a further elaboration from Hamlet that either is or is not interrupted again by Polonius. Or, Hamlet's sounds prompt Polonius into a second premise, which Hamlet ruptures with a complex language joke that Polonius ignores, denying the rupture any continuation and completing his own premise. The Folio text with its two interruptions, both instigated by Polonius, paints him as a rude disrupter always trying to gain power over those who obfuscate his purposes, namely Hamlet. Rowe's text with three interruptions demonstrates two men who are vying with each other to continue disparate premises. Finally, Jowett's punctuation in the *New Oxford* with two interruptions, one by Polonius and one by Hamlet, has Hamlet potentially correct Polonius's rude microinterruption, re-establish hierarchy, and stop Polonius from further rude interruptions. No matter the punctuation, investigating these interruptions establishes that the quality of the relationship between Hamlet and Polonius is at stake in this brief exchange.

While modern texts most often uses a dash for interruptive pointing, and modern editions of earlier texts use it as the preferred pointing to indicate the moment of rupture, the example from *Hamlet* demonstrates that this cannot be the only approach to examining interruptions within a text.[20] Dashes are a guide only and demonstrate an author's, compositor's, printer's, publisher's, or scribe's sense of interruption within the dialogue, but they do not account for all microinterruptions within a text. Beyond punctuation, the readers, audience members, and editors must use grammar and context to further distinguish moments within texts that are interruptive. Again, the early texts of Hamlet (Q1 and Q2) use full stops for Polonius's first interruption of Hamlet, though the moment, as confirmed through later editions, is clearly interruptive. Any examination of microinterruptions necessitates combining an examination of the original texts and their punctuation with a further consideration of the dialogue to see if moments not marked with dashes contain microinterruptions.

Microinterruptive texts

Volpone, *The Tempest*, and *The Humorous Lieutenant* are all plays that invest in the intensive use of dialogic microinterruptions. Table 1.1 offers a breakdown of interruptions across the three plays. The table significantly illustrates how Jonson and Fletcher invested their texts with more microinterruptions than Shakespeare, both on average and dispersed across the scenes of these plays. While Shakespeare's play has interruptions and significant ones at that, he as a writer seems much less interested in either indicating microinterruptions or writing them into dialogue. While interruption may be 'the key to dramatic originality in *The Tempest*',[21] Jonson and Fletcher are more originally and engagingly interruptive playwrights. Jonson and Fletcher have a strong investment in employing the dialogic structure of the microinterruption within their texts. Perhaps this alertness to the way that dialogue may overlap led Dryden to his assertion that Fletcher 'understood and imitated the conversation of gentlemen much better' than Shakespeare or Jonson.[22] What follows is a further elaboration of the numbers of microinterruptions found within each individual text. Through the explication of the numbers and details therein, I aim to demonstrate the relation of each text to the other texts.

Jonson's *Volpone* (1606) is the earliest of the three plays and is overall the most interruptive as evidenced by number, average, and scenic distribution. The play exists in two important early editions, the Quarto published in 1607 by Thomas Thorpe (Q1) and the Folio published in Jonson's *Works* of 1616 by William Stansby (F1); both provide a good text full of dashes and interruptions. While some have argued for the primacy of the Folio over the Quarto, Richard Dutton through his analysis of exclamation marks and dashes has demonstrated that the groupings found within the changes between the versions cannot clearly demonstrate authorial intervention.[23] He concludes, 'in the great majority of changes between Q1 and F1 it is impossible finally to say whether the printer or Jonson was responsible.'[24] Therefore, we should look to the dashes in both texts before looking for the interruptions that are indicated through other pointing. The Q1 text contains 186 dashes that indicate interrupted speech; the F1 text, which eliminates some but adds others, contains 189 interruptive dashes.[25] However, several microinterruptions

Table 1.1 A Comparison of the Microinterruptions in Volpone, The Tempest, *and* The Humorous Lieutenant

	Volpone	*The Tempest*	*The Humorous Lieutenant*
Total Interruptions	255	75	158
Lines/Interruption	12	26	17
Average # of Interrupt./Scene	6.5	8.4	5.8
Median # of Interrupt./Scene	5	5.5	7
Line Count	3037	1977	2648
Most Interrupt. in a Scene: # (Scene, Rate of Lines/Interrupt.)	35 (3.7, 8)	32 (2.1, 10)	20 (1.1, 19)
Lowest number Lines/Interrupt.: # (Scene)	4 (5.10)	10 (2.1)	4 (2.5)
# of Scenes without interruptions	9	1	5
Dialogue interruptions: # (% of total)	161 (63%)	28 (37%)	121 (77%)
Action interruptions: # (% of total)	12 (5%)	2 (3%)	8 (5%)
Self-interruptions: # (% of total)	82 (32%)	45 (60%)	29 (18%)
Most interrupted character: Name # (% of total)	Mosca 60 (34%)	Gonzalo 13 (42%)	Celia 24 (20%)
Most interrupting character: Name # (% of total)	Volpone 34 (20%)	Sebastian 10 (32%)	Leontius 24 (20%)
Most self-interruptive character: Name # (% of total)	Mosca 25 (30%)	Prospero 17 (38%)	Leontius 9 (31%)
Character involved in most interruptions	Mosca 109 (43%)	Prospero 21 (28%)	Leontius 51 (32%)

(especially self-interruptions) are not punctuated with dashes. The text upon examination possesses 255 microinterruptions, which means that there is an average of seven microinterruptions per scene or one microinterruption for every twelve lines of dialogue.[26] The play contains nine scenes without any interruptions, and *Act Three*, Scene Seven has the most interruptions for any single scene (thirty-five). However, *Act Five*, Scene Ten and *Act Five*, Scene Three have the highest rates of interruptions, with four lines per interruption and five lines per interruption respectively.[27] These numbers lay out the various ways in which Jonson's text is interruptive through its intensity of deployment and scenic distribution.

Shakespeare's *The Tempest* (1611) is the next chronologically, and while it demonstrates a high rate of usage for Shakespeare, it is the least interruptive of the three plays. The original text, unlike Jonson's, does not give much guidance to the number of interruptions found within the play. As stated earlier, the play was first printed in the 1623 Folio but had only one dash in that text, and while interruptive to a reader, that dash only reflects Crane's typical use of dashes in connection to stage directions.[28] The dialogue of the play, however, indicates seventy-five, significantly less than *Volpone*. However, with fewer scenes and fewer lines, *The Tempest* becomes more like *Volpone* with an average of eight interruptions per scene and an overall rate of twenty-six lines per interruption. The most interruptive scene is *Act Two*, Scene One, which has thirty-seven interruptions and a rate of eight lines per interruption, both of which are significant compared to the numbers for the whole play.

The final play chronologically is Fletcher's *The Humorous Lieutenant* (1619). As printed in the B&F F1, it has 115 dashes that indicate interrupted speech, the most of any play in that collection and possessing more than *The Tempest* but fewer than *Volpone*. The average number of microinterruptive dashes found in Fletcher's other solo-authored plays in the Folio text is fifty-two, meaning that *The Humorous Lieutenant* uses over double the average number of dash-indicated microinterruptions. The dialogue, as grammar and situations indicate, contains another forty interruptions marked with various pointing, which means the B&F F1 text alone has 155 interruptions, which is double the number found in *The Tempest*. Fletcher's play, however, also exists in another early version, a manuscript by Ralph Crane from 1625 (MS). The MS includes four interruptions without dashes in dialogue not found within B&F F1, and two interruptive dashes in similar dialogue, which is an unusual piece of Crane punctuation. These numbers add up to a maximal text that contains 159 dialogue-level interruptions, or one interruption for every seventeen lines of text.[29] The play averages six interruptions per scene and has five scenes without any microinterruptions. *Act One*, Scene One has the most interruptions in a single scene with twenty, but *Act Two*, Scene Five, and *Act Four*, Scene Six, have the highest rate of interruptions with the lowest number of lines per interruption: four and five, respectively.

This breakdown illuminates these plays in two ways. Firstly, it indicates that these texts invest in an approach to examining shifts in power relationships between characters at specific moments. Through their investigation of the social relations of the characters and their interruptive dialogue amid those negotiations, all three plays illustrate a ruptured interpellative process of identity formation. Secondly, it points towards an auricular world in which grammatical completeness becomes rarified. The audience of these plays would experience language not as a logical or complete whole but rather through broken, ruptured phrases that intermingle through the dialogue's interruptive construction. Both of these aspects are most apparent in the scenes with the lowest number of lines per interruption, where the audience becomes bombarded with characters interrupting each other. These similar scenes ultimately demonstrate the playwright's differing usages of microinterruptions and their investments within power dynamics among characters.

Volpone: *Act Five*, Scene Three

Act Five, Scene Three of *Volpone* dramatizes the moment when the inheritors discover that Mosca has been made Volpone's heir after Volpone fakes his death. It brings the play back to the original problem in *Act One*, when the audience first met this same parade of would-be inheritors. In *Act Five*, the audience watches their final rebuffing at the hands of the servant that they all assumed was working for them. Jonson balances the structure of the scene as the characters enter one at a time to find Mosca itemizing the horde of gold and jewels and stuff. Each one is certain of their personal gain only to have Mosca ignore them. Once the wannabe inheritors get Mosca's attention, he personally rebuffs each in the order of their appearance, and does so by highlighting their own indiscretion. While the final half of the scene has some significant manipulations of self-interruptions as Mosca mocks Voltore, the first half of the scene develops a Jonsonian rhythm of dialogic microinterruptions that illustrates his own sense of the power game that plays out through dialogue. Jonson, unlike either Fletcher or Shakespeare, locates the power of the scene and the controlling identity in the interrupted servant. This scene then demonstrates the manner in which power is invested and maintained within the speaker of the premise despite the several attempts of the rupturers to claim their own ascendancy. Therefore, Jonson demonstrates the subversive potential for power within the seemingly subjugated.

The beginning of this scene lays out the structural dynamic with which Jonson imbues his microinterruptions. As stated earlier, this scene has a two-action layering that structures the initial premise: Mosca is itemizing his inheritance, while Voltore, Corbaccio, Corvino, and Lady Would-Be each try to interrupt that action. The scene begins with Voltore's entrance, and he immediately interrupts Mosca's counting:

VOLTORE: How now, my Mosca?
MOSCA: [*Writing*]   'Turkey carpets, nine—'
VOLTORE: Taking an inventory? That is well.

(5.3.1-2)[30]

The first exchange demonstrates the dynamic between the two characters quite insightfully. Voltore enters and asks a clear question of the erstwhile servant. Mosca, however, completely ignores the question and continues his work, which prompts Voltore's first rupture. In this rupture, he attempts to get Mosca's attention by halting Mosca's progress, thereby controlling the situation. He does this in a self-centred manner by aligning his interests with Mosca's, assuming that their interests are the same. Voltore acts as if Mosca's choice to ignore Voltore is on Voltore's behalf, and, therefore, despite its potential rudeness, Mosca's lack of acknowledgment is still commendable or 'well'. This set-up allows for the audience to begin their ridicule (in this scene at least) over the narcissistic lawyer, who attempts to rewrite a situation in a manner that best serves himself.

The microinterruption demonstrates the self-focused nature of the interrupter. Mosca's choice to not allow the rupture to overtake the premise illustrates Mosca's power in the scene. Furthermore, it might be considered a turning point for the character. Mosca is the most interrupted character in the play, and while the earlier interruptions all play into his subservient position compared to the other characters, here his control of the continuation demonstrates the alteration in the power dynamics. This understanding holds true even if we consider Mosca's earlier subservience as an act, because this moment too is another part of Mosca's play. The intuited layers of the action and the character make Mosca's investment in microinterruptions part of the play's delight in this form.

The second microinterruption follows the first by reiterating both Mosca's continuation, now as a premise again, and Voltore's rupture, though this time more forceful, leading towards the final ridicule. Voltore again asks a question in his rupture, but is not answered:

MOSCA: 'Two suits of bedding, tissue—'
VOLTORE: Where's the will?
        Let me read that the while.

(5.3.3-4)

The premise and rupture are the same, but the continuation here is less assured as he asks for the will. His desire to verify what he has assumed indicates a slight shift in the power relationship, but the overall relationship does not change as Mosca does not hand over the will until line 14 after everyone has arrived. The dynamic that these first two interruptions establish—Mosca itemizing, inheritor ruptures, Mosca ignores—creates a patterned foundation for the subsequent interruptions, one by Corbaccio and another by Voltore. All of these four initial microinterruptions in the scene demonstrate the shifting power dynamics of the play as it hurtles towards its conclusion. The inheritors perceive success and read their success into the lack of acknowledgment, while the lack of acknowledgment plays out the power dynamic that readers and audience members understand from their knowledge of the trick.

The fifth microinterruption in the scene, while seeming to be different, also mimics this dynamic and demonstrates a larger methodology for Jonson's use of interruptions. Mosca continues to itemize; however, this time Volpone interrupts:

MOSCA: 'Eight chests of linen—'
VOLPONE: [Aside]   Oh.
    My fine Dame Would-be, too!

(5.3.11-12)

Volpone interrupts Mosca from his position as onlooker, commenting on the action and interrupting his servant's counting. However, as an aside, this moment is not an interruption for the characters on stage but is so only for the readers and audience members. The characters cannot hear Volpone, and so the power dynamics for those within the scene are not altered. But, for those reading or watching the scene, a clear power dynamic emerges as we perceive Volpone reading the situation similarly to Voltore and the others. Volpone tries to examine another facet of the trick, commenting upon Lady Would-Be's arrival. However, it is not her but Corvino that speaks next, indicating that Volpone's rupture, even for the outside reader/spectator, does not colour the continuation at all. His power has diminished now that he has signed Mosca over as heir, but Volpone does not perceive this diminishment. Without knowing it, he is just like the other would-be inheritors. By having Volpone interrupt part of the cataloguing just like Voltore and Corbaccio, Jonson hints at the way in which the play will conclude: with Mosca tricking Volpone.

The next two interruptions further play out the manner in which the Volpone/Mosca power dynamic becomes central to the microinterruptive structure of the scene. After Mosca hands over the will, the scene continues:

CORBACCIO: Is that the will?
MOSCA: 'Down-beds and bolsters—'
VOLPONE: [Aside]   Rare!
    Be busy still. Now they begin to flutter;
    They never think of me. Look, see, see, see!
    How their swift eyes run over the long deed
    Unto the name, and to the legacies,
    What is bequeathed them, there—
MOSCA: 'Ten suits of hangings—'

(5.3.15-20)

The first microinterruption here, like the earlier one by Volpone, is of an on-looking Volpone interrupting the cataloging Mosca to direct the attention of the audience. The directional language here is apparent and forceful, especially as only the audience members can perceive it. Volpone tells us what to look at, what we should notice, even having the thrice iterated command of 'see' end with an exclamation mark.[31] The excited Volpone has interrupted his servant and delivers a speech to control the perceptions of the audience.

This speech ends with the first time that Mosca interrupts another character in this scene, and it does so in an odd manner. The dash clearly indicates that a microinterruption occurs; however, Volpone's grammatical sense is complete in a way that could almost insinuate no interruption. Furthermore, if Volpone is completely aside, there is no way for Mosca to know that he is interrupting his master's enjoyment of the inheritors reading the new will. This dash though is clear in both texts, and as Jonson was 'unusually alert to print's symbolic possibilities',[32] this indication of interruption is important for a reader as well as an audience member. If this moment is to be interruptive, it works in two potential ways. One possibility for the rupture is that Volpone's aside is not so complete, as we will see with Antonio and Sebastian, in that Mosca overhears or perceives his master. In this reading/performance, Mosca as a character clearly and overtly makes a move to wrest power from the gloating Volpone, refocusing the scene on himself and on his new-found wealth. This version demonstrates a more conniving Mosca, who is aware of his situation. It is a Mosca who wields power in ways that work towards asserting his own ascendancy. The other possibility is that Mosca does not hear Volpone, but, as with Volpone's previous asides, Mosca ruptures his master's speech in a way imperceptible to him but clear to both an audience and, with the dash, a reader. In this presentation, Mosca does not perceive the power transfer embedded within the dialogue, but Jonson presents it in a way for interpreters to perceive the shifting balances of power within the scene. Even in this version, Volpone would be aware of Mosca's rupture as he cedes speaking rights to his servant. What both approaches demonstrate is Jonson's use of microinterruptions to change the power dynamic of the play, to illustrate the way in which Mosca employs language and performance to his personal ends that are ultimately different from Volpone's. In this way,

Jonson's punctuation 'is congruent on a micro level to construction of the plots on a macro level'.[33] This structure foreshadows the conclusion of the play when Mosca forces Volpone to give him significant portions of his wealth.

Throughout this scene and the shifting power structures, Jonson crafts a dynamic that inverts the understood power structures of the play and of the interruptive schema. While the rest of the play dramatizes an interrupted Mosca, whom the other characters seemingly overpower, in this scene that relationship becomes itself interrupted: now, Mosca's being interrupted, or the repeated effort to interrupt him, is a sign of his power and control. This scene's dialogue then renders the previous scenes anew as the character relationships differ and the game for dominance once more inverts. So too, we can see here a radically different approach to power dynamics than we will see in either Shakespeare or Fletcher. Jonson's interruptee possesses the greatest amount of power and constructs his identity paradoxically through his seeming lack of power. While Fletcher will also have the interrupters attempt to control the identity of the interruptee, his scene ends with a reification of the community, whereas Jonson's scene revels in its disrupted revelation of inverted power, destroying the interrupters' assumptions. This inversion portrays a contrasting approach that defies communal interpellation of identity from the interrupter or hierarchical moral schemas. Jonson's power resides within those that least seem to wield it.

The Tempest: *Act Two*, Scene One

Unlike Jonson's inversion of power, Shakespeare's microinterruptions in *The Tempest* characterize Antonio and Sebastian, solidifying a moral hierarchy. In *The Tempest*, when Gonzalo tries to console the grieving Alonso, Antonio and Sebastian mock the older man's statements through a series of interruptions. Lynne Magnusson concludes that Sebastian and Antonio's 'comments attack every mode of discourse that satisfies the mind's inclination to accept whatever conforms to its uncritical longings for coherence, intelligibility, idealization'.[34] Her striking analysis connects this interruptive move to Prospero's own self-interruptions, but here I would like to spend more time unfolding her assertions by further exploring the interruptions in this scene, illustrating how Shakespeare approaches the power dynamic by isolating his villains. Shakespeare invests in the competitive nature of dialogic microinterruption by pushing Sebastian/Antonio to the margin as disruptive agents.

Unlike scenes where grammatically incomplete sentences and dashes attest to the presence of microinterruptions, Shakespeare's scene contains no dashes in the early text and few moments of incomplete grammar; therefore, the number of interruptions present in the scene becomes debatable. In the first 100 lines, ignoring the two self-interruptions, Rory Loughnane, the editor of the play for *The New Oxford Shakespeare*, indicates only eight dialogic microinterruptions.[35] In the Folio text, all of the speeches in this segment conclude with either a full stop, a question mark, or an exclamation point, except for three speeches that have no concluding punctuation. It appears as such with the lines in bold that have no terminal pointing:

> *Gon:* **Well, I haue done: But yet**
> Seb: He will be talking.
> Ant: Which, of he, or Adrian, for a good wager,
>   First begins to crow?
> Seb: The old Cocke.
> Ant: The Cockrell.
> Seb: Done: The wager?
> Ant: A Laughter.
> Seb: A match.
> Adr: Though this Island seeme to be desert.
> Seb: Ha, ha, ha.
> Ant: So: you'r paid.
> Adr: Vninhabitable, and almost inaccessible.
> *Seb:* **Yet**
> *Adr:* **Yet**
> Ant: He could not misse't.[36]

As those moments are interruptive, one might argue that those are the only microinterruptions indicated by the Folio, creating an even more conservative number than Loughnane.[37] Conversely, considering both the context of the scene and the structural relationship between the two groups of courtiers, one might arrive at a maximal number of twenty-one microinterruptions within these first 100 lines.[38] The scene, therefore, has a total of three, eight, twenty-one, or some other in-between number of microinterruptions.[39]

Shakespeare begins the scene with an interruption, and he uses that form to demonstrate a moralizing schema of good and evil in the play. Like the scenes by Fletcher and Jonson, Shakespeare's scene functions on two levels: one group is involved in one action, while another group interrupts that action. In this first plane of action, Gonzalo and Adrian attempt to console the grieving Alonso, and in the second plane Sebastian and Antonio mock those attempts. The interactions between these two planes create the series of microinterruptions that drives the scene, which ultimately illustrates Shakespeare's investment in highlighting the separateness of the characters. Antonio and Sebastian's dialogic ruptures indicate their desire to rupture larger structures (such as their later contemplation of regicide), and so allow the audience to consider the natures of these men. The ostensibly good characters in the scene do not interrupt each other and rather are the victims of the sarcastic interference of the villainous duo. While this analysis may seem reductively to reiterate Coleridge's assertion that the scene shows 'the tendency of bad men',[40] an interruptive analysis that uses a formal reading of the characters and the power dynamics implicit in their interruptions demonstrates how Shakespeare builds up Coleridge's observations. Furthermore, this scene with its intensity of interruptions illustrates more broadly Shakespeare's use of microinterruptions.

The first microinterruption of the sequence exemplifies the typical microinterruption in this series by demonstrating the power relationships inherent in the form. The rudeness, the boldness, or the subtlety of Sebastian becomes encoded within the presentation and the performance of this moment as are the obliviousness, the dotage, or the insistence of Gonzalo. After Sebastian notes that Gonzalo will continue trying to console Alonso, the old courtier speaks up, but only manages to get out, 'Sir—' before Sebastian ruptures with, 'One. Tell' (2.1.17). Before Gonzalo can even begin to create sense out of his statement, Sebastian halts the forward progression to highlight his own accuracy in assessing the situation. He counts the word as if it is a strike on a clock. The power dynamic, however, depends specifically upon an edition or a performance. To begin at one extreme, David Bevington's edition of Sebastian's interruption employs the dash to indicate the rupture but then precedes Sebastian's line with the emendation: '[*aside to*

Antonio]'.⁴¹ By instructing a reader to see the line as completely aside to Antonio, Bevington erases most of the power dynamic invested in the microinterruption as Gonzalo is only interrupted for an audience or reader. This aside means that Gonzalo does not perceive the rupture and that the pause for Sebastian to speak is only his own self-interruption as he prepares to continue addressing Alonso. The Arden edition by Virginia Mason Vaughn and Alden T. Vaughn offers the other extreme by giving no added stage direction (2.1.17). This choice allows readers to see the moment where Sebastian wrests speaking privilege from Gonzalo, demonstrating his sense of power over the older courtier. In this version, which contains multiple potentialities, Gonzalo hears his interrupter and must account for Sebastian's commentary before continuing. This account means that Sebastian's rupture colours Gonzalo's continuation. In Bevington's polite version, Gonzalo is ostensibly not interrupted and his continuation has no inclination of any rupture as his premise continued as he expected.

The New Oxford Shakespeare demonstrates a middle way that clarifies addressee while leaving the question of the power relationship more open than in crafting an aside. Loughnane adds the stage direction '[*to Antonio*]' before Sebastian's rupture.⁴² This stage direction without the indication of aside, which would exclude Gonzalo, clarifies that Sebastian intends to address Antonio, but acknowledges that the two are participating within the larger scope of the scene. How much Gonzalo hears or does not hear is up to a reader's imagination or a performance's choice. This iteration demonstrates a subtle Sebastian willing to defy but doing so more indirectly. Gonzalo must account for this rupture as he can potentially hear it, but he can ignore it as well. Interestingly, Loughnane alters Gonzalo's continuation through two unique emendations: a stage direction and a dash. When Gonzalo begins his next speech, the *NOS* text reads first '[*to Alonso*]' and then starts the dialogue with a dash and a lower case 'w': '—when every grief is entertained'.⁴³ In this version, the speech continues as unaffected by the rupture as possible with a firm reconnection to the addressee and a textual indicator of its connection to the previous speech. While Loughnane's stage direction for Sebastian opens up the possibility for Gonzalo's reaction, his choices surrounding Gonzalo's line limit those and direct the continuation to assert Gonzalo's control, asserting a new premise. As with the choice of punctuation then, editor's choices about stage directions influence a text's presentation of interruptions in a way that can alter the potentialities of that text.[44]

One final possibility to be considered here is a theatrical one. T. W. Craik has offered that Sebastian's line 'Tell.' should be considered as an imperative mood stage direction, meaning that the word is a direction for the actor playing Sebastian to 'tell' or keep counting.[45] If Craik is right, the moment becomes more complicatedly interruptive as Sebastian repeatedly interrupts Gonzalo by continuing to count. This stage direction would mean that the scene would continue with a further series of interruptions as Gonzalo could barely speak without Sebastian indicating for how long he had spoken. This stage direction would seemingly cease when Sebastian wittily quips 'A dollar', indicating that he has ceased counting and is now trying a new approach. Reading 'Tell.' as a stage direction for continued action would not only increase the interruptions, it would make it more akin to Jonson's Praeludium to *Cynthia's Revels*.[46] No edition or performance that I am aware of has adopted this approach; however, the possibility of it remains in the text, and it accords with the dynamics within the rest of the scene. Allowing Sebastian to continue to interrupt and count during Gonzalo's short two lines would only further characterize him as being outside the central discourse of the scene proper as each number would be as unsuccessful in altering the course of the scene as the last. However, it would possibly disrupt the communication of Gonzalo's meaning as the continued vocalizations would break open Gonzalo's statement and separate the words from their syntactical structure. Both in its intense disruptive possibility and in its lack of efficacy, the reading of 'Tell.' as a stage direction intensifies the function of the other interruptions within this scene.

The importance of the first interruption's status as aside or not becomes even more significant in light of the second interruption. Gonzalo continues:

GONZALO: When every grief is entertained that's
   offered, comes to th'entertainer—
SEBASTIAN: A dollar.
GONZALO: Dolour comes to him indeed. You have
   spoken truer than you purposed.
                                                    (2.1.18-22)

Unlike the first microinterruption, which demonstrates the problems of interruptions and encodes various amounts of potential information about Sebastian and Gonzalo, the second interruption presents a clear continuation. Sebastian's rupture here is spoken to the entire on-stage audience. Instead of inserting a sarcastic side comment, he attempts to wrest sense and meaning from Gonzalo's statement. Sebastian's rupture creates its own continuation by concluding Gonzalo's sentiment in a comedic way through punning on the meaning of 'th'entertainer'. However, Gonzalo's continuation expertly demonstrates his own wit as well as his control. He changes the monetary joke into a rectified version of his own continuation that furthers the pun and completes his sense, concluding his line by even acknowledging the rupture. In such an acknowledgment, Gonzalo demonstrates his control of the situation by returning to the premise and altering the rupture to meld it into his original sense. So too, his explicit comment on the rupture demonstrates his ability to navigate the derision leveled at him by Sebastian.

In both this moment and the first, Shakespeare highlights Sebastian as an agent of derailment, attempting to control the language of the situation and to deride the older courtier. However, Gonzalo's navigation of these ruptures demonstrates a containment of the rupture and an ability of the premise to survive such impingements. The next five interruptions (lines 25, 28, 37, 40, and 42) all follow similar articulations, further demonstrating the failed attempts to control the scene by Sebastian and Antonio. In fact, the men even create a game of interrupting Adrian and Gonzalo, anticipating both new premises and necessitating further ruptures, none of which succeed in altering the course of the conversation.

After line 42, most modern texts indicate only one more dialogic microinterruption before Alonso's speech at line 108. However, considering that either Sebastian or Antonio rupture the first seven times that either Gonzalo or Adrian attempt to speak, one might infer that the fourteen subsequent speeches where Sebastian or Antonio speak directly after Gonzalo or Adrian should be also considered as interruptions. For example, consider the following exchange:

ADRIAN: It must needs be of subtle, tender, and delicate temperance.
ANTONIO: Temperance was a delicate wench.

SEBASTIAN: Ay, and a subtle, as he most learnedly delivered.
ADRIAN: The air breathes upon us here most sweetly.
SEBASTIAN: As if it had lungs, and rotten ones.
(2.1.44-50)

No modern editor ends either of Adrian's lines here with a dash to indicate interruption, which can be justified through grammatical sense. Adrian has completed his thought; therefore, unlike the earlier lines in the scene, these are not so obviously interruptive. However, the form of the scene overall allows for a different reading in which these lines are not complete. In fact, all of the same complications figured into the earlier exchanges are extant in these exchanges too.[47] Looking at the sequence as presented earlier demonstrates the clearly interruptive manner of the speeches. Adrian has not finished his thoughts in line 45 and so continues to describe the island in line 49, but in both instances he only gets out one sentence before first Antonio and then Sebastian stop him from further description through their desire to comment. This structure is interruptive even if the grammar is complete; therefore, the rest of this sequence should indicate that when Antonio or Sebastian speak after Gonzalo or Adrian that is an interruption. They attempt to wrest the scene from the other courtiers and recolour the description of the island in their own perception. They insist upon the superiority of their point of view and continue trying to assert their own prerogative.

A reading of this scene as such, perhaps in an edition with dashes at all such moments, indicates the profusion of interruptions within the first 100 lines of the scene. Furthermore, while highlighting the many and frequent attempts to grab power by the power-hungry courtiers, it would actually demonstrate the way in which their attempts to wrest power from Gonzalo and Adrian are ultimately impotent. Their sarcastic descriptions and destructive analyses are ineffective: Gonzalo continues to domineer the scene. The first major shift in power occurs when Alonso finally interrupts Gonzalo at line 108, which silences the old courtier for almost thirty lines. The King then is the only character present who truly has power, and Gonzalo's speeches indicate that relationship through a reading of the interruptions. Only when Ariel puts Gonzalo and the others to sleep do Sebastian and Antonio finally have the power to converse as they would like.

This reading illustrates how Shakespeare's sense of power struggles, demonstrated through his extensive use of interruptions, is a hierarchical and competitive one. Such usage leads to characters whose dismissals and ruptures emphasize them as villains. Unlike Jonson's subversive Mosca, Antonio and Sebastian mark out their identities through their interruptions, in a way that ultimately self-interpellates. While their interruptions compete with Gonzalo and might offer audiences two alternatives to assessing the court's situation, the frame of exposition that Prospero constructs around them in the preceding scene already begins to delineate their position. The rude posturing that the interruptions continue leads towards the understanding of their characters as villainous, which emerges completely once the others are asleep and they have the scene to themselves. Importantly, Antonio and Sebastian's many ruptures are impotent as the nexus of power emanates from the hierarchical peak of the King, and perhaps from the author above him. Such a construction forces those who rupture to be outside of the community; the second half of the scene literally isolates them and allows what germinated within their interruptions to sprout into an openly malignant character. Shakespeare, unlike Jonson whose ruptures seem to reveal power but ultimately reveal the opposite, uses ruptures destructively as negative constructs that attempt to destroy a premise. The lack of interruptive success reifies the importance of the premise's unity, leading the audience towards witnessing the interrupters' attempt at regicide that ends the scene.

The Humorous Lieutenant: *Act Four*, Scene Six

While Jonson inverts the power dynamics and Shakespeare hierarchically reifies them, John Fletcher offers another approach in which the interruptions actually build community. In the latter half of *The Humorous Lieutenant*, Fletcher writes his version of an interruptive conversation, like those in *Volpone* and *The Tempest*, where the audience witnesses the eponymous Lieutenant's accidental protestations of love for the King within a public and male space. This play from the beginning dramatizes the interaction of public and private spaces, and this scene in particular demonstrates the breakdown of the Lieutenant's private interior as it erupts into public protestations of love for the King. Leontius's abrasive side commentary repeatedly quashes these protestations. In this way, the issue of power in the play through interruptions becomes central as the Lieutenant's identity is at stake and both Leontius and the Lieutenant vie for supremacy. Admittedly, much of the humour here lies in the homophobic joke that the Lieutenant cannot possibly 'love' the King in the manner that he purports. This joke though further emphasizes the Lieutenant's subjected experience within the power dynamics of this play. In fact, throughout the play, the Lieutenant is deprived of subjective agency and power while those around him, especially Leontius, wield it over him.[48] In this scene, the Lieutenant is once again the subject of mockery, but the power dynamics—through a cohesive use of interruption—do not establish a hierarchical imbalance. The Lieutenant as one of the central characters of the play possesses theatrical power, in that the audience surely likes to watch him, but the play repeatedly, as does this scene, denies him social power and emphasizes his lack of it. Leontius's direct engagement with the Lieutenant creates a scene that while highlighting social power disparities also demonstrates a method of cohesion and care across the imbalances that the interruptions reveal.

 The first interruption is during the Lieutenant's apostrophe to the King and illustrates the power imbalance between the Lieutenant and Leontius. The Lieutenant's premise follows an earlier line about his love for the King, but he does not get far before Leontius ruptures him:

LIEUTENANT: O never King—
LEONTIUS: By this hand, when I consider—
LIEUTENANT: My honest friend, you are a little sawcy.[49]

The Lieutenant attempts to express his devotion for the King, but Leontius stops him, an action that their entrance prefigures.[50] Leontius's rupture achieves its end in that the Lieutenant's continuation becomes itself a rupture for Leontius's rupture, which has then become a new premise as he intends to explicate what he now sees. Leontius's original rupture does not achieve its larger goal of returning the Lieutenant to his former self or reminding him of 'the wars' (4.6.1), and the Lieutenant's rupture only functions momentarily as the continuation allows the first Gentleman to comment, 'I told you you would have it' (4.6.10). These first two interruptions and their cascading interrelationship demonstrate the soldiers' combative communication. Even as the Lieutenant attempts to avoid Leontius in order to extol his love for the King, he participates in the dialogue through his interruption, asserting a sense of his own power within the situation. The Lieutenant oversteps his bounds by cutting off his superior, though with a kind word. Such an epithet—'my honest friend'—even if slightly sarcastic highlights how the Lieutenant has stepped beyond his bounds in rupturing the premise of a superior. The two quick interruptions highlight the combative nature not only of the soldiers within this scene but also of microinterruptions more generally.

Leontius tries to divert the Lieutenant from his growing humiliation in delivering all the subsequent microinterruptions, which underscores his regained control of the situation. In fact, the series of four ruptures demonstrates four differing approaches to dialogic microinterruptions and transforms the power battle into a constructive and unifying space. The first of these ruptures immediately follows the aforementioned dialogue, and is an attempt to continue the premise:

LIEUTENANT: When mine owne worth—
LEONTIUS: Is flung into the ballance, and found nothing.
(4.6.10-11)

Leontius grammatically completes the premise, but in doing so he invites mockery by transforming the premise into a joke, echoing Sebastian's approach in *The Tempest*. By seeming to create unity through grammatical sense, the rupture paradoxically produces less unity, though perhaps produces more comedy. Leontius does not allow the Lieutenant's behaviour to complete, but through verbally interrupting the praise for the King, he asserts dominance to control the situation. The second rupture offers another approach as it clones the syntax to echo the premise in a mocking way:

LIEUTENANT: And yet a souldier—
LEONTIUS: And yet a scurvy one.
(4.6.12)

Leontius's isocolonic rupture parallels the syntax, creating a coherency alongside the original while using that syntactic similarity to highlight his intention to mock the speaker. Unlike the previous rupture, this parallel rupture allows for some continuation as it does not complete the premise but recolours it within its own terms. This approach as well as the previous one is aimed at the on-stage audience more than at the Lieutenant directly, meaning that the ruptures here are more destructive and mocking than helping. In both of these microinterruptions, Leontius employs syntax—that completes or that echoes—to attempt to regain control of the situation through mocking the Lieutenant. At this point, the scene then follows what Shakespeare constructs in *The Tempest*, but Fletcher changes the dynamics in the subsequent interruptions, while Shakespeare does not.

In the second half of the sequence, Leontius's ruptures begin to work with the Lieutenant and not against him, altering the general's approach. The third rupture neither completes nor echoes; instead, it gives clarification through description:

LIEUTENANT: One that has followed thee—
LEONTIUS: Faire and far off.
                                        (4.6.13)

This exchange moves towards a dialogue in which the two conversants acknowledge each other. It resembles less the combative interruptive monologue structure found previously in this scene and exemplified by Sebastian and Antonio in *The Tempest*. Unlike the first two instances where the rupture recolours the premise in a domineering mode, the third iteration, while still attempting to dominate by not allowing premise completion, demonstrates how Leontius engages the Lieutenant's statement. His clarification ridicules the premise, but it does so by taking the premise seriously and clarifying it through elaboration. To do so, he also turns his attention more fully towards the Lieutenant, making him the audience for the ruptures. In this turn, the dialogue illustrates how Fletcher employs the seemingly destructive microinterruptions to unify his characters, moving them towards cohesion. The final rupture of the sequence shows an explicit alteration that breaks down the dual structure of the scene as Leontius's rupture actually answers the premise:

LIEUTENANT: Fought for thy grace—
LEONTIUS: 'Twas for your griefe, you lye sirha.
                                                    (4.6.14)

With this rupture, Leontius fully engages the Lieutenant through second-person address and closes the dual structure of the scene by unifying the sideline interruption he has been delivering with the Lieutenant's attempts at love poetry. He gets the Lieutenant's direct attention by demonstrating to the Lieutenant his own ridiculousness. The express charge that the Lieutenant has lied, an indication that the Lieutenant has ruptured veracity, makes the Lieutenant leave behind his apostrophe and engage the conversant on stage with him. This admonition from Leontius provokes the Lieutenant because it charges him with an interruption of the truth. Leontius claims that the Lieutenant's presentation of reality is contrary to his own perception; the Lieutenant, therefore, ruptures the expectation that Leontius possesses. The difference in perception that the charge of lying evokes demonstrates the potential interruption of perception that differing points of view entail. In the world of the play, this rupture that emphasizes another rupture engages the Lieutenant to halt his premise and acknowledge Leontius.

Additionally, the shift in Leontius's approach parallels the Lieutenant's own shifting approach as he moves away from descriptions of himself and begins addressing the absent king directly with second-person pronouns. The intensifying personalization increases the necessity for Leontius to break the spell that the Lieutenant is under. The disunity that Leontius tries to create through his belittlement of the Lieutenant's ridiculous love offers an attempt at unifying the Lieutenant to his former self. Ultimately, this destructive interruptive conversation—ending in Leontius's invocation of falsehood, which gets the Lieutenant's attention—demonstrates Fletcher's approach to using dialogic microinterruptions. Fletcher's Leontius is like Gonzalo in his position next to the King; however, Leontius's ability to speak truth to power coupled with his ability to commiserate and unify with those below him illustrate an understanding of a communal distribution of power. His interruptions may interpellate the Lieutenant's identity, as they do throughout the play, but he too is a member of that community, whereas Antonio and Sebastian rupture in a way that marks them as outside of the community.

This scene, even with the Lieutenant's premises being ruptured, demonstrates how characters can use these forms to achieve junction through disjunction. After the Lieutenant exits, Leontius has a short speech in which he comes to understand the Lieutenant's situation. This speech demonstrates Leontius's affection for the Lieutenant despite his mocking tone. In fact, the interruptions might have given the Lieutenant space to save his reputation, as he was not allowed to complete his adoration for the King.[51] The allowance of Leontius to continue interrupting illustrates societal information about his status and his ability to subject those around him through controlling their identities. Through this status-building implementation, the question of dominance emerges. Leontius interrupts more than any other character, and he has more self-interruptions than any other character. This fact means that his character possesses a sense of power that allows him the ability to interrupt the other characters. His continuous interruptions become indicative of his character that boldly ruptures premises. While this may seem like Sebastian or Antonio in *The Tempest*, Leontius's actions support the social structures of the play. His interruptions range from the socially acceptable, as in 4.6, to his frequent attempts to control both the King and the Prince in their passions. His position allows for mobility and connects him to both sides of the plot. He then acts like a Mosca that moves throughout the varied groups; though unlike Jonson's fly, Fletcher's lion uses interruptions to strive for continuation that creates community. Leontius' unstable social identity indicates the play's own interruptive uncertainty about the status of societal identities. Leontius and his interruptions of the Lieutenant create a societal cohesion based upon dominant interpellative ideologies, as adjudicated through Leontius himself. This situation exemplifies Fletcher's convoluted paradoxical situations that he often leaves unresolved.

Conclusion

These three examples demonstrate some of the ways dialogic microinterruptions unveil power structures and characterization within a play. Looking at only three scenes with high rates of interruptions illustrates not only the undergirding structure but also the potential variety of ends that this form facilitates. While Jonson queries the underlying power structures of such relationships and Shakespeare employs them to highlight the antagonism in dialogue, Fletcher brings such disruptive forms into a manner of unity. While dialogic microinterruptions can investigate interruptive structures of power in a game of dominance, as the previous scenes have demonstrated even to their various conclusions, not all such microinterruptions need do so. I end with one final scene from Fletcher, in which he explores another way to craft dialogic microinterruptions. Unlike 4.6, which has Leontius controlling the identity of the Lieutenant, in an earlier scene, Fletcher demonstrates a methodology for interruptions to create community out of the power struggles encapsulated within them.

Act Two, Scene Five of *The Humorous Lieutenant* takes place in a domestic space both governed and peopled by women (unlike the aforementioned scenes) and through its series of interruptions creates a coherency through the power struggle inherent in microinterruptions. In this scene, Leucippe, the bawd, solidifies her plan with the Governess to lure Celia to the court. The first interruption occurs as Leucippe presses the Governess for specific information about the relationship between Demetrius and Celia. After bringing up 'carnall copulation', Leucippe avows that 'we are women,/And may talke thus amongst our selves' (2.5.6,7-8). Despite attempting to create a safe space based upon gender, the Governess resists Leucippe's insistence on being salacious. Her diffidence prompts Leucippe's impatience:

> GOVERNESS: But truly, that I ever knew the gentlewoman
>   Otherwise given, then a hopefull gentlewoman—
> LEUCIPPE: You'll grant me the Prince loves her?

(2.5.10-12)

The premise is the Governess's attempt to illustrate the goodness of Celia. After Leucippe's brash assertion of 'carnall'-ity, the Governess accedes that Celia seems to hope for something better but implies a defense as she refuses to relay details. Such reluctance brings Leucippe to a rupture in which she changes tactics. Leucippe recolours the conversation to allow the Governess to consider the situation from the vantage point of the Prince's actions. The rupture achieves Leucippe's goal as the Governess answers, 'There I am with ye' (2.5.12). By rupturing the Governess's diffident premise, the bawd achieves intimacy with her conversant, thereby gaining access to her knowledge. Leucippe creates a female space that she then ruptures, demonstrating the way such interruptions qualify this type of conversation.

This interruptive sequence invites more interruptions as the next one is Leucippe's self-interruption, quickly followed by the Governess's, which leads into a series of three more. These cascading interruptions create a rhythm moving back and forth between the two women:

> LEUCIPPE: I should think now,
> (Good woman let me have your judgment with me,
> I see 'tis none of the worst: Come sit down by me)
> That these two cannot love so tenderly—
> GOVERNESS: Being so young as they are too—
> LEUCIPPE: You say well—
> But that methinks some further promises—
> GOVERNESS: Yes, yes[. . .]
>
> (2.5.16-22)

Leucippe interrupts herself, the Governess interrupts Leucippe, Leucippe interrupts the Governess, Leucippe interrupts herself again, and finally the Governess interrupts Leucippe.[52] This series condenses several interruptions into one moment. The Governess now feels comfortable enough to interrupt Leucippe, her social superior. Despite the potential faux pas, Leucippe's interruption acknowledges the Governess's, but then she must interrupt her appended praise to move back towards the initial conversation. The back and forth interruptive quality, despite seeming unproductive, leads to the admission about the marriage. In this pattern, Fletcher illustrates how these women use interruptions as a conversational device to create trust and constructively communicate by breaking into each other's speech through acknowledging the other's presence.

What this final scene overall demonstrates is a less-antagonistic model of a sometimes-antagonistic form, and something not found within either Jonson or Shakespeare. Fletcher uses the possibilities within this quotidian form to highlight the way in which everyday people speak, and while not disavowing the power struggle that this form insinuates, his interruptions present that struggle within a productive situation that achieves a sense of community. Reciprocal identity is at stake for both characters and neither fully controls the situation or the other's subject formation. Shakespeare's scene ends with an interrupted murder, and Jonson's with further interruptions of Volpone by Mosca as Volpone unwittingly plots his own downfall, but Fletcher shows a way in which the power struggle lends itself to a unifying goal. Through identifying each other, we all participate actively in the formation of identities within the community. Fletcher transforms the quotidian into the artistic, which is another way of putting Eugene Waith's idea that Fletcher melds the familiar and the remote,[53] and furthermore underscores both Fletcher's ideas about tragicomedy and his affinity for the genre and its interruptive potentialities. His positive outlook then contrasts heavily with his predecessors and ultimately takes a form about rupture and makes it into one of agreement.

2

Self

What is the nature of the self-interruption? Like dialogic interruptions, self-interruptions are micro in scale and possess the same tripartite form. However, the space between premise and rupture is more significant and more marked in self-interruptions than in dialogic microinterruptions. To reiterate from the previous chapter, dialogic microinterruptions consist of a line of dialogue by a character cut short (premise), a line of dialogue by another character (rupture), and a third line of dialogue by either character (continuation). Within this form, the rupture is easily identified, and as the last chapter explored, the relationships between conversants become a central focus. A self-interruption is completely contained, in that only one character is responsible for all three parts. Without having the voice of another character stopping the line of the character, the self-interruptive character must stop their own language; therefore, this stopping requires some sort of change of thought to make the speech suddenly alter, whether with additional information, a clarification, or a brand-new thought. Because of this process, the rupture has an internalized origin that highlights the space between premise and rupture.[1] While dialogic microinterruptions are about power dynamics between characters, self-interruptions are about the creation of inwardness and interiority of a character. As Katharine Maus has stated, 'in a culture in which truth is imagined to be inward and invisible, and in which playwrights seem perversely to insist upon parading the shortcomings of their art, theatrical representation becomes subject to profound and fascinating cries of authenticity.'[2] The self-interruption seems to be one of those cries of authenticity and is one of the 'dramatic techniques' to 'further aggravate the relationship between spectacle and truth'.[3]

The connection of interiority to this form highlights character creation and audience interpretation. Self-interruptions in dramatic literature then are similar to Wolfgang Iser's 'blanks' that function as 'a tacit invitation to find the missing link'.[4] Inviting the audience to perceive the interiority of the character emphasizes the audience or the reader's participation and creation of that interiority itself. The self-interruption, therefore, is a site of such productive interpretive energies, where 'we speculate on the omission, we guess at the contents of the gap'.[5] Self-interruptions are moments that both defy and offer unity in a character. So too, such moments are where the playwrights 'in constructing life [advertise] vacuums which demand filling, which imagination duly fills'.[6] Again, as Iser calls the blank 'a paradigmatic structure',[7] we must see the self-interruption as the most character-driven iteration of such a structure.

To explore briefly, the rich variety of self-interruptive potential and to help point out the interiority of the self-interruptive rupture, I turn once more to *Hamlet*. Hamlet's first soliloquy (Q2 1.2.129-159) demonstrates the methodology for understanding the structure within the complicated presentation of self-interruptions. In the thirty-one lines of this speech, Hamlet could potentially interrupt himself thirteen times. While others may find more or less than I (the Arden third series edition indicates only five with dashes), the speech contains several moments of self-interruption as Hamlet works through his complicated response to his father's death and his mother's marriage. After noting how hasty his mother's marriage was and then describing her as Niobe, Hamlet laments:

>   Why, she—[8]
> O God, a beast that wants discourse of reason
> Would have mourned longer—married with my uncle,
> My father's brother[. . .]
>
>   (1.2.149-52)

Here, the premise is obvious as is the self-interruption. The premise is 'why, she . . . married with my uncle', and the fact that the break occurs between subject and verb makes the rupture and the self-interruption clear. What becomes interesting is the use of the oath 'O God', to create a rupture in his dialogue. The apostrophic interjection points to the rupture in the speech, while only hinting at the thought that has led Hamlet to divert his syntax. The rupture seems to be a backward-moving thought, connecting to the previous image of the lack of a properly elongated period of mourning, even as he tries to move on with his overall thoughts in denouncing the marriage of mother and uncle. The interjection as rupture signals the potential subtext of the moment, making a reader connect the language into coherence that lends the character of Hamlet a sense of personhood and interiority. The sense that his emotions overcome him and force him to exclaim, to change thoughts midsentence, and to return to previous thoughts, all make him seem to possess an active mind that is interior, that is behind or beneath his language. The interruption as a form creates the sense of that interiority through the missing text of the speech, missing text that the interjection overlays yet indicates, points toward and stands in for.

Self-interruptions generally break into three broad types: emotional, manipulative, and comedic, each of which has a particular connection to inner workings and inter-workings. By inner workings, I mean the connections and relations within a character that the interruptions suggest. Inner workings are the thoughts or ideas that self-interruptions elide. Inter-workings are the connections between the self-interrupter and their audiences. They are the various affects that such moments evoke both intentionally and unintentionally. Emotional self-interruptions are when any emotion from a character becomes so forceful as to overtake the character's ability to speak in logical syntax, thereby creating the rupture for the self-interruption. These interruptions while dramatizing the dynamic interruptive inner working within a character actually go outside of the character to affect the inter-working between the character and the audience. The effect of the emotional self-interruption is to cause the audience to supply missing linguistic information that has been subsumed by an affective response; the inter-working leads to a contemplation of the inner working. The second type is a conscious copy or imitation of the emotional self-interruption, manufactured by the characters who interrupt themselves, specifically so that they can use the seeming interruption for manipulative ends. Such deceitful characters use corrections, aposiopesis, and feigned emotion in self-interruptive inner workings to manipulate the emotions of other characters. These faux interruptions dramatize the inter-workings between audience and character found in the emotional self-interruptions, but require an *on-stage* audience to supply missing information to create particular affects in the receiving character. Finally, comedic self-interruptions occur when characters (either intentionally or not) interrupt themselves for humorous purposes. These moments point towards inner workings that are disordered and illogical and often connect to a character's status. Unlike the emotional interruptions, a comedic interruption is almost completely internal in its supplying of ruptured language, but this inner working is structured to elicit a singular affective response in its inter-working: laughter. These self-interruptions ultimately create larger tonal commentary through their iteration of the same structure of inner- and inter-working found in the other two.

This chapter will break down these types of self-interruptions, examining both the form's usages and indications and the approaches employed by the three playwrights of this study. Of course, the three types have some overlap; therefore, the creation of rigid distinctions is not my aim. However, using these types allows a consideration of how these playwrights approached the idea of theatrical interiority in differing situations. While the self-interruption always gestures back toward that inaccessible interiority of character, it also, in an extension of dialogic microinterruptions, moves outside of the tripartite system to affect an outside party. If dialogic interruptions are contained systems, more or less, the self-interruption internalizes that contained system in order to generate an external affect—pity, fear, jealousy, laughter—on the part of the audience, whether on stage or off.

Emotional self-interruptions: Egeon, Celia, and Memnon

In *The Arte of Englishe Poesie* (1589), George Puttenham termed 'aposiopesis' as 'the figure of interruption', connecting it to four causes: fear, shame, anger, and distraction.[9] While the final example is an action microinterruption (as the arrival of another character or a bird flying overhead occasions the interruption), the other three are all based upon the emotional outburst of the speaker. In this way, the 'figure of interruption' is allied with the emotions overtaking the logical rhetoric of speech. This usage of self-interruptions is perhaps the most widespread and most recognizable, occurring in many examples throughout many plays. As Puttenham's language suggests, the outburst of emotion characterizes interruption and makes it a 'figure of defect'.[10] This section examines these emotional outbursts and explores the way in which such defective devices can actually demonstrate significant and important aspects of character as well as authorial style. To do so, I will briefly look at Shakespeare's Egeon in *The Comedy of Errors* before examining two examples from Jonson and one from Fletcher.

At the beginning of *The Comedy of Errors*, Egeon cuts off his speech with a clear emotional self-interruption. The Duke encourages him 'to say in brief' how he arrived in a place where his nationality condemns him to death (1.1.28). Despite desiring immediate death, Egeon delivers a speech of sixty-four lines outlining his tragic journey. However, before completing it, he stops, 'But ere they came—O, let me say no more!/Gather the sequel by that went before' (1.1.94-5). Egeon's self-interruption is an obvious example. In reliving the experience of losing his wife and one of his children, he has come to a point where he feels unable to continue the story. Egeon's emotions are foregrounded as the text renders the character overcome by his sorrow. His premise is cut off in the middle of the syntax, the rupture is an unspoken emotion represented by the ecphonesis 'O', and the continuation is his desire that the audience infer the rest of the story. As exposition, the audience needs the rest of the story, and so it must continue, which the Duke also demands, even later declaring that Egeon, in a reversal of his initial directive, 'dilate at full' everything that happened (1.1.122).

This emotional self-interruption both illustrates the inner working of character that self-interruptions elicit through a relationship between surface and depth and demonstrates how such an emotional cut-off plays into a larger construction of inter-working. More so than the other two types of self-interruptions, emotional self-interruptions invest in the connections between layers within a character—the connection between an inaccessible interiority that is hidden and an accessible, verbal exteriority on the surface. As examined earlier, the character develops an interiority through his demonstration of emotion that is ineffable. He cannot continue thinking about his lost family and relating the long story of the separation, even if both on- and off-stage audience need the information. His passive construction, 'let me say no more', indicates the power structure of the scene. He is possessor of the story but the Duke is ultimately in control, and it is at the Duke's behest that Egeon begins and ends. This dash[11] and 'O' develop the sense of Egeon as a character with depth and interiority, despite the fact that the rest of the play treats him as a flat character, not allowing him any change or greater sense of difference, only reappearing in the final scene to effect the conclusion.

Beyond the emotionality at play in these two lines, they also play with the audience's experience of the play's beginning. Firstly, the cut-off creates a brief moment of suspense as Egeon has reached a climax; the self-interruption bolsters the audience's attention, a part of its inter-working. Furthermore, it plays into the almost tragic nature of the opening scene. While the title identifies the play's genre, the first scene could begin a tragedy, especially as it promises death for the central character. However, the Duke's change of interest—from 'say in brief' to 'dilate at full'—indicates how Shakespeare subtly introduces comic ideas within the seemingly tragic frame. So too, the self-interruption— with its emotionality, obvious ploy for suspense, and necessity for continuance—becomes almost anticipated and, therefore, an obvious marker of comedy. Consequently, the self-interruption plays into a larger scenic construction here helping to infuse the tragic sensibility with a hint of the comic register. The tension that the self-interruptions play out are ones of dramatic irony, a staple of Shakespearean interruption, in that the title and the Duke's responses undermine the emotional tenor of the tragedy implied through Egeon's emotions.

In contrast to Shakespeare's dramatic irony, Jonson gives the most extreme version of a self-interruptive speech that almost negates the relationship between exterior and interior as it focuses only on the character's intense fear. In *Act Five*, Scene Three of *Catiline His Conspiracy*, Volturcius is caught with rebel forces and forced to reveal what he knows about Catiline's plans. He gives the following speech 'with feare and interruptions' as a marginal stage direction indicates:

> I was sent with letters—
> And had a message too—from Lentulus—
> To Catiline—that he should use all aides—

Seruants, or others—and come with his armie,
Assoone, vnto the citie as he could—
For they were readie, and but staid for him—
To intercept those, that should flee the fire—
These men (the Allobroges) did heare it too.[12]

> Vol. Then, I knew all. But truely I was drawne in
> But t'other day. Caes. Say, what thou know'lt, and feare not.
> Thou haft the *Senate* faith, and *Confuls* word,
> To fortifie thee. Vol. I was fent with letters———
> And had a meffage too——from Lentvlvs———
> To Catiline——that he fhould vfe all aides———
> Seruants, or others——and come with his armie,
> Affoone, vnto the citie as he could———
> For they were readie, and but ftaid for him———
> To intercept thofe, that fhould flee the fire———
> Thefe men (the Allobroges) did heare it too.
> All. Yes, *Fathers*, and they tooke an oath, to vs.
>
> *He anfweres with feare and interruptions.*

FIGURE 2.1 *Volturcius's speech. Ben Jonson,* Catiline, *in* The Workes of Benjamin Jonson *(London, Will Stansby, 1616), sig. Rrr4r. The John Work Garrett Library, Sheridan Libraries, Johns Hopkins University.*

His speech illustrates his anxiety over revealing his involvement in the conspiracy, fearing the punishment for his actions. To highlight this moment, Jonson (in the 1616 Folio text)[13] specifically presents the speech, as transcribed earlier and seen in Figure 2.1. The use of the nine dashes adds self-interruptions, which the stage direction of 'with feare and interruptions' clarifies, and the final parenthetical of 'the Allobroges' could almost be another self-interruption. The Folio's long line breaches, as Jonson elsewhere calls them, are unmistakable and might even signify huge breaks in reading or performing the text, significantly disrupting the delivered information. The modernized em dash mentioned earlier shows a more moderate version that provides shorter pauses/breaks as Volturcius tremulously delivers his information. However, if we remove that punctuation entirely, we can consider that this speech does not need these self-interruptions at all. Consider the following version of the same speech:

> I was sent with letters,
> And had a message too, from Lentulus

To Catiline, that he should use all aids,
Servants or others, and come with his army
As soon unto the city as he could.
For they were ready and but stayed for him
To intercept those that should flee the fire.
These men, the Allobroges, did hear it too.

Punctuated thus, the speech makes sense, does not break off, and possesses only some moments that could be potentially self-interruptive, but are not clearly so. Therefore, Jonson's use of the stage direction along with the placement of specific dashes creates the emotional self-interruptions that characterize the entire speech, a speech otherwise devoid of emotional content, only delivering messenger information. The speech's lack of interruptions beyond the dashes and the stage direction indicates the great extent to which acting can make choices to place interruptions, especially self-interruptions, anywhere. No grammar within the speech, or verbal sounds, like Egeon's 'O', indicates a cutting off of speech in an interruptive manner. In fact, the speech is full of information that is necessary for the audience. The interruptions are essentially paratextual; they are added to, and outside of, the verbal content, rather than built into the linguistic structure itself.

The stage direction combines the issues of emotionality with the idea of self-interruptions as Volturcius answers with both 'feare and interruptions'. The specification of both qualities unites them as the speech could be delivered without interruptions though with fear; conversely, it could be delivered with interruptions for another affective end. However, Jonson specifies the end of the speech to illustrate the extreme fear of the character. His stage direction indicates both form and quality, uniting the two into a singular affective structure. Despite his fear and his nine separate interruptions, which are given no specified length,[14] the speech completes, the thought concludes. Ultimately, this speech follows the Jonsonian pattern with interruptions. Volturcius, unlike Egeon, does not stop, but he continues through his interruptions. His continuation is simply the grammatically logical constructions that complete the information within the speech. His emotionality is therefore additive to the interruptions—'feare *and* interruptions'—but is not constitutive of it. The emotion that self-interruptions usually illustrate and the interiority that they indicate is here obscured as Jonson controls the interruption through insistence on the continuation, meaning that the continuation completes the premise with only the vaguest hint of influence from the rupture itself. This is typical of Jonson's controlling practice. Interruptions are an additive form but not one that controls or guides any speech, moment, or character.

The most significant self-interruption in the Jonsonian canon, though, is Celia's speech to Volpone, a speech that is similar to Volturcius's fearful one. Celia's monologue occurs after Volpone's song in *Act Three*, as she attempts to repulse the would-be seducer, trying to defend her chastity. While Karen Pirnie examines this speech as a site to explore the complexity of editing Jonson, Richard Dutton disagrees with Pirnie's assumptions, arguing that the compositor is just as likely responsible for the changes.[15] This debate centres on the punctuation: the 1607 Quarto prints this speech using a series of dashes, but the 1616 Folio uses commas, colons, and semicolons instead. Below is the first printing of the speech in the Quarto, replete with dashes; though unlike Volturcius's fearful speech, Celia's possesses no stage direction and are not the sustained breach but are mostly made of two short 'en' dashes (see Figures 2.2 and 2.3). In only twenty-one lines, the speech contains seventeen dashes as punctuation marks, almost a dash for every line, constituting 38 per cent of the entire punctuation in the speech. The dashes are an important aspect of the moment, evoking a sense of Celia's character for the reader of the speech that potentially harkens back (or forward) to Volturcius's speech, which includes the stage direction clarifying the use of the pointing device. While the Folio Celia may also interrupt with her commas and semicolons, such interruption becomes less clear to a reader than the dash with its sense of incompletion, and readers familiar with the earlier text would note a change. While Dutton makes this change an argument about nothing 'more than aesthetics', insisting that Jonson himself did not make the changes, I argue that the change, while aesthetic, is significant and therefore worth consideration.[16]

If Jonson changed the punctuation (as Pirnie asserts), then his revised vision of Celia was one that was not particularly emotional and fearful. However, if Jonson is not responsible for the changes, we must consider that the Q represents the Celia that Jonson intended, which gives the reader a character full of interiority but losing control as she pleads for her honour. Two issues emerge in

> ## THE FOXE.
>
> Whil'ſt,we,in changed ſhapes,act *Ouids* tales,
> Thou,like *Europa* now, and I like *Ioue*,
> Then I like *Mars*,and thou like *Erycine*,
> So, of the reſt, till we haue quite run through
> And weary'd all the *fables* of the *Gods*,
> Then will I haue thee, in more moderne formes,
> Attired like ſome ſprightly Dame of *France*,
> Braue *Tuſcan* Lady, or proud *Spaniſh* Beautie ;
> Sometimes,vnto the *Perſian Sophies* Wife ;
> Or the *grand-Signiors* Miſtreſſe ; and,for change,
> To one of our moſt arte-full Curtezans,
> Or ſome quick *Negro*, or cold *Ruſſian* ;
> And I will meete thee, in as many ſhapes :
> Where we may,ſo, tranſ-fuſe our wandring ſoules,
> Out at our lippes, and ſcore vp ſummes of pleaſures,
> > *That the curious ſhall not know,*
> > *How to tell them, as they flow ;*
> > *And the enuious, when they find*
> > *What there number is, be pind,*
>
> CEL. If you haue cares, that will be pierc'd-- or eyes,
> That can be open'd-- a heart, may be touch'd--
> Or any part , that yet ſounds *man*, about you--
> If you haue touch of holy *Saints*--or *Heauen*--
> Do mee the grace,to let me ſcape--if not,
> Be bountifull, and kill mee--you do knowe,
> I am a creature, hether ill betray'd,
> By one, whoſe ſhame I would forget it were--
> If you will daigne mee neither of theſe graces,
> Yet feede your wrath,Sir, rather then your luſt--
> (It is a vice, comes nearer manlineſſe--)
> And puniſh that vnhappy crime of nature,
> Which you miſcall my beauty--Flea my face,
> Or poiſon it, with oyntments, for ſeducing
> Your bloud to this rebellion --Rub theſe hands,
> With what may cauſe an eating leproſie,
>   H 3   E'en•

FIGURE 2.2 *Celia's speech. Ben Jonson,* Volpone *(London, Thomas Thorpe, 1607), sig. H3r. Harry Ransom Center, the University of Texas at Austin.*

comparing this speech to the one in *Catiline*. Firstly, the dashes remain in both the 1611 Quarto of *Catiline* and the 1616 Folio, and those possess authorial purpose if we agree with David Bevington that Jonson's hand is clear in the presentation of the 1611 Quarto.[17] Therefore, the idea that a fearful person would need to stop in

> **THE FOXE.**
>
> E'ene to my bones, and marrow— Any thing,
> That may diſ-fauour mee, ſaue in my honour.—
> And I will kneele to you, pray for you, pay downe
> A thouſand howrely vowes, Sir, for your health—
> Report, and thinke you vertuous— V o l p. Thinke me cold,
> Froſen, and impotent, and ſo report me?
> That I had *Neſtor's hernia*, thou wouldſt thinke.
> I do degenerate, and abuſe my *Nation*,
> To play with oportunity, thus long:
> I ſhould haue done the act, and then haue parlee'd.
> Yeeld, or Ile force thee. C e l. O, iuſt God. V o l p. In vaine-
> B o n. Forbeare, foule rauiſher, libidinous ſwine,
> Free the fore'd lady, or thou dy'ſt, Impoſtor.
> But that I am loath to ſnatch thy puniſhment
> Out of the hand of *Iuſtice*, thou ſhouldſt, yet,
> Be made the timely ſacrifice of vengeance,
> Before this *Altar*, and this droſſe, thy *Idoll*,
> Lady, lets quit the place, it is the den
> Of villany; feare nought, you haue a guard:
> And he, ere long, ſhall meete his iuſt reward.
> V o l p. Fall on mee, roofe, and bury mee in ruine,
> Become my graue, that wert my ſhelter. O,
> I am vn-maſqu'd, vn-ſpirited, vn-done,
> Betray'd to beggary, to infamy—
>
> ACT. 3, SCENE. 8,
>
> Mosca. Volpone.
>
> WHere ſhall I runne, moſt wretched ſhame of men,
> To beate out my vn-luckie braines? V o l p. Here, here,
> What? doſt thou bleede? M o s. O, that his well-driu'n ſword
> Had beene ſo curteous, to haue cleft me downe,
> Vnto the nauill; ere I liu'd to ſee
>   My

FIGURE 2.3 *Celia's speech continued. Ben Jonson,* Volpone *(London, Thomas Thorpe, 1607), sig. H3v. Harry Ransom Center, the University of Texas at Austin.*

the middle of grammatical units because emotions erupt through the language is something that Jonson used for his readers across publications. Secondly, the only difference between the Quarto and Folio versions of Volturcius's speech is the addition of a stage direction, which clarifies the meaning of the dashes—that they are interruptive moments of extreme emotion for the character. This addition signals, if Jonson oversaw the revisions in the Folio as Bevington argues,[18] that Jonson thought the dashes themselves were not clear enough in their intentions and that a stage direction to a reader would indicate the proper reading of the speech's pointing. This reading of *Catiline*'s texts offers two competing theories for the punctuation of Celia's speech. The retention of Volturcius's dashes with a new stage direction may indicate that Jonson liked such punctuation, meaning we should retain them as a Jonsonian aspect. Conversely, Jonson perhaps liked Volturcius's dashes but not Celia's and wanted to eliminate the connection between the characters. One final consideration is that *Volpone* was printed before *Catiline* in the Folio;[19] therefore, Jonson might have seen the printed change to Celia's speech, and while he did not fix it, he added a note to Volturcius's so that the similar speech did not receive the same treatment. While this theory is only speculation, it represents a Jonson of 'waning' interest in fixing the Folio though still somewhat involved.[20] Ultimately, Celia's punctuated quarto speech is the more Jonsonian in that his distinctive use of the new punctuation is born out in the statistics of his usages as presented before. Furthermore, the two versions demonstrate the complexity of self-interruption and the spectrum of potentiality that all dramatic texts encode in such moments. Just as my repointed version of Volturcius's speech demonstrates a not-highly interrupted version, so too the 1616 Folio illustrates a Celia that does not interrupt herself and is ultimately only interrupted by Volpone.

Both presentations offer aesthetic and performative choices that are worth considering, but Celia's emotional self-interruptions impact the reading of her character, suggest important inner workings, and underscore the power that she does and does not wield. Celia embodies a character that has been severely interrupted and controlled throughout the play. Her voice has been one that is rarely heard, with only twenty-four speeches in the entire text. This speech is her longest and threatens to break down throughout as she stops and starts. It occurs as Celia's husband has left her to be sexually assaulted by Volpone, who has assailed her with speeches and songs despite her protestations. The overall structure of the speech demonstrates a heavier use of self-interruptions at the beginning of the speech with shorter intervening phrases. As Celia continues, her phrasal units in between interruptions become longer. To illustrate this shift, I have re-lineated the following speech adding a line break at each dash:

> If you haue eares, that will be pierc'd—
> or eyes, That can be open'd—
> a heart, may be touch'd—
> Or any part, that yet sounds man, about you—
> If you haue touch of holy Saints—
> or Heauen—
> Do mee the grace, to let me scape—
> if not, Be bountifull, and kill mee—
> you do knowe, I am a creature, hether ill betrayd, By one whose shame I would forget it were—
> If you will daigne mee neither of these graces, Yet feede your wrath, Sir, rather then your lust—
> (It is a vice, comes nearer manlinesse—)
> And punish that vnhappy crime of nature, Which you miscall my beauty—
> Flea my face, Or poison it, with oyntments, for seducing Your bloud to this rebellion—
> Rub these hands, With what may cause an eating leprosie, E'ene to my bones, and marrow—
> Anything That may dis-fauour mee, saue in my honour—
> And I will kneele to you, pray for you, pay downe A thousand howrely vowes, Sir, for your health—
> Report, and thinke you vertuous—

This breakdown illustrates how the speech comprises two equal parts when considered in interrupted units (eight short segments of length between two to nine words, and nine long segments of length between five and nineteen words).[21] The first half of the speech builds rhetorically as Celia catalogues potential aspects that Volpone may possess, all nestled within a larger if/then structure. The dashes in these moments illustrate a struggling rhetorician, grasping at images and heaping them on in a basic form of *accumulatio*. Her elision of words in the subsequent phrases also rhetorically demonstrates her desperation as she attempts to find some approach that may affect her potential rapist. The two notable climaxes of the speech are the shortest phrase when she invokes Heaven and the turn into the second half of the speech when she begs for death. Both of these moments illustrate her building up to a significant point and then breaking off and changing strategies.

As demonstrated earlier, the ruptures are the breaks themselves, and, therefore, the stimulus for the transformation cannot be easily indicated within a written dramatic text. Such causes remain the domain of the actor or the director; however, these interruptions cause the reader and audience to perceive that this character possesses an interiority as she struggles with her situation, emotionally pleading with her captor. So too, these moments create various versions of what that interiority might be for the character. We can imagine two Celias: either a Celia that uses 'or Heauen' to reach an emphasized point and appeal to the highest authority or a Celia that deflates at the thought that even Heaven might not appeal to this man before her. And such descriptions are not the limitations of the potentiality that the microinterruptions give the character within the speech. No language is particularly missing from her speech,[22] and so these moments are not specifically aposiopoetic, rather they give the sense of her stopping her image to deliver another image. In this way they point towards a mind that is working in the present moment. They indicate that the interiority of the character is at stake in this moment, which in fact it is. The use of the dashes, which attempts to show a desperate mind at work, demonstrates a character who is full of emotions and who ultimately delivers a coherent argument, though in fits and starts.

One briefly interruptive moment highlights the complicated inner workings and inter-workings of the speech as Jonson crafted it, even if it does not achieve the effect that Celia desires. The most striking line in the speech is: '(It is a vice, comes nearer manlinesse—)'. With its doubly interruptive punctuation, the line sets itself out as being particularly revealing of the mind at work. Celia gambles with Volpone by trying to get him to beat her through castigating his manliness. The reflexive moment that is embedded within parentheses and dashes indicates to the reader, and perhaps the actor, that the character here is pulling out tangential information by interrupting the flow of the overall thought itself. Significantly, the interjection is the shortest line in the second half of the speech, further marking it out from its surroundings. Therefore, as she is gaining some composure and crafting longer phrases without interruptions, she briefly interrupts to reinforce her argument for inciting violence.

As this speech indicates, Jonson uses interruptions in a manner that ultimately does not alter the meaning or change the significance of the moment. The interruption is ornament that indicates more, a device added onto the texture of the speech, but that does not govern the speech. At no point does Celia go on a tangent or allow an interrupted thread to become the new focus of the argument. Each unit follows the unit before by amplifying or clarifying or adding to or altering the already-stated premise. Again, in this structure we can see an author who indulges in the sense of interruption, and in the potential for interruption—at any point Celia might just break off into emotion or change course—but who ultimately returns to the logical structure of the speech as laid out. The premise survives in Jonsonian interruptions, even if we do not clearly see the full premise until after the delivery of the total speech. The rupture breaks for a moment but then returns to deliver the information as necessitated by the situation and by the hand of the crafting authorial voice. Ultimately then, Jonson's approach to the emotional self-interruption only adds paratextual emotion to the already-existing text. In this way, Celia's and Volturcius's speeches both work perfectly well with or without self-interruptions, and while the choice to use the self-interruptions changes the aesthetic and performative colouring of the specific moments, the outcome and the speech's inherent control mean that Jonson remains in control of the message. We may conclude the debate over the punctuation of Celia's speech to say that both ways are Jonsonian and that the second is inherent in the first and the first only colours differently the same iteration of the second. Jonson fully prizes premise and its continuation over rupture even as he heavily deploys ruptures.

John Fletcher illustrates a contrasting type of emotional self-interruption, especially in the character of Memnon in *The Mad Lover*. In crafting an 'anti-Hamlet' that brings up 'echoes of and responses to' Shakespeare in parodic fashion,[23] Fletcher provides the titular character with a soliloquy that considers the implications of death and suicide.[24] After being stricken dumb upon seeing the princess Calis, Memnon the 'mad lover' contemplates death as he is about to deliver his heart, literally, to her:

—'Tis but to die,—dogs doe it, ducks with dabling,
Birds sing away their soules, and babyes sleep 'em,—
Why doe I talke of that that is treble vantage?
For in the other world she is bound to have me,—
Her Princely word is past:—my great desert too
Will draw her to come after presently,—
'Tis justice, and the gods must see it done too.
Besides no Brother, Father, kindred there
Can hinder us,—all languages are a like too;
There love is everlasting, ever young,
Free from diseases, ages, jealousies.
Bawdes, beldames, painters, purgers die, 'tis nothing,
Men drowne themselves for joye to draw in Juleps
When they are hot with wine;—In dreames we doe it;
And many a handsome wench that loves the sport well
Gives up her soule so in her lovers bosome;
But I must be incised first,—cut and open'd,—
My heart—(and handsomelie)—taine from me:—staie there,—
Dead once,—stay, let me thinke agen, who doe I know there?—
For els to wander up and downe unwaited on
And unregarded in my place and project
Is for a sowters soul, not an old Souldiers.—
My brave old Regiments:—I there it goes,—
That have bin killd before me, right—[25]

I have supplied a modern-punctuation acting edition here of the speech, in which I posit the locations of the most obvious self-interruptions in Memnon's soliloquy; all the dashes in the aforementioned text are editorial. Unlike the Folio presentation of Celia, which gives her 'wit' and 'self-control' simply by removing interrupting dashes,[26] the earliest and most authoritative edition of *The Mad Lover* does not use any dashes but also does not indicate self-control.[27] This lack of interruption pointing means that the text itself must manifest where the interruptions might be. In my estimation then, the speech contains roughly twenty interruptions in twenty-four lines, which makes it similar in usage to the Quarto punctuation of Celia's speech.[28] As I will demonstrate, Fletcher amplifies the disorderly way in which emotions can create self-interruptions and crafts a soliloquy that remains singularly unfinished either rhetorically or dramatically.

The speech itself emerges from an interruption as the character begins mid-thought. His entrance onto the stage and his beginning to speak to the audience open himself up but hint at the unavailable presence of his previous thoughts and ideas. When Memnon asserts, "'Tis but to die', he clearly echoes such characters as Hamlet,[29] but unlike Hamlet he does not enter with a beginning in mind. Hamlet's famous line, 'To be or not to be', follows itself with the clear delineation of what it is: 'that is the question'.[30] While the audience, from this question and statement, surmises the thoughts that have come before it, Hamlet's line lacks the immediate interruptive quality that Fletcher gives the general with the syntactical phrasing of "'Tis but to die'. His statement's commencement on a pronoun opens up the lack of clarity in the construction, which is further interrupted in the contraction with the verb itself. Unlike Hamlet's 'that', which has a clear antecedent, the audience has to remember back to the general's situation to construe his meaning for "'T', the unspecified referent for what 'is but to die'. By constructing the first phrase in this interruptive mode, the playwright forces both reader and audience to grant the character a profound sense of interiority. In this manner, one interrupted letter without clear antecedent ruptures the stage picture and creates the fictional presence embedded within the grammatical and syntactical absence of the language itself.

The speech continues in this interruptive mode, not following up the statement about dying with further philosophy or even clarification but only with an interruption and additional imagery. The speech in its initial list engenders a methodology for Fletcher's emotional self-interruptions, in which the character's thoughts drive the speech without strong logical or rhetorical construction. Yet those thoughts are the subtext that the author does not provide, which is only provisionally available to an audience. Hence, the self-interruptive structure illustrates the manipulative power of the author over the audience in crafting a sense of interiority out of absence, and a sense of presence out of disrupted matter. Memnon continues his speech: "'Tis but to die, dogs doe it, ducks with dabling,/Birds sing away their soules, and babyes sleep 'em,/Why doe I talke of that that is treble vantage?' (2.1.1-3). That first interruption between 'die' and 'dogs' demonstrates Fletcher's playful manipulation of the emotional interruption. Again, he does not follow up the statement with clarification but rather goes to a listing of various creatures who also experience the same situation. In fact, the only logic connecting across the rupture is the alliteration flowing from the word 'die'.[31] That alliteration continues from die to dog to ducks and dabling, then from the second syllable of dabling to birds and babies. The formal logic of the alliterative list is clear enough, and who is to say that formal features like alliteration are less important to linguistic thinking than referential features like logic? But the semantic content of the list seems somewhat arbitrary as crafted. While an internal logic could be surmised—emphasizing that death comes even to small defenseless creatures—that logic would only be the purview of the Stanislavskian subtext, provided to cover over the rupturous and interrupted connection within this highly self-interruptive speech.[32] Memnon breaks from his list to reaffirm his commitment through the use of erotesis, but once more a reader or audience member would be at a loss to question the logic of his conclusion. The 'treble vantage' that Memnon cites does not conclude from his list of animal deaths nor does it clearly follow in the subsequent lines, even though he does enumerate some potential advantages. The manner in which Memnon breaks off from subject to subject, freely following his thoughts through lists, illustrates the disparate mix of Fletcher's style that has provoked comparisons to both Walt Whitman and Harold Pinter.[33]

Towards the end of the speech, Fletcher amplifies the self-interruptions by contrasting the use of the conjunctions that often are missing. As a piece of grammar, conjunctions are the ties that override the self-interruption and craft logical connections between what otherwise would be disparate thoughts. In doing so, they give the semblance of logical consistency to speech and language. However, in Memnon's speech, his language is most self-interruptive when he uses or overuses conjunctions. In fact, the middle section of his speech, while it has long lists, has no moments that are particularly self-interruptive; each item seems to relate to the previous as he rolls out his images. However, at the end of the speech, he has a few lines with several conjunctions and self-interruptions:

> But I must be incised first,—cut and open'd,—
> My heart—(and handsomelie)—taine from me:—staie there,
> Dead once,—stay, let me thinke agen, who doe I know there?—
> For els to wander up and downe unwaited on

And unregarded in my place and project
  Is for a sowters soul, not an old Souldiers.—

  (2.1.17-22)

Here, the conjunctions are amplified, as are the interruptions. The quick deployment of several interruptions as he first contemplates the actual excision of his own heart amplifies the emotionality of the moment as the character considers the physical reality of his own death and not the abstract potential thereof. He begins with a reversal of the previous thought, 'But', and then continues with the physical action of being cut open, which he stops to add redundant information, before beginning a new grammatical phrase that is immediately interrupted with a qualifying phrase before being completed. In this almost rapid-fire deployment of self-interruptions, the character's text illustrates the lack of logical coherence that the character seems to possess at this moment. The text's suggestions of the myriad self-interruptions create the character's emotionality. But unlike Celia's deportment that can be found with the removal of pointing or that builds even with the dashes (as her phrases become longer), Memnon, who starts with several self-interruptions, begins to spiral. So too, his interruptions take hold of his speech. As opposed to Hamlet's grand conclusions at the end of his suicidal soliloquy,[34] Memnon is left contemplating who might also be in the afterlife to keep him company. In this conclusion of what is erstwhile a grand soliloquy about suicide and death and love, Fletcher disrupts the coherence of a logical argument and rather follows the continuations of the ruptures within the self-interruptions that Memnon's speech generates. The fluidity of the images and the language present a character not finalized or formalized but more chaotic, and perhaps, in that lack of coherency, less finished, though maybe more human.

  Emotional self-interruptive speeches elide linguistic information that becomes supplied through the work of an actor, an audience member, and/or a reader. These outside participants in the aesthetic experience become the affective object of the self-interruption in a way that dialogic interruptions do not possess. Dialogic microinterruptions remain internalized within the system of the participants in the dialogue, but self-interruptions reach out into the affective plane that grabs the aesthetic participant. As viewers and readers, we supply what might be missing, the vocalizations and the thoughts of the emotional character, and so the emotional self-interruption becomes a distinctly affective aesthetic phenomenon that engages the outside spectator through the positing of the internal life of the character by eliding linguistic text.

Manipulative self-interruptions: Iago

What emotional self-interruptions do through affective means, manipulative self-interruptions achieve through suggesting missing logical connections whether accurate or fallacious. The tension within the realm of the logical and the affective is the purported end of the manipulative self-interruption that pretends to the same origin as the emotional self-interruption but rather begins from a more calculated position of creation by the character. In this way, the affective move to the audience that the emotional self-interruption achieves is rather intended for another character as audience and not for the outside audience. The outside audience or reader can approach the manipulative self-interruption from a place of irony through their superior information as they have a privileged perspective on the situation.

The most obvious user of manipulative self-interruption is Iago in Shakespeare's *Othello*. His entire plan is based upon elision that lures Othello into suppling missing information. Iago has been the focus of much modern criticism, leading Edward Pechter to state that we are within an 'Iagocentric' turn.[35] Iago has been deemed 'an amateur of tragedy in real life', full of 'motiveless malignity', and potentially 'dangerous' as well as 'attractive'.[36] This need to intuit Iago's motive and mind continues with the move towards cognitive studies and its inroads into literature.[37] My examination of Iago will consider these approaches, but rather than figure out the interior workings of Iago, I explore his methodology within his self-interrupted language that creates the sense of the psychological interior that critics continue to debate. Through such an analysis, I show how Othello's responses to Iago's self-interruptions replicate the responses that an audience member might have to emotional self-interruptions. In this manner, we may see how the manipulative self-interruption derives its power from the inter-working between actor and audience just as the emotional one does, but this time the intended audience is even more forcefully and explicitly the one on stage. This removal of our own emotional engagement in the creation of the character within the ruptures allows for a critical distance that incites the reflective aesthetic distance necessary for irony, specifically dramatic irony, as we are aware of the trap into which Othello falls.

Act Three, Scene Three, is replete with Iago's manipulative self-interruptions, which demonstrate his methodology for ensnaring Othello. Not all of them are particularly obvious, and like Memnon's aforementioned speech and some of the dialogic interruptions discussed in the previous chapter, they often do not have the accompanying punctuation to indicate the interruptive nature of the text.[38] As Othello and Iago enter the scene, they see Cassio taking his leave of Desdemona, and the following exchange occurs:

IAGO: Ha, I like not that.
OTHELLO: What dost thou say?
IAGO: Nothing my Lord; or if—I know not what.

(3.3.34-36)[39]

The manipulation here is quite clear to the off-stage audience, but Iago's aposiopesis, in which he demurely iterates that he is unsure of what he said or saw or thought, creates the curiosity that drives the rest of the scene. Madeline Doran calls this moment 'the small hole in the dike which, persistently widened by Iago, will let in the destroying flood'.[40] Iago does not cut himself off after the first half of the statement; rather, he begins to explain some thoughts about what he said and why it might be more than nothing, but *then* cuts himself off. The purposeful lingering of the phrase 'or if' creates the sense of lack of completion and allows the auditor's mind to begin its imaginative work to fill in the void that the dash now represents. The premise of this self-interruption is more important than even the missing rupture. Without the initial hint of something else contrary to nothing, which the 'or' represents, and the possibility of that existence of contrariness found in 'if', the audience, both on- and off-stage, would have nothing to build on in the intervening rupture. The continuation of 'I know not what' is obviously disingenuous and goads Othello to continue the conversation, focused on finishing the premise that Iago ruptured. The desire for completion or wholeness in the thought contrasts Othello to Iago, who delights in the ruptured nature of the self-interruption and the power that it wields. In this one moment, we begin to see the effect of the manipulative self-interruption. Significantly, Othello, the intended target of the aposiopesis, is hit quite clearly, while the off-stage audience is left with the dramatic irony that knows what Iago wants Othello to intuit. We see both the falsified completed premise and the underlying completed premise. That is to say that the manipulative self-interruption interrupts on two levels: one for the on-stage auditor and one ironically for the off-stage auditors. The rupture for both is the same, but the premises and perceived continuations are vastly different. Within this singular moment, Shakespeare aligns the audience with Iago, as we look through his ruptured language into the machinations that he deploys to ensnare Othello. Thus, the manipulative self-interruption creates distance between the characters and the off-stage audience in a way that the emotional self-interruption does not.

Furthermore, Othello's response—'Was not that Cassio parted from my wife?' (3.3.37)—indicates that Othello did hear Iago, which he affirms later in the scene, but wants Iago to unfold his mind fully to him. While Paul Cefalu argues that Othello suffers from mindblindness in that he cannot read into other people's minds in the way that Iago can,[41] Iago's self-interruptions and Othello's pressure around them indicate that he is verifying that which he heard surrounding the rupture. The breaking off of the text indicates clearly to Othello that there is another thought being left out, and he pursues it, which plays directly into Iago's trap. In fact, he later follows up these previous hints on Iago's part, noting:

> And for I know thou'rt full of love and honesty
> And weigh'st thy words before thou giv'st them
>   breath,
> Therefore these stops of thine fright me the more.
> For such things in a false disloyal knave
> Are tricks of custom, but in a man that's just
> They're close [dilations][42] working from the heart,
> That passion cannot rule.
>
> (3.3.121-27)

Othello may be unable to 'model Iago's mind',[43] but he clearly perceives that something is going on inside it. Even if he lacks the intuition to piece together the implications, he knows that the implications exist and that he lacks the ability to perceive what those implications might be. His self-awareness only takes him so far, in that he has misjudged Iago as 'just' and 'honest', but here he demonstrates that he is fully aware of Iago's mind at work and that the self-interruptions, the 'stops' or 'close dilations', indicate something important. The ability for an audience to perceive Othello's weakness here and to realize that the image of the 'disloyal knave' that uses self-interruptions as 'tricks of custom' once more brings the audience back to the level of dramatic irony in which they perceive the working out of Iago's desired outcome through his use of self-interruptions.

The scene continues with Iago delivering more and more self-interruptions as he reveals bits and pieces of thoughts to Othello, driving him towards enraged jealousy. In the sequence leading up to Iago's suggestion that her Venetian identity will lead her to stray, Iago has a series of speeches whose self-interruptions are not indicated through dashes or grammar. However, these lines possess a manipulative movement, as Iago shifts topics to reiterate his identity to Othello and his lack of desire to speak. These lines are full stopped, but Othello notes before that stops are also interruptive for Iago. Many of these speeches are also structured with the conjunction 'But'. While conjunctions are almost antithetical to interruption (because they create a connection to the syntactical structure as I note earlier), here they create hesitancy and hint at Iago's reluctance. For example, in talking about Desdemona and her father, Iago states:

> She that so young could give out such a seeming
> To seel her father's eyes up, close as oak –
> He thought 'twas witchcraft. But I am much too blame,
>
> (3.3.207-07)

While the Arden 3's dash here provides a moment of potential self-interruption, the stronger break is after 'witchcraft'. There, Iago invests this moment with a sense of self-interruption as he moves away from suggesting Desdemona's sorcery and towards a sense of his own guilt in having to reveal these thoughts to Othello. The manipulation then overcomes the typical indicators of non-interruption. Furthermore, 'But', while a grammatical conjunction, functions as a disjunction in that it denies the previous thought, articulating an inter-working in which the assertion is reversed for an intended effect. Moreover, the earlier interruptions in this sequence have created a pattern in which we, and Othello, are more likely to discern a self-interruption in the disjunctive conjunction. Iago indicates that there is more to be thought about Desdemona's witchcraft, but that instead of considering those further thoughts, he would rather insure himself of Othello's pardon. In this almost non-interruption, Iago creates the sense of the interruption that drives Othello to consider the unspoken rupture about witchcraft and Desdemona. His power over Othello that he clearly demonstrates in this scene stems directly from his ability to craft interruptions and interruptive forms. In this manner, we might think of Iago like a playwright who 'in staging scenes and manipulating people, [and] in creating illusions'[44] harnesses the power within the interruptive form of dialogue just as Shakespeare or any other playwright does.

Of course, Othello is not the only victim of Iago's self-interruptive manipulations. The audience members and readers of the text are as well. In Iago's two early monologues, he employs several self-interruptions that lack an on-stage audience to create dramatic irony, which means the off-stage audience becomes both audiences. This doubling of audience highlights the problems attendant upon this play and the criticism of this character with his 'motiveless malignity'. In his soliloquy at the end of 2.1, Iago peppers his speech with self-interruptions that are not emotional. They seem to be manipulative, but are so only for the off-stage audience, which is precisely the point. He begins:

> The Moor, howbeit that I endure him not,
> Is of a constant, loving, noble nature,
>
> (2.1.286-87)

The interruptive parenthetical—'howbeit that I endure him not'—suggests Iago's necessity to discredit any kindness towards Othello.[45] His statement then almost provides a generous assessment of a person, but does so after the rupture of the reiteration of his hatred, which reminds the audience to see the following description within a negative consideration. Othello's 'constant, loving, noble nature' is not a point of praise, and actors often indicate this by turning the apparent praise into a sneer. After once more bringing up the accusation of Othello's cuckolding him, Iago adds:

> And nothing can or shall content my soul
> Till I am evened with him, wife for wife . . .[46]
> Or, failing so, yet that I put the Moor
> At least into a jealousy so strong
> That judgement cannot cure:
>
> (2.1.271-275)

This passage of interruptions is remarkable in almost veering towards the nature of the emotional self-interruption. The focus on his hatred, a strong emotion, leads towards such a suggestion. His interruptions at 'or shall', 'for wife', 'failing so', and 'the Moor' all indicate a discombobulated mind not that dissimilar from Memnon. However, considering Iago, one must remember that even in this soliloquy, he has an audience that is present for him, and, therefore, he seems to be acting out his role. The interruptions here want the audience to read into the motivations that might or might not be behind his dislike of Othello. They lead us towards giving Iago an interiority, or a Theory of Mind, that could be rationally understood if we had access; however, these interruptions are as completely manipulative as are the ones surrounding Othello, and the audience here is left as the mindblind target, knowing that there should be more, but unable to see anything beyond the black ink on the white page. We then are as duped as Othello, but our duping is that we think we can—through our superiority over the drama, in a position of ironic distance—have the power to determine the truth behind the characters and to gain access into them. Ultimately, we, like Othello, only perceive what Iago/Shakespeare wants to reveal. In the end, we can only 'demand . . . nothing' from the page, as 'what you know, you know', for those ruptures 'never will speak word' (5.2.300-01).

Shakespeare is of course not the only of the three playwrights to use manipulative self-interruptions (Mosca in *Volpone* has several significant moments); however, in focusing on Iago, I want to demonstrate one place where Shakespeare focused his interruptive energies through the importance of dramatic irony. Shakespeare's interruptions are often less about what happens to the stage characters and more invested in making sure that the off-stage audience is ahead of the game. He elevates us to an ironic distance that has led critics and theatregoers to return to him time and time again because in his world we are privileged. Iago then reflexively becomes unique in his denial of our status. While he gives us plenty of ironic moments, as I have demonstrated (and more abound, see 4.1 e.g.), he also through Iago's self-interruptions removes our privilege and our access. In this way, he finds a playful and productive space in which to challenge his own characteristic approach to interruptive structures by having them complicate their own genesis and production.

Comedic self-interruptions: Mistress Quickly

One final mode of self-interruptions is comedic. These usages are often quickly deployed, illustrate wit, and are almost completely self-contained outside of the affective response that they intend to engender. Like the manipulative self-interruptions, comedic ones intend to affect both on- and off-stage audiences, while being mostly controlled by the speaker themself. As Laura Salisbury explains, 'What makes a comic instant funny rather than paradoxical ... is the fact that its transgressions must be understood as improper, its incongruities brought together within comprehension.'[47] This delineation moves towards an explication of the comedic self-interruption: the moment becomes comedic as its continuation creates an incongruity with the premise that the audience must then put back together into a coherent whole. In affixing the form back together over the rupture, comedy emerges. Salisbury concludes, 'even reduced to the barest formalism, comedy only pierces and punctures expectation as it transgresses internalized or felt laws of propriety, whether they are social, sexual, physical or linguistic.'[48] Her idea illustrates the manner in which the unseen/unheard rupture of the comedic self-interruption becomes almost externalized. It is only through making the interruption complete and through perceiving where the rupture broke with the expectation that one can see the comedy in the moment. Even if the comedy is unwitting on the part of the speaker, the audience's perceptions of and realization of the rupture that breaks a perceived decorum coheres the form and gives it comedic force. Therefore, comedic interruptions are like emotional self-interruptions when the speaker does not realize the joke they have made and like manipulative self-interruptions when the speaker makes the joke deliberately. Their own perceived intentionality becomes central to the affective working of the self-interruption as those that perceive their affective power in comedic language have power in the situation over their ability to willingly transgress the boundaries through their self-interruptive ruptures, while those that unknowingly make these jokes become powerless and the object of the joke as they do not comprehend the transgression. In this way, the unknowingly comedic self-interrupter's identity itself becomes the joke that is cohered into a whole over the rupture through their ignorance of transgression, whereas the knowing self-interrupter creates the sense of their control over the rupture and their ability to elicit a response.

To demonstrate these issues within comedic self-interruptions, I turn to Mistress Quickly in Shakespeare's *The Merry Wives of Windsor*.[49] Quickly's comedic self-interruptions, both intended and not intended, reflect how the structure of the interruption within the character's speeches becomes aligned with the larger moment in the play's narrative, refocusing the comedic value of the scene by amplifying the ruptured expectations that become comedic through their coherence into whole utterances. In *Act One*, Scene Four, Quickly deals with several suitors to Anne Page including her master, Doctor Caius. Quickly's recurrent self-interruptions illustrate a comedic mode based upon tempo in its theatrical development. The men are desirous for immediate satisfaction and information, while Quickly's language, counter to her name's suggestion, dilates and expands, interrupting to add context and commentary, that, in its lack of speed, develops a comedic sensibility around the female servant. Her role both exemplifies and questions the status of the female servant as she embodies the misogynistic stereotype of a chatty woman who cannot remain focused, while also allowing her to control the situation through her possession of information.

The scene has a double structure—like the scenes of dialogic microinterruptions—as Quickly talks to the suitors while also dealing with Caius. As Quickly first engages with Simple, Master Slender's servant sent on his behalf, she explains her desire to help Slender's appeal to Anne:

> But notwithstanding, man,
> I'll do you your master what good I can; and the very
> yea and the no is, the French doctor my Master—I may
> call him my master, look you, for I keep his house, and
> I wash, ring, brew, bake, scour, dress meat and drink,
> make the beds and do all myself —
>
> (1.4.86-91)

Quickly aims to explain that Caius, the French Doctor, is also in love with Anne Page; however, her self-interruption impedes the delivery of that specific information as she decides instead to explain her relationship to her 'master'. The rapid diversion based on one lexical word, which culminates in a lengthy list of the various chores for which she is responsible, illustrates the quick and the slow in Quickly's self-interruptions. Her move from one thought to the next is ruptured so quickly that an audience or a reader might have a moment in which to question where the idea derived. The joke resides in her explications. Before the rupture, she elaborates on the situation at full, which creates a tension between the sense of her delivery from the text and the actual text itself. Her response is not quick, but the movement from thought to thought is. Within her interruptions, she even lightly self-interrupts to draw attention to her self-interruptions. By adding, 'look you', she demands attention from her audience despite the fact that she has moved away from the premise of the conversation itself and is exploring a thirty-two-word continuation unrelated to the premise.

Her power within this moment emerges through Simple's response as he continues the ruptured continuation without moving the conversation back to the premise. He responds, ''Tis a great charge to come under one body's hand' (1.4.92-93). In following her continuation and not returning to the premise, Slender allows Quickly's rapid self-interruption to control the conversation, moving it around to subjects as she pleases. In fact, she responds to his assertion, by stating:

> Are you avised o'that? You
> shall find it a great charge, and to be up early and down
> late; but notwithstanding—
>
> (1.4.94-96)

Her response enhances Slender's agreement to follow her lead and even takes up his language before rapidly self-interrupting once more: this time not to a new topic but to return to her list of chores and duties to Caius. In doing so, she wrests the conversation back from Simple as she controls the dialogue through her self-interruptions. The ability of the character to use the internalized self-interruptions, part of a monologue, to then control the dialogue illustrates the power of language that Quickly possesses. The tension throughout her language, as it is rapid and slow at the same time, creates the comedic tension but also imbues her with a sense of power over the other characters, both master and male alike. The end of Quickly's line in fact reinterrupts herself in order to return to the original conversation, but in her own time. After drawing Simple into the explication of her duties as a servant, she then wrests the conversation back to the matter at hand, using the same conjunction as before 'but notwithstanding'. Here the self-interruption's continuation is a return to the initial premise after almost sixty-three words of digression fully in control of the female servant. She chooses when to reveal the information necessary for Simple to take to Slender. She controls the dialogue through her interrupted monologue.

Her subsequent self-interruption follows up this sense of control by commenting on the power of language and the comedic tension therein. In returning to her premise, she explains:

> but notwithstanding—to tell you in your ear, I
> would have no words of it—my master himself is in
> love with Mistress Anne Page; but notwithstanding
> that, I know Anne's mind—that's neither here nor
> there.

(1.4.96-100)

Her first self-interruption of this section is to comment upon what she is about to explain. She uses her conjunction, 'but notwithstanding', indicating a return to the issue of Caius and Anne, but she stops short of explaining her point by insisting that she 'tell[s him] in [his] ear', thereby insinuating that further secrecy is necessary. However, as the moment is already an aside, only available to the audience and the two characters (Caius is busy writing a letter), her extra layer of security is then exaggerated and prolongs her delivery of information. Furthermore, she interrupts this interruption with the additional information that 'I would have no words of it'. In adding this odd warning, perhaps an explication of needing to say it in his ear, she illustrates a desire to control language that cannot exist. Her need to deliver the language, the words, directly into his ear, becomes unavailable as the offstage audience needs the information she is about to impart, and, therefore, she must give the idea words for the information to be communicated. Her interruption calls attention to the staged situation and to the language that she uses to deliver information as she paradoxically expresses a desire not to reveal language while only able to reveal the idea through the medium of words themselves. However, her medium of words, as she recurrently demonstrates, is one that can be interrupted, diverted, and digressed, and through such tangents can be controlled by the speaker.

While a later speech reiterates these complex comedic issues, once more demonstrating her desire to control and rupture (1.4.139-44),[50] her final line in this scene brings together the whole complicated self-interrupted character of Quickly and the power of the comedic self-interruption. After Fenton's exit, she states:

> Truly an honest Gentleman—but Anne loves him not.
> For I know Anne's mind as well as another does.—Out upon't, what have I forgot?
>
> (1.4.153-55)

In the moment of asserting her ability to know another person's mind, Quickly suddenly loses her own and interrupts her thought to comment upon her own lack of control over her own mind. Shakespeare uses the self-interruption as a comedic device to make Quickly look like a bumbling silly servant/woman; however, the structure illustrates how complicated it is to know, or even try to know, another's mind. Quickly's assertion of mind-knowing is therefore countered through her inability to know herself. Her self is at stake in the self-interruptions, as the readers and audience members attempt to see the subtextual mind of the character that has self-interrupted throughout the scene and, thereby, controlled dialogue through monologue. The comedic closure to this scene of self-interruptions through a self-interruption about knowing a mind highlights the complex presentation of self-interruptions themselves. They tantalizingly invite us to consider the interior mind that resides beyond the textual language presented to us as spectators; however, this moment reminds us, in a comedic vein, that such an apprehension of character is an unknowable object. There is nothing but 'out', and the 'forgotten' thought in Quickly's utterance is nothing more than the line that she has forgotten something, a something that never existed except in an inaccessible interiority that we as audience must provide.

This moment, therefore, not only highlights Shakespeare's comedic usages of self-interruptions but also demonstrates how he uses these moments to further illuminate one-sided power dynamics. Comedic self-interruptions seem to be internalized, controlled systems that lack the affective outreach that emotional or manipulative ones possess; however, like their counterparts, they too illustrate how self-interruptions invite a conception of interiority, but only through a contemplation of the comedic coherence that they proffer after their ruptures disconnect. While these self-interruptions may be for a laugh, a powerful affective response in itself, they also articulate structures within these texts that work on the audience as we approach the characters' interiorities.

Conclusion

As we have seen, interruptions are always about relationships: either between characters, between text and audience/reader, between author and text, between author and hypothetical audience, between author and precedent, or between audience and history. Interruptions question the nature of seemingly established relationships and resituate the dynamics of a relationship through negotiation of the encountering parties. Interruptions constitute a struggle, an active dynamic encounter, and an investigation of them uncovers the methodologies by which authors examine the struggles between their characters, themselves, and their texts.

All three types of self-interruptions examined in this chapter possess a triadic affective structure. This structure emphasizes the intense scrutiny of interiority that we offer to characters upon reading or seeing them. Despite seeming like the most contained microinterruption focused solely on inner workings, self-interruption is only important or significant through its inter-workings with its audiences, which may or may not possess a similar approach to comprehending the character. Whether the interruption derives from fear or necessity, from manipulative energies or comedic control, these structures demonstrate the power that the playwright wields in crafting these moments. In this way, the power dynamics invested within the self-interruption become about the struggle for control of meaning that plays out between the playwright and the audience with the text and the actor as intermediary. Importantly though, we cannot think of the text or actor as complacent or caught entities, as their own histories and interventions affect and effect the outcome of the meaning development in this power struggle. Through punctuation and subtext to name two central poles, the text and actor can alter, drive, impede, or accelerate an interpretation of any particularly interruptive moment. However, what these specific types of interruptions reveal is the manner to which we invest within the character the interiority and the subjectivity that we ourselves desire. The gaps in the text, which are only ever absent, are paradoxically always present as we fill them up with subtext. Egeon's tragedy, Celia's anxiety, Memnon's confusion, Iago's manipulation, and Quickly's control all illuminate how self-interruptions develop the relationship between the audience/reader and the actor/character/text. The self-interruption then is therefore a rupture that exposes the matrix through which we develop the idea of character.

3

Action

Hamlet instructs the players with the often-quoted line: 'Suit the action to the word, the word to the action' (3.2.17-18). Linking the bodily language to the oral language—the language of action and the language of words—Hamlet reminds the actors, and the audience, of the deep-rooted connection between these two halves in the theatre. However, in printed play texts, we regularly encounter words that are actions and actions that are words, suited to each other and representing something different from the dialogue. These sites are called 'stage directions,' a phrase that is as complicated as that which it represents.[1] These pieces of textuality, whether we term them 'stage directions' or *didascalia*, interrupt dramatic dialogue. They are action interruptions, rupturing the expectation of spoken dialogue by inserting gesture, movement, music, and guidance. Stage directions, and other *didascalia*, are 'fundamentally mutable, enigmatic, and various'.[2] Additionally, they provide a theatrical point of contact within the dramatic script.[3] While we cannot know what theatre makers in the past did or what contemporary theatre makers would do with the stage directions as printed, these moments—when the action interrupts the dialogue—are expressions of a 'complex power relationship'[4] within the text that, when attended to, present dramatic and theatrical information about a play for both reader and producer.

    This chapter explores moments when non-linguistic theatrical occurrences (mostly entrances, exits, and sounds) rupture the dialogue.[5] Just as self-interruptions obscure the rupture, implying it through subtext, action interruptions combine the rupture with the continuation. For example, at the end of 1.1 of Fletcher's *The Mad Lover*, Chilax's final line reads, 'Come let's together,/I'le see your tricks, and as I like 'em—*Exeunt*' (1.1.339-40). Here, the rupture is the movement of the men offstage, breaking off the conversation mid-thought. The continuation is their continued absence from the stage. We never learn what Chilax will do if he likes the Fool and Page's tricks. The combination highlights the constructed nature of these interruptions, reminding the reader or the audience member of the author's controlling hand. Action interruptions, such as Chilax's exit, are not indicative of Chilax's lack of desire to be on the stage; rather, it shows Fletcher's scenic construction in which the conversation seemingly continues without the presence of the audience. The characters exist in a world offstage, while we are planted within the venue of the playhouse and only experience what the playwright brings into that space. Action interruptions combine rupture with continuation and emphasize the performative nature of the texts. These interruptions provide theatrical opportunities for staging that are myriad in possibility but are also limited through the guiding form of the text itself.

Such moments signal an interplay of power among the fictive world of the play, the performative world of the theatre, and the dramatic world of the printed script. At the centre of this interplay, we find the figure of the editor. As discussed in the previous two chapters, editors possess significant power of presentation for these texts as gatekeepers for modern readers and performers. We can never access the earliest performances or original (manuscript) texts of these plays and, therefore, must rely on later textual manifestations; however, the interference of editors in stage directions, like their interference in pointing, is an accepted alteration in early modern drama.[6] Too often, though, editors reconfigure these moments to recreate a scene that makes sense to them, sometimes removing action interruptions to follow their own sense of dramaturgy. I am perhaps advocating for an 'unediting' approach, as Leah Marcus has explored, through an understanding of interruptions as a particular form.[7] In this I mean that we should explore these moments in their earliest version as they are and evaluate those texts alongside later editorial emendations. Therefore, actions interruptions not only reflect an author's sensibilities of theatricality but also of editorial evaluation of these playwrights.

The simplest form of an action interruption is the entrance. When a character enters, their entrance ruptures the dialogue that is taking place. I begin with an examination of the entrance as rupture itself within Jonson's classical scenic structure in his published texts. Examining the problems of these divisions demonstrates the tensions within Jonson's texts of readerly approaches versus performative technique. I then turn to the entrance of spirits in Shakespeare, an unexpected occurrence that always has ramifications for plot and character, especially with his use of Banquo's ghost in *Macbeth*. I end with Fletcher's use of offstage female songs, especially in *The Woman's Prize, or The Tamer Tamed*. These songs shift a scene's focus to an inaccessible location that takes over the dialogue. In these ruptured moments, Fletcher provides a space for female characters in his plays to engage power through performance. What all three of these cases ultimately explore is the powerful role of the editor. By moving from Jonson through Shakespeare to Fletcher, we see the differentiation of editors from a totalizing respect in the case of Jonson, down to misunderstanding in the case of Fletcher.

Jonson's scenes

Entrances are the most ubiquitous of action interruptions; in fact, a drama cannot exist without characters entering the stage. Their inherent conventionality means that their own interruptive nature becomes obfuscated as we accept them as an integral part of drama. However, some entrances are not expected, and their interruptive nature becomes glaringly apparent to either an audience or a reader. Entrances, therefore, present a site of interruption that exits do not always contain. Unlike the atypical moment in *The Mad Lover*, most exits indicate where the character is going to and possess the quality of completion rather than an irruptive quality of creation.[8] The rupture that entrances possess—bodies taking up space, ink marking up a page—provides the audience with the material that makes the dramatic text possible. By placing these characters into the space before the audience, the text allows for the drama to unfold.

The interruptive entrance finds further import when aligned with another important dramatic form: the scene. Typically, the early modern page presented scenes as occurring either between cleared stages or when a new character entered.[9] Both definitions offer a 'frame of perception', as Bruce R. Smith terms it,[10] even if that frame remains debatable and problematic. The cleared stage logic is one that prizes the exit: it is a frame about completion, demarcating units that possess a sense of ending because of the exit. However, the other logic, the so-called French scene, which derives from classical texts,[11] demarcates a new frame based upon entrances. In uniting the already-interruptive form of an entrance to the division of the scene, the French scene possesses an inherently interruptive logic in dividing up the sections of a play.

Ben Jonson's usage of the French scene disrupts that convention to allow for greater authorial control over his constructed frames. While many early modern English plays are not divided up by scenic structure at all, Ben Jonson carefully crafted his texts with scenes that seem to rely upon the neoclassical precedent.[12] This section will examine Jonson's usage of the French scene as a division of text, arguing that his usage is not consistent and, thereby, emphasizes the interruptive logic of the entrance-driven French scene. His inconsistencies allow for disruption of expectations, and therefore highlight the use of interruption for authorial control. This differentiation highlights not only the ever-present tension of theatrical performance and printed text within all drama of the period[13] but also Jonson's particular creation of his own dramaturgical spaces to deal with that *frisson*.[14] These ideas are best exemplified in the scenic structure of *The Alchemist*, a play full of interruptions and reversals.

Examining the scenic structure of *The Alchemist* provides two insights. Firstly, the scene divisions are not predicated upon entrances or exits, thereby exposing the overly facile idea of the simple 'French scene'. Secondly, they are authorially crafted units intended for the reader of the script and which would have little to do with the presentation of the theatrical performance. Jonson's scenic art relied upon the convention of the French scene, which provides neither entrance stage direction nor exit stage direction, but only gives an Act and Scene numbering followed by a list of the characters involved in that division. His plays range in number from fifty-eight such scenes in *Sejanus* down to twenty-three in *The New Inn*.[15] While *The Alchemist* possesses only twenty-seven such scenes, it does have one of the longest streaks of continually occupied stage space, made of eight French scenes.[16] As Peter Holland and William Sherman note in their introduction, 'Jonson's choice of a classical model for scene division, marking a new scene when a character enters or leaves the stage, poses a difficulty for editors.'[17] This statement presents the accepted consideration of Jonson's scenes as well as the problems that it incurs. To make the text legible to a current reader, Holland and Sherman, as have all previous twentieth- and twenty-first-century editors, add the words 'Enter' and 'exit', which otherwise appear infrequently in the marginal stage directions.[18] Sherman, in his textual essay on the play, dismisses the marginal stage directions as looking more like 'notes to the reader' rather than 'instructions for an acting company',[19] which is precisely what they are. Stage directions are text that is always a note to the reader, whether that reader is in a theatre or a library. They craft or reproduce the theatrical performance on the page, suggest what could take place on a stage, and provide action apart from the dialogue.

The very first scene break in the play, between *Act One*, Scene One, and *Act One*, Scene Two, suggests not only a seemingly normative approach but also one integrated within an interruptive frame. After the trio of Subtle, Face, and Doll burst onto the stage amidst a fight, Doll finally calms them down by reminding them of their collective ambition. Subtle then says, 'Who's that? One rings' (1.1.180).[20] This sound marks the first of several visitors over the course of the play. Notably, unlike the other entrances, Dapper's entrance here is preceded by a ring, a sound drastically different from the knocks that pervade the text otherwise (especially in Jonson's marginal stage directions).[21] This atypical auricular cue initiates the sequences that follow, and while it ruptures the conversation, stopping Face from further praising Doll, the continuation is immediate as the characters respond and prepare to entertain their first dupe. Furthermore, the sound precedes the entrance of the character as well as the break in the text. The audience then expects Dapper's appearance, having been prepared by Doll's spotting him outside and Face's recognition from her description. Even the play-acting for Dapper begins before the scene break and Dapper's entrance:

FACE: [*Raising his voice*]   God b'wi'you, sir.
    I pray you, let him know that I was here.
    His name is Dapper. I would gladly have stayed, but—
                1.2
DAPPER: [*Within*] Captain, I am here.
FACE: Who's that?—He's come, I think, Doctor.
    [*Enter* DAPPER.]
Good faith, sir, I was going away.
                                  (1.1.197-1.2.2)

Holland and Sherman's direction for Face to raise his voice at the end of the scene helps readers see that Face is now acting a part. The scene break could go before this line, as it aligns with the pretended narrative that dominates the following scene; instead, it anticipates that scene. The scene break is highly interruptive as it cuts into Face's line, stopping his goodbyes to the Doctor and inserting Dapper into the stage grouping. But what ruptures the line? From a theatrical point of view, it is either Dapper's voice, as Holland and Sherman edit it, or it is his entrance, as the logic of the French scene and F.H. Mares edit it. Mares uses the emended direction '[*Enter to them*] DAPPER' to bring Dapper into the stage space: voice, body, and all.[22] Both presentations of course 'work' for either a theatrical performance or a readerly one. We can easily imagine hearing Dapper and then seeing him (reflecting the anticipatory ring announcing his arrival just moments before) or seeing him talking immediately as he walks in. No matter the choice, the imagined theatrical moment is that the character of Dapper ruptures Face's exit, with the continuation bringing him into the scene, where he remains.

However, for readers of this text, Dapper does not interrupt the moment. His presence has already been heralded in the fictional world via the ring and Face's identification of him. Instead, readers of the first Quarto, Jonson's first Folio, *The Cambridge Edition of the Works of Ben Jonson* (*CWBJ*), or any other text of the play see the line 'I would gladly have stayed, but —' interrupted by a series of numbers: 'ACT. I. SCENE 2' in the Quarto, 'Act I. Scene II.' in the Folio, or the minimal '1.2' in the *CWBJ*. These textual pieces are not inherently obvious or necessary. And while they are not stage directions, they are certainly *didascalia*. In one radical edition, W. Gifford does not provide this demarcation. There, the rupture is the speech prefix of 'Dap.', his voice and character entering the play world, rupturing the false exit.[23] In creating the separation of 'Act I. Scene II.', Jonson and the editors that have followed him create a division within the text that presents the previous dialogue as a specific unit, followed by a connected but differing unit of dialogue. The continuation in the system (we are still in Act I) provides connectivity, but the advancement (Scene II) and the intrusion into the middle of a speech mean that this break interrupts and thereby reframes the passage. These demarcations seem to be French scenes, especially as Q, F, and Mares present them, providing a new grouping of characters with an entrance. In this way, they function as an action interruption. So too, if we think of scenes as Smith's 'frames', they are here functioning as open brackets: they open onto a new unit, but they are not necessarily closing anything.[24] This presentation allows no end to the frame. In this way, we may note that Doll exited before the change in frame, but no new frame was provided when the stage would be occupied only by Face and Subtle. So, what does this demarcation provide? Because Dapper might not enter here and because his entrance is already heralded long before we encounter 'Act I. Scene II.', the break ultimately seems less concerned with entrances. These divisions are not the neoclassical French scenes that scholars want to equate with Jonson. These breaks cause so much editorial strife because they are idiosyncratically authorial, specifically Jonsonian scenes, crafted into units of his own logic and division, which are concerned with action and character not with cleared stages or entrances. Therefore, Jonson interrupts your reading of his text to demarcate and divide the text into a unit of his authorial crafting.[25]

While this tension here is debatable (again, Mares has Dapper enter), in a later scene Jonson provides several marginal directions that disrupt the idea that entrances are the logic for the scenic structures. The Jonsonian unit 'Act II. Scene III.' has 13 per cent of all the marginal directions in the text.[26] This scene is the first part of gulling Sir Epicure Mammon, which has several exits and re-entries for Face, as Subtle asks him to check on alchemical processes occurring offstage. Neither Q nor F indicates Face's exits or re-entries during the long sequence of alchemical information; however, late into this scene, a marginal stage direction appears, 'Dol is seene.', which is quickly followed by 'Face returns.', 'He goes out.', and 'Face againe.'.[27] This sequencing of action from Doll's entrance, which gathers attention through Face's entrances and exits, provides a separate unit from the previous two-thirds of the scene, which have focused on the alchemical conversations between Subtle and Mammon and on Surly's disbelief. Her appearance changes the narrative with repercussions for the rest of the play. Once Mammon sees Doll, he becomes obsessed with her and wants her almost as much as he wants the philosopher's stone. The shift for all of the characters in entrances, tactics, and goals creates a new unit within the larger framework of 'Act II. Scene III.' However, Jonson does not rupture the scene. Despite this moment easily calling for at least one French scene, Jonson leaves it as part of the larger continuity, even though adding a division here would make this scene more equal to the lengths of the other scenes in the play. Therefore, entrance-wise, theme-wise, and lengthwise, this should garner a division, an interruption, just as the moment is itself interruptive, but Jonson avoids the textual division. This lack of a scene break indicates Jonson's use of his own logic in crafting these scenes that goes beyond easy entrances or straightforward themes; rather, he is intent on establishing his control over the reception of the text. As this scene leads to the blowing up of the furnace as well as Surly's decision to adopt the Spanish disguise, Jonson gives it space and emphasis, allowing it to meander along. So too, the prolonged alchemical discussion itself highlights Jonson's own knowledge of alchemy while also cementing the overall effect for an audience of being bombarded with information. The authority invoked here, alchemically and authorially, controls the interruptions that take place in the text.

The Act divisions in the play also demonstrate thwarted expectations, which further indicates Jonson's control, even to the point of crafting uneven breaks in both performance and printed text. *Act One* and *Act Two* both end with the expectation of a cleared stage. At the end of *Act One*, the trio anticipate the arrival of Mammon, and *Act Two* begins with only Mammon and Surly on stage. This shift, and our first scene without any of the trio, makes the cleared stage for the interval obvious. At the end of *Act Two*, Face leaves to confront Surly, and *Act Three* begins with the arrival of Tribulation and Ananias. This is another clear break.[28] The act break between *Act Four* and *Act Five* also has an obviously cleared stage as Lovewit arrives outside of his house just after being spotted by Doll. The usage of an act interval would have most likely been expected of a play being performed at the Blackfriars Playhouse. Plays written for the Blackfriars Playhouse use the five-act structure to provide interval breaks, and as this play was obviously meant to be performed in the Blackfriars, it would possess such breaks.[29] Intervals were necessary for candle upkeep and also allowed for talking by audience members;[30] however, the regularity required for such maintenance remains unclear. Therefore, the early playgoers to *The Alchemist* most likely had several breaks in which to stretch their legs, show off their clothes, and discuss the performance. However, the textual division between *Act Three* and *Act Four* does not provide the same indication of the cleared stage that the other three suggest. While classical precedent of the French scene meant that act breaks were for cleared stages,[31] as we have seen, Jonson was crafting his own idiosyncratic sense of divisions that are more strongly unified by thematic affect than around clear-cut theatrical actions.

Just as *Act One* ends with Mammon's arrival, so too the end of *Act Three* reiterates this stage picture with Doll spying him before he enters the stage space. After securing Dapper and filling his mouth with gingerbread, Face quickly prepares to meet with Mammon as Lungs:

> SUBTLE: Only the fumigation's somewhat strong.
> FACE: Sir Epicure, I am yours, sir, by and by.
> [*Exeunt.*]
> 4.1 [*Enter*] FACE [*and*] MAMMON.
> FACE: Oh, sir, you're come i'the only finest time—
> MAMMON: Where's master?
>
> (3.5.81-4.1.2)

Holland and Sherman provide an act break that one might expect: both Subtle and Face exit, and then Face re-enters with Mammon, a re-entry that works with an act interval. They provide an extensive note not only justifying their decision to treat the act break as a cleared stage but also noting that other editors have left it more open, even insisting that the action is continuous (3.5.82SDn). Their assessment concludes, 'If act breaks were marked by act-music in the King's Men practice of staging by this date . . . then it would be odd for only one act-break not to be so marked. But it would be improbable for Face to stay onstage during the act-music' (3.5.82SDn). It would indeed be odd for the act break to not have music, but the question is who would know that it was an act break? An audience would not have recourse to a text to know when the act break should occur. By line numbers alone, the acts in *The Alchemist* are extremely regular (512, 758, 525, 742, 496), with *Act Two* and *Act Four* each covering about 25 per cent of the text and the other three acts cover 17 per cent each. The vacillation between 500-line and 750-line units might be a rhythm that an audience member could notice. Twenty-five minutes, then a break, thirty-eight minutes, then a break, twenty-five minutes, then a break, and so on. However, while the numbers demonstrate an equality, they in no way can vouch for an audience being aware of such discrepancies. This is to say that the ending of *Act Three*, especially Face's line directly to Sir Epicure, seems more like the several Jonsonian scene breaks that move onward and less like the three other act breaks in the text. If we imagine a performance that did not include an act break here but ran on, then the audience would be barreling towards the arrival of Lovewit and the breaking up of the entire enterprise.[32] The overly long middle section would allow for the amplification of the farcical nature of entry and exit, leading towards the furnace explosion, the fight with Surly, and Lovewit's arrival, the three destructive actions that conclude this middle section.[33] If Jonson intended this act break not to break in performance, then he manipulates his audience by crafting the sense of a break but then allowing for no reprieve, driving the action ever onward. He not only provides his readerly audience with the neoclassical formation to create its own balanced logic, but also insinuates the driving continuity through the immediate repetition of characters and speakers, again acting more like a Jonsonian scene break than one of the previous act breaks. This construction is pervasively under the control of Jonson the playwright, who interrupts our expectation of breaks in the indoor theatre to create uneven sections in performance and questionable breaks in the printed text.

 Ultimately, the play hinges on such control, as the explosion in 4.5 is also an act of authorial control. Does the furnace actually explode, or is it part of Subtle's fiction? Neither audience member nor reader can ever ascertain the truth of that sound. In the theatre, quite literally, nothing explodes, and the direction, 'A great crack and noise within', leaves open the possibility of a real explosion without the narrative reality of what exactly it means or is. The direction does not take the form of theatrical necessity as in 'the sound of . . .', indicating the creation of that sound from an offstage perspective. Nor does it indulge in complete fictive fantasy as in 'the furnace explodes . . .'; rather, the construction remains somewhere between the two. So too, Jonson's divided printed texts remain somewhere between a readerly drama and a theatrical book. This is not a prompt copy, but it is also not meant to be divorced from its theatrical origin either. Perhaps the best way of understanding these scenic constructions is that Jonson makes 'a fresh scene with each major turn of the action'.[34] Jonson interrupts the development of typical acts and scenes in both theatrical and printed vocabularies by engendering his own approach based upon both classical forms and character/action development. He once more ruptures expectations as he controls the outcome, crafting texts to suit his vision of the play to be read. Therefore, as readers encounter these interruptive breaks, denoting acts and scenes, they must assess the information being supplied within these ruptures, immediately leading into a continuation of action as the printed words barrel forward. As William Sherman sums it up, 'the printed page offers a new occasion for staging of a different kind in which author, reader, and patron all have starring roles.'[35] Though as the interruptive forms indicate, the first among these for Jonson was the author.

Shakespeare's spirits

Just as scene breaks and other *didascalia* represent a liminal space between reading text and performance, certain characters within drama further elicit such indeterminate space. Ghosts are one such type, as they are 'both reality and representation, both theatrical fiction and performing actor'.[36] Just as 'a stage ghost is visible to playgoers and yet often invisible to fellow characters, never fully the disembodied spirit it represents nor merely the ordinary body of an actor',[37] so too the stage direction is never fully part of the literary text, often moved without comment by editors, nor fully part of the theatrical text, indicating only action to be performed and often moved without comment by directors and actors. Stage ghosts then perhaps are an embodiment of *didascalia*. Shakespeare in particular presents spectral others within moments of interruption. The Ghost in *Hamlet* stands as exemplar, where the Ghost is expected but the audience is lulled into narrative stupor only to experience a rupture through the entrance of an other-worldly presence. There, the tension between the narrative/literary and the theatrical/dramatic becomes literally embodied in the liminal construct of the Ghost.

Shakespeare regularly uses ghosts to interrupt narratives as they are unfolding. He used ghosts in five plays: *Richard III*, *Julius Caesar*, *Hamlet*, *Macbeth*, and *Cymbeline*, and in four of the five encounters they are immediately noticed and identified.[38] In *Richard III*, Prince Edward speaks upon his entrance, identifying himself as Richard's victim (5.3.119-20), and Richard wakes after the whole procession perturbed and dismissing the event, saying he 'did but dream' and that 'there's none else by' (5.3.179, 183). As Caesar's ghost enters, Brutus says, 'How ill this taper burns. Ha! Who comes here?' (4.3.273). The entrance causes instant disruption, and after the half line of him noticing the candle, he sees and responds to the Ghost. Horatio first cuts off Marcellus with 'Peace, break thee off' (1.1.39), then says 'But soft, behold' in the middle of his own story (1.1.125), and later informs Hamlet with 'Look, my lord, it comes' (1.4.38).[39] As soon as the ghosts in *Cymbeline* vanish, Posthumous awakes recalling the vision of his family, calling 'sleep ... a grandsire' who 'begot/A father' for him (5.4.93-94). The only example, aside from *Macbeth*, where the characters do not immediately notice the ghostly presence is in *Hamlet* when the Ghost appears in Gertrude's closet (3.4). Hamlet delivers a line, 'A King of shreds and patches' (Q2 3.4.99), after the stage direction for the Ghost's entrance but before he reacts to seeing the Ghost by saying, 'Save me' (Q2 3.4.100).[40] In Shakespeare's typical dramaturgy, then, as soon as either audience or reader engage these spirits, the characters on stage do too, enveloping them within the dramatic and theatrical worlds.

Macbeth's ghost, however, is an outlier. In *Macbeth*, Shakespeare presents a ghost who lives outside of the space in which he arrives. Its placement within the scene stands out because, unlike every other instantiation of ghosts in Shakespeare, Banquo's ghost appears in a stage direction long before any character notices his presence. As soon as the other ghosts enter, they are acknowledged. Banquo, however, enters long before Macbeth reacts to seeing him. Because of these differences, editors since the eighteenth century have been uneasy with the *Macbeth* stage direction, moving it closer to Macbeth's reaction. While this alteration may create a more alarming effect for a reader or may strengthen the dramatic irony surrounding Banquo,[41] the movement also effects a lessening of Shakespeare's interruptive impact and building of suspenseful dramatic irony in this scene of eerie suspense. This moment exemplifies Shakespeare's investment in interruptions as form for dramatic irony through its delayed delivery of reaction.

In *Act Three*, Scene Four, of *Macbeth*, Banquo's ghost twice disrupts the festivities that Macbeth has planned to celebrate his kingship, but the placement of these disruptions has led to confused editorial emendation. The Folio text, the earliest surviving version, places the stage direction directly after Lady Macbeth's line:

>   *Lady.* My Royall Lord,
> You do not giue the Cheere, the Feast is sold
> That is not often vouch'd, while 'tis a making:
> 'Tis giuen, with welcome: to feede were best at home:
> From thence, the sawce to meate is Ceremony,
> Meeting were bare without it.
>
>   *Enter the Ghost of Banquo, and sits in Macbeths place.*
>
>   *Macb.* Sweet Remembrancer:
> Now good digestion waite on Appetite,
> And health on both.
>   *Lenox.* May't please your Highnesse sit.
>
> (TLN 1293-1303)[42]

The italicized direction is further highlighted as it is separated from the dialogue by two blank lines of text. In offsetting the direction thus, the mise-en-page calls attention to the stage direction's rupture of the dialogue. After Lady Macbeth comments on Macbeth's surly attitude, the Ghost of his victim suddenly arrives. A reader may wonder how the king will react, what will Macbeth do. Instead, he replies to his wife: 'Sweet Remembrancer:/Now good digestion waite on Appetite,/And health on both' (TLN 1300-02). While a reader may ponder if they missed something, the scene continues for over ten more lines until the first indication that Macbeth has seen the Ghost. This delayed response seems to lessen the interruptive impact of introducing the preternatural character.[43] The audience will not be shocked or astounded when the Ghost is recognized by the protagonist because we have already seen him enter and seen him move about the space. This problem, this lack of an action interruption here, led Shakespeare editors of the eighteenth and nineteenth centuries to move this stage direction to differing locations to create their conception of the appropriate 'jump scare'.[44]

The Folio placement, however, early and unacknowledged, achieves its own particular effect, especially in performance. That early entrance creates a prolonged rupture in which the expectations of the audience lie suspended, as we await the moment in which the continuation might hit. To break it down within the language of interruptions: the premise is the banquet and the giving of cheer to which Lady Macbeth enjoins her husband, and the rupture is the

Ghost's entrance with its prolonged unacknowledged status. This stage direction and its placement reflect Shakespeare's continued preoccupation with interruptions that provide and amplify dramatic irony. The reader and the spectator have almost ten lines of text in which they are aware of the problems attendant to the scene that no character notices. This bit of irony amplifies the suspense and the tension, leading towards the eerie affective release once Macbeth acknowledges the Ghost and begins his outbursts.

That continuation though is also couched within a performative moment as the initial indication from Macbeth that he sees the Ghost neither is in a stage direction nor is it verbal. When Macbeth claims he has no seat, Lennox replies, 'Heere my good Lord./What is't that moues your Highnesse?' (TLN 1314-15). This reaction takes on the silent yet active performance that the Ghost insinuates into the scene. Like the Ghost's continued silence, Macbeth is initially silent in his reaction and disengages from the party. The continuation does not occur until Macbeth addresses the Ghost. At that moment, he decides to openly confront the spirit and alter the course of the banquet. This entrance then ruptures the entire party and completely dominates the premise, eventually resulting in the complete breakdown of festivities. It also demonstrates how action on the stage achieves power over language. The Ghost is always silent, and Macbeth's outbursts and his attempts to control the Ghost only further indicate to the audience (both on- and offstage) how little power he possesses. The interruption of the Ghost with its Folio placement further exemplifies Shakespeare's connection of interruption to dramatic irony while also, through Macbeth's delayed and ineffectual ranting, reveals Macbeth's losing of power.

This stage direction has not always remained where the Folio text places it, demonstrating editorial attempts at control. Despite the performative and interruptive context within which the Ghost ruptures the banquet, editors have moved it in order to emend the text. The impulse to move the stage direction, like all editorial emendations, derives from a desire to eliminate error.[45] For example, Nick de Somogyi provides an extensive note in his edition of the play for *The Shakespeare Folios* series. While he abides by the Folio placement, he adds, 'The Folio positioning of this extraordinary stage-direction risks confusing a reader'.[46] He even hypothesizes that the placement of the stage direction in the manuscript must have confused the compositor, leading to the supposedly 'odd' placement. George Steevens, whose edition uses the Folio placement, noted this moment as one to excite an invested reader:

> I have repeatedly met with thin flakes of piecrust between the leaves of our author. These unctuous fragments, remaining long in close confinement, communicated their grease to several pages deep on each side of them—It is easy enough to conceive how such accidents might happen;—how aunt Bridget's mastication might be disordered at the sudden entry of the Ghost into the Queen's closet, and how the half-chewed morsel dropped out of the gaping 'Squire's mouth, when the visionary Banquo seated himself in the chair of Macbeth.[47]

The moment embroils itself within a readerly affect that stupefies the senses and makes the reader unaware of their other bodily functions. Steevens perceived no problems with the entrance being affective for readers as is, using it to prove Shakespeare's terrifying qualities through readerly interaction.[48] Examining the editorial tradition through this stage direction indicates the complicated methodologies of power implicated through action interruptions and their engagement of text and performance. The liminal space that they occupy means that their clarity is rarely precise and more often contentious than not. Moving these texts, either for emendation or clarity, claims a level of power over them by the editor, even if that power is being wielded within the service of creating a more perfect text.

The first editors of *Macbeth* continued the Folio placement by placing the stage direction for the Ghost's first entrance after Lady Macbeth's line: a placement that held, aside from one oddity, until the second half of the eighteenth century. Nicolas Rowe (1709), Alexander Pope (1725), Lewis Theobald (1733), Thomas Hanmer (1743), and Samuel Johnson (1765), among others, all kept the First Folio (F1) placement of the direction.[49] So too, William Davenant's theatrical adaptation (pub. 1673), purportedly reflecting stage practice of the late seventeenth century, kept the placement (though he did shorten Lady Macbeth's line). Readers as well as theatregoers of the late seventeenth century and into the eighteenth century, therefore, would have experienced this moment in the same way.[50] However, Edward Capell in his 1768 edition began a trend that would last for over 100 years. Capell's edition was an attempt to look through the accumulated editorial histories and assess what the earliest texts provided.[51] As Alan Galey and Rebecca Niles put it, 'Precision was a fundamental aspect of Capell's plan'.[52] Despite his rigour for investigations of textual emendation, stage direction placement did not receive the same sort of respect.[53] Unlike the editors before him, many of whom he rejected because of their interference, Capell moved the Ghost's entrance forward by four lines, placing it after Lennox's line, 'May't please your highness sit?'.[54] Nowhere, not even in his posthumously published notes,[55] does he explain his decision to move this entrance. The alteration makes the ghost appear just before/as Macbeth begins to speak about Banquo's absence. While this move eliminates, perhaps, uncertainty for a reading audience, it dampens the peculiar impact that the Folio placement provides. Capell's placement accords in some sense with Shakespeare's other ghosts, as he enters and is immediately, even if ironically, discussed or recognized. Because of this connection, we might see the logic of the move. However, it is a move that focuses on readerly clarity and not performative clarity.[56]

Shakespeare editors after Capell all agreed with him. Although a few editors between 1773 and 1786 followed the Folio, most, including Edmund Malone's 1790 edition, did not. Malone provided copious notes in his volume, but, like Capell, he provides no justification for moving this stage direction from the Folio placement to its position after Lennox's line.[57] This edition solidified this new position for the entrance, creating an orthodoxy for the nineteenth-century editions of Shakespeare. One dissenting voice in the Victorian era was Thomas Keightley, who in 1864 moved it even closer to Macbeth's reaction. He placed it after Ross's line, 'Please't your highness/To grace us with your royal company?',[58] thereby having the ghost enter just as Macbeth notices that the table is full, uniting the rupture of the entrance with the continuation. This placement reduces the reader and audience's knowledge over the on-stage characters. It removes their ability to perceive information that no one else, not even Macbeth, perceives. It places us more directly into the same space as the characters on the stage. This construction is, however, the less Shakespearean construction of an interruption. Shakespeare typically uses interruptions to give power to his audience, rupturing the expectations of characters but not necessarily of the audience.[59]

The twentieth century saw the return of the Folio placement, which generally has remained, aside from one notable exception.

Kenneth Muir's Arden 2 edition of the play offers yet another reading of this stage direction. Muir placed the entrance in the middle of Macbeth's speech:

> MACBETH: Here had we now our country's honour roof'd,
> Were the grac'd person of our Banquo present;
> *The Ghost of* BANQUO *enters, and sits in* MACBETH'S *place.*
> Who may I rather challenge for unkindness,
> Than pity for mischance!
>
> (3.4.39-42)

Muir in some respects provides the most interruptive option as the Ghost's entrance literally ruptures Macbeth's text, emerging between the lines. This ghost comes immediately upon being called by name. Such placement, from an interruptive consideration, gives the Ghost the power over Macbeth both physically and verbally, pulling focus from Macbeth's speech. It might even in a performance drown out the end of the line, or perhaps make the offstage audience not hear the line as they shift their attention, thereby further rupturing the scene. Again, this placement, as do the other non-Folio placements, provides myriad opportunities to explore the dynamic between Macbeth, the Ghost, and the audience.

In another unique move, Muir, unlike so many previous editors, justifies his decision:

> The Folio marks the entrance of the Ghost after Lady Macbeth's last speech. This may be either a premature direction to give plenty of warning to the actor, or it may merely indicate that on the Elizabethan stage the ghost would have some distance to walk. According to Forman's account the Ghost entered as Macbeth began to speak of Banquo. I have marked the entrance accordingly. Wilson adheres to the Folio entrance, other editors have marked it at 43 and 45, but the favourite place is after 39. The Ghost appears when summoned.[60]

While Muir's explications are grounded in a sense of the theatrical, he regards the Folio placement as inherently wrong and problematic, needing explication. He only accounts for two possibilities, both of which dismiss the placement as not adhering to the necessities of the reading text or of the story being told. Either it is a cue or it represents the size of the stage. What is inherent in the second suggestion, but does not merit consideration in his dismissive tone, is that if the Ghost needed that time to walk over the large stage, he would still be visible to the offstage audience. Therefore, the entrance would have an effect that surely Shakespeare would have understood as he had been working at the Globe for several years before writing this play.

As the note indicates, Muir's justification derives from his reading of Simon Forman's account. Forman saw the play performed on 20 April 1610 and mentions the Ghost's entrance. He remembers it thus:

> The next night, being at supper with his noblemen whom he had bid to a feast to the which also Banquo should have come, be began to speak of noble Banquo and to wish that he were there. And as he thus did, standing up to drink a carouse to him, the ghost of Banquo came and sat down in his chair behind him. And he, turning about to sit down again, saw the ghost of Banquo, which fronted him so . . . .[61]

Forman provides a memory of the staging, clearly indicating the impact that the moment had on him in the audience. While Muir notes the connection that Forman makes between Banquo being mentioned and the Ghost appearing, he perhaps puts too much pressure on the exactitude of Forman's memory. Forman, after all, also said that Macbeth and Banquo were 'riding through a wood' at the beginning of the play.[62] The imaginative work of the play seeps into Forman's recounting, and so, with the Ghost's entrance, the immediate connection between being named and appearing also seems to have united, whether that was part of the original staging or not. Notably, Forman is the only early account of this moment in the theatre, describing a performance that took place during Shakespeare's lifetime. The Folio text is posthumous, and in several respects presents a version of the play that postdates Shakespeare. However, we should not read Forman as if he were recording everything precisely. For example, the drinking of the carouse does not occur for the first entrance, but does so for the Ghost's re-entrance, which, while still happening before Macbeth sees the Ghost, is only two lines before Banquo is mentioned and four lines before Macbeth reacts.[63] The final observation to make about Forman's account though is that he records seeing and taking in the Ghost before Macbeth sees the Ghost. He remembered the Ghost, and he remembered seeing the Ghost before Macbeth did. Forman as audience is aware of the Ghost's presence and makes the dramatically ironic connection before the character on stage can react to the apparition.

Ultimately, Muir sums up his analysis with 'the Ghost appears when summoned'.[64] He argues that no matter what the placement (and he mentions all of the placements that I have noted so far), the Ghost must arrive when named. That is true in one conception of the scene, one that perhaps leans overly hard on Forman's account. However, the Folio and the bulk of the editorial tradition have tended to let the Ghost arrive earlier than summoned. Almost all other twentieth-century, and all twenty-first-century, editions of the play have reverted to the Folio's placement of the Ghost's entrance. They may or may not note that this could be moved in performance or could be closer to Banquo being named, but even if they note it, they opt to retain what the earliest printed text encodes. While this choice may signal Marcus's 'un-editing' influence, it also accords with Shakespeare's other uses of interruptions. The Ghost is an unexpected guest, not appearing in the sources, who ruptures the dinner party; however, Shakespeare emphasizes the power of the Ghost over the scene through his early entrance and continued silence. Beyond the Ghost is the offstage audience who can see the Ghost and Macbeth and the reactions all around. Importantly though, if our expectations were ruptured, if we, like Steevens' Squire drop our 'unctuous fragment' in fright over the Ghost's appearance, we also have time to compose our reaction and to respond to the entrance before any character on stage does so. We know who's sitting in Macbeth's chair, even if he does not, and that provides a fuller conception of dramatic irony, removing a jump scare and engaging us with Macbeth's response. The ghost's early entrance is an action interruption for Macbeth, not for the audience. We are not meant to be frightened like Macbeth; we are instead meant to see how Macbeth responds. In this way, we may begin too to understand why this ghost is so different and yet so similar to the earlier stage ghosts. He may not be immediately recognized, but we are not meant to be as fully aligned with Macbeth, perhaps, as with Brutus or Hamlet. Yet this distance in the affective response due to the early entrance allows for the unexpected nature of the Ghost's arrival. The other ghosts have candles and sleep and previous sightings that alert us to their possibility. Banquo's ghost walks right in and sits down.

If we take the Folio stage direction as an authorial one, then the scene as crafted has an interruption, though perhaps not for a reader or an audience member. The interruption is for Macbeth, and we are outside of Macbeth, an effect that Shakespeare is careful to craft throughout the play (e.g. the dagger). When editors move the stage direction, they craft a stronger action interruption, allowing the banquet part of the scene to be prolonged and allowing the reader or audience member to be shocked at the Ghost's arrival, but they lessen what seems to be Shakespeare's or at least the Folio text's crafted creation of a scene of dramatic irony. We are supposed to see and know more than Macbeth does, this moment included. When editors lessen that effect in favour of other effects, they risk making the text less Shakespearean and perhaps a bit more Fletcherean or even Middletonian.[65] Overall, this is a play of supernatural interruption; the dramaturgy throughout, where a Scottish history play is interrupted by a supernatural tragedy, undergirds Banquo's ghost's arrival. It is a play of the human disrupted by the otherworldly, but only for its character not for the audience, who start with the other-worldly—*Act One*, Scene 1 is the witches—and always, via dramatic irony, know a little bit more.

Fletcher's songs

The examinations of Jonson and Shakespeare have explored interruptive ramifications of entrances in connection to texts both authorial and editorial. Fletcher's plays provide several such entrances; however, one particularly unique methodology in crafting these interruptive moments for Fletcher is his coupling of them to offstage music. Even more specifically, Fletcher tends to dramaturgically craft moments of offstage female song that invades a male stage. Fletcher used music throughout his career, with every solo-authored play calling for at least one moment of music or song.[66] In three different plays, Fletcher crafts moments when offstage female characters sing in a way that disrupts the male conversations occurring on the stage.[67] In *Women Pleas'd* (1620), Silvio hears a song that encourages him to continue on courageously.[68] In *The Chances* (1617), Constantia sings offstage, affecting first two servants and then Don Frederick and Don John. Later in the play, when the men are searching for her, they stumble upon a group of women riotously singing within a house.[69] Finally, in *The Woman's Prize, or The Tamer Tamed* (1610), which is Fletcher's response to Shakespeare's *The Taming of the Shrew*, a group of men hear riotous music and are regaled with a servant's report of the actions inside before hearing a song and then confronting the women as they emerge above.[70] These four moments all disrupt the masculine conversation on the stage and direct attention to an offstage female voice; however, this interruptive form of non-linguistic theatrical action, that is, music and song, rupturing dialogue has created confusion for editors over where to place these occurrences. The following section will focus on the moment in *The Woman's Prize* as indicative of the textual problem incumbent upon interruptive music. Considering the placement of the direction for music as well as the women's song indicates the relative interruptive power of the women. While the earliest texts truly disrupt the male space, making the entrance unexpected, editors soften that rupture and move the song later in an attempt to clarify, which only succeeds in reducing the women's power. Fletcher, as with his other interruptions, tends to favour the rupture and the unexpected, placing character and audience on the same level. This musical moment of joy and celebration, as placed in the earliest texts, does just that.

The Woman's Prize is probably Fletcher's best-known solo play and exists not only in three seventeenth-century versions, but also has been regularly edited up to the twenty-first century. The two earliest texts of the play, the Lambarde Manuscript (Folger MS j.b.3, hereafter referred to as MS) and the 1647 Beaumont and Fletcher Folio (B&F F1), both place the stage direction for the song in the midst of the dialogue occurring on the stage (see Figures 3.1 and 3.2). The two earliest versions of the play, therefore, indicate that the song interrupts the dialogue. Jacques is reporting about what he spied in the house (premise), the song begins (rupture and continuation), and the men attempt to reassert control (further continuation). The song here is both rupture and continuation because, even though neither early edition includes lyrics, the idea that a song would be occurring indicates a prolonged moment of musicality. After hearing this song, the men cannot return to discussing what they think they know, but instead are poised to begin their encounter with the group of ensconced women. This situation contrasts with the one that occurs only moments before in which only music comes out of the above.

110 INTERRUPTIONS IN EARLY MODERN ENGLISH DRAMA

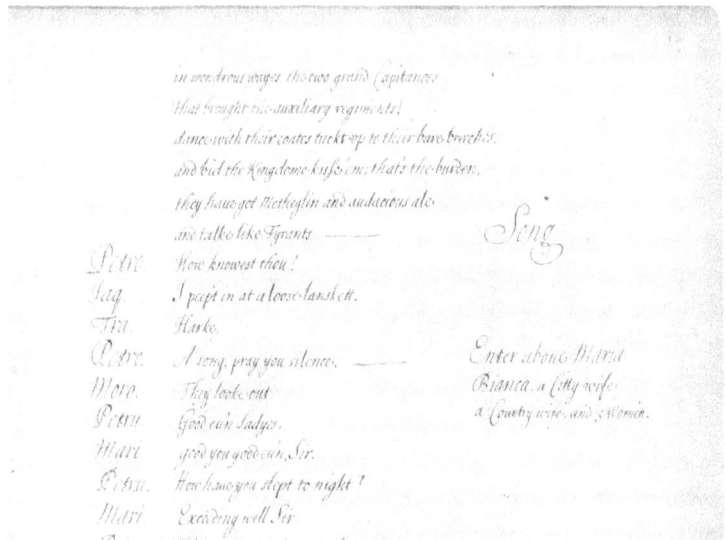

FIGURE 3.1 *The direction for the women's song. John Fletcher.* The Woman's Prize, *Fol. 90r. Call #: Folger MS j.b.3. Used by permission of the Folger Shakespeare Library under a Creative Commons Attribution-ShareAlike 4.0 International License.*

> They have got Metheglin, and audacious Ale,
> And talke like Tyrants.
>   *Petron.* How knoweſt thou?
>   *Jaq.* I peep't in   *Song!*
> At a looſe Lansket.
>   *Tra.* Harke.
>   *Petron.* A Song, pray ſilence.   *All the women above.*
>   *Mor.* They look out.
>   *Petru* Good ev'n Ladies.
>   *Mar.* Good you good ev'n ſir.
>   *Petru.* How have you ſlept to night?
>   *Mar.* Exceeding well ſir.

FIGURE 3.2 *The direction for the woman's song. John Fletcher.* The Woman's Prize, *in* Comedies and Tragedies, *written by Francis Beaumont and John Fletcher (London, Humphrey Moseley, 1647), sig. Ooooo2r. Florida State University Special Collections and Archives.*

While Tiffany Stern claims that the word 'song' in early modern plays should be considered 'scribe directions' as they represent something that 'cannot be performed' and 'is not, then, a direction for an actor' even if editors make them one,[71] she is mistaken. A song, while indicating something about the text that follows, also indicates a particular staged action that an actor needs to accomplish. Despite Stern's denigration of editors, their impulse to help readers see the action with 'Song' as printed/written in the early texts of the play demonstrate that word's status as stage direction and, importantly, as action direction. 'Song!' means that here the women must sing.[72]

Importantly, both early editions illustrate the theatrically interruptive nature of this stage direction and this moment. The MS places the stage direction after a long rule or dash at the end of Jacques' line, 'and talke like Tyrants', which itself does not include any final pointing.[73] While the absent period could be a simple omission, it also signals the possibility that Jacques has not finished describing what he has seen. We can easily hypothesize him continuing to deliver salacious details. Regardless of the pointing, the song breaks out over the description in a manner reminiscent of the entrance of Hamlet's ghost. Here the theatrical performance supersedes the narrative description as the music raucously overtakes the dialogue. The dash here, while specifically situating the rupture and pointing to the action, further helps to emphasize the idea of interruption. While scribes seem to use dashes in manuscripts to indicate stage directions as opposed to a modern conception of broken off dialogue, the punctuation's use as interruption in dialogue was beginning to be well accepted, especially after Ben Jonson's intense usage of them in his *Works* (1616).[74] Therefore, as a readerly text the dash here both points towards action while also indicating the way that stage directions break the 'boundaries' of the linguistic text.[75] Especially as the subsequent two speeches do not respond to the song itself, we can imagine the staging in which the song is occurring above and the men below, especially Petronius and Jacques, attempt to retain power by finishing their conversation. The action interruption here illustrates the ineffectual attempts by Petronius and Jacques to regain that control, and Tranio eventually points out the song with his 'Hark', and Petronius responds, 'A song. Pray you silence'.

The B&F F1 text moves the song later by placing it in the same line as Jacques' 'I peep't in' but offers more theatrical fluidity in having the stage direction float in the right-hand margin. The lack of a dash in B&F F1 and its sharing of a line with part of a speech further suggest interruption, though perhaps an open choice of exactly when that interruption occurs. The compositor though takes the moment to emphasize this occurrence through the unique usage of the exclamation point here, emphatically rendering the rupture as the women begin to sing upstairs. This text's inconclusive floating permits readers to stage their own possibilities for the emergence of music. Its placement though ends, as does the MS, with Tranio's recognition of the sounds and Petronius's line 'A Song, Pray silence'.

The subsequent printing of the play, in the 1679 *Fifty Comedies and Tragedies* by Beaumont and Fletcher (B&F F2), demonstrates how this moment coalesces rupture and continuation. This version prints the lyrics to this song for the first time, and all subsequent editions of the play have followed suit (see Figures 3.3 and 3.4).

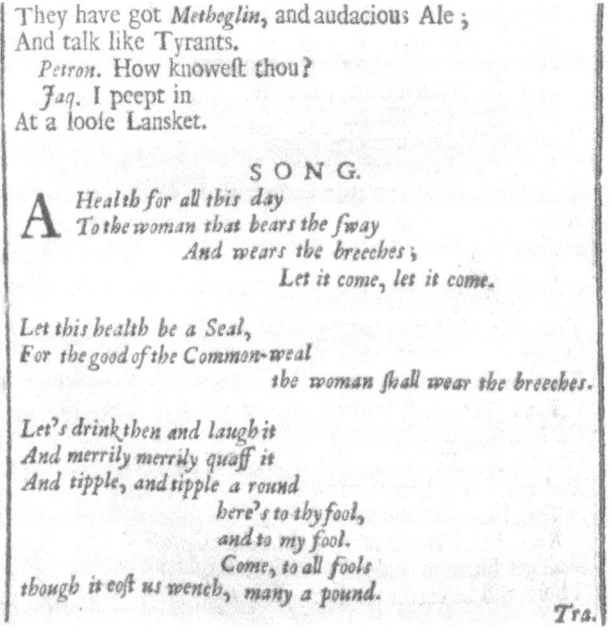

FIGURE 3.3 *The woman's song with lyrics. John Fletcher,* The Woman's Prize, *in* Fifty Comedies and Tragedies, Written by Francis Beaumont and John Fletcher, Gentlemen, *(London: John Martyn, Henry Herringman, and Richard Marriot, 1679), sig. Gg3v. Special Collections and University Archives, University of Maryland Libraries.*

By seeing the lyrics of the song incorporated into the text, the reader (as would the audience member) experiences the way that the rupture leads into a continuation that subsumes the premise. The men lose their power of conversation in light of the song coming from the women's chambers. Overall, the effect here from the text is clear: the men's discussion of the women is ruptured by the women's song, a not-fully linguistic action (especially as presented in the earlier versions of the play without lyrics)[76] that disrupts the drama of the dialogue by insinuating a theatrical moment that further emphasizes the importance of performance. Maria's whole attitude after all is an interruptive performance, intended to stop Petruccio from behaving as he has, and thus to produce a new Petruccio. Furthermore, B&F F2 continues a trend of moving the song later in the exchange, now placing it after Jacques' entire line but before Tranio's 'Hark'. This placement differs from B&F F1 slightly but likely stems from the printing of the song's lyrics, which could not all fit in the space to

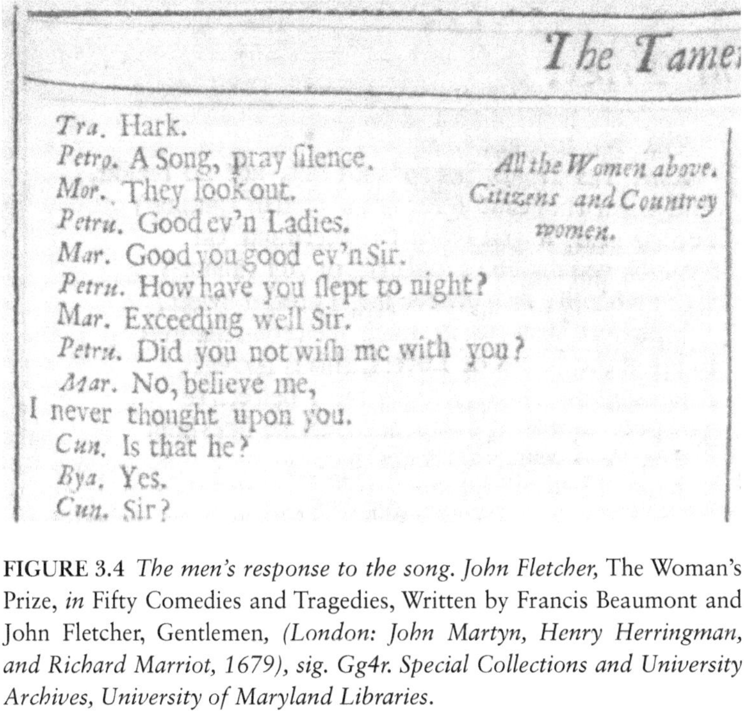

FIGURE 3.4 *The men's response to the song. John Fletcher,* The Woman's Prize, *in* Fifty Comedies and Tragedies, Written by Francis Beaumont and John Fletcher, Gentlemen, *(London: John Martyn, Henry Herringman, and Richard Marriot, 1679), sig. Gg4r. Special Collections and University Archives, University of Maryland Libraries.*

the right. Furthermore, the compositors might have thought it best to keep Jacques's line all together and then present the song, allowing Jacques to finish delivering his information before the women sing. While this may be efficacious to the printing of the lyrics, and while the lyrics help us to consider the continuation embedded within the action rupture, this placement reduces the interruptive nature of the moment. By allowing Jacques not only to finish his line but also to complete the dialogue segment of his reporting, this text presents the song as interruptive only in the sense of the women breaking out over what the men are speaking about. It follows on the heels of the narrative, but does so in an orderly way, which the printing house has regularized. The MS and the B&F F1 not only allow for open interpretation of a key theatrical moment but also emphasize that the women begin their singing *before* Jacques finishes his dialogue. In many ways then, B&F F2, while providing the reader with more Fletcher, reduces the Fletcherean strategy of placement. Fletcher's interruptions are repeatedly unexpected and embrace the rupture, allowing them to drive continuations. This play is of course no different. Here, he takes on both Shakespeare and Jonson and redefines the battle of the sexes by taming Shakespeare's own character.[77] Just as the play ruptures this tradition, so too this moment of song and theatrical playfulness breaking out over the dramatic dialogue illustrates a Fletcher engaged in staging his plays, having his female characters wrest power and privilege from their erstwhile dominators. The song then when most overlapping and most interruptive works best to underscore the text's proto-feminist engagement.[78]

The lessening of the interruptive impact found in B&F F2 only worsens as modern editors applied their own idiosyncratic, uneven, and often unexplained habits to the placement of this song. After B&F F2, the two eighteenth-century editions of the play (1711, 1750) reprint the placement of this song as found in F2. At the end of the century, in 1778, the edition, attributed to George Colman the elder,[79] became the first to do what all subsequent editors (except one) have done. In 1778, the song, for no clearly explained reason, was moved to follow Petronius's line, 'A song! Pray silence'. Interestingly, the song is the catchword at the bottom of the page and appears in full on the top of the facing page. Perhaps the move then was an efficacious one for printing: a desire to keep the song as an entire unit as opposed to printing only the title and one line. Regardless of the impetus for Sherlock as printer or Colman as editor to move the song, their move established an editorial normative up to Lucy Munro's New Mermaids edition in 2013. The only edition to differ in this placement is Waller's edition for Cambridge in 1910, where he follows B&F F2, which is the copytext for all plays in that series.[80] Therefore, out of the ten editions of the play between 1778 and 2013, only one places the song in a position found in one of the three early editions; the other nine follow the late eighteenth century and place it after Petronius's line. George Ferguson notes, 'This song is difficult to place in the dialogue';[81] yet despite the difficulty, he gives the song and its placement no further thought or consideration in any apparatus.

The logic behind the move governing the critical consensus seems to be that Petronius's line, 'A song, pray silence', means that first he hears a song and then asks for Tranio, Jacques, and the other men below to listen. This reading is logical and makes sense to editors, especially those with a sense of propriety and an understanding that text must be delivered one piece at a time. Theatre, however, allows for the breaking of politeness, and more than one person or group of people can overlap speech on stage. Significantly, by moving the song to after the two lines that note the song, it is no longer an interruption, especially not a Fletcherean one. The men below now hear and anticipate the song, and through Petronius's line, they also permit it. The men then control the presentation of the song by giving the women space to present it. As already demonstrated, the moment as an action interruption, which all early editions of the text present, participates in the riotous outburst of the women as they hold their strike. They control the stage despite the men below trying to do so. When editors move this song, they give the men the control by keeping the power situated within the patriarchy that listens below.

The most confusing edition relative to the placement of this song is Fredson Bowers', namely because he claims that 'the position of stage-directions in relation to the lines of the dialogue is that of the copy-text in so far as typographically possible'.[82] However, Bowers moves the song and the stage direction to a place that accords with the editorial tradition but not with copy text. It would surely have been 'typographically possible' to place the song at least where B&F F2 does, which is closer to the cue in B&F F1 than to where Bowers places the song, namely after Petronius's line. Ultimately, despite noting that his copy text (B&F F1) only gives a marginal notation and no lyrics, he does not mention or explain his choice in moving the placement.[83]

As a step towards fixing the song placement, Lucy Munro's New Mermaids edition hints towards moving the song but then reifies the misogynistic control inherent in removing the interruption. Munro uses the MS as her copy text,[84] and she actually places a stage direction for the song where one occurs in the MS.[85] We might view this as an achievement, a move towards giving the women the power to rupture the male congregation that has come to rupture their party. Munro even notes that the word 'Song' here might be 'an instruction for [it] to begin'.[86] In doing so, she offers for readers the possibility of the interruptive moment. However, her full note subsumes this possibility, and the placement of the lyrics accords with the other editors from the past two centuries. It reads:

> The direction appears here in MS, and at l. 44 in F; these may be anticipatory directions indicating that the song is imminent, or an instruction for it to begin. Petronius' comment at l. 46 suggests that the song has already begun by this point, but that the lyric only becomes clear when the men fall silent.[87]

Her final reading of Petronius's line and her choice to place the lyrics after this line, for all of her suggestions, miss the power of this moment as interruption. She shies away from boldly defying the editorial tradition and instead sees Petronius's line as a kind one in which he and the others become silent in order to hear the song that has begun. The consideration that this group of angry men silently give the stage to the rioting women only further suggests the insidious paradigm through which editors place their trust in the patriarchy.

Two considerations address the editors' concerns and make sense of an anomaly that the editors have created. First, if Petronius's line comes as it does in the MS, B&F F1, and B&F F2, which is to say, if it comes *after* the song and not before it, then what is he saying? Clearly, Petronius, the father who calls both of his daughters 'whore', and begins this scene saying, 'I had rather see her carted',[88] is not the type to quiet everyone down to listen to a group of rabble-rousing women. As such, this line is not to the men at all; rather, it is an admonition to the women up above. Petronius is not politely demurring to his comrades to be quiet so they can hear what song is being sung above their heads. He is irately yelling at his daughter and her compatriots, demanding they be quiet and docile and feminine. We here should note an echo to the play's other predecessor: Jonson's *Epicene, or The Silent Woman*. While it is not Moroso who clamours for silence here as in Jonson, Petronius's misogyny in this text is as strong as that in Jonson's. Petronius's line is an admonition to the women after they have disrupted the men's conversation. The women invade the men's inquisitive intrusion with signs of their own bacchanalia. Reading Petronius's line as an admonition to the women further makes sense of an editorial problem that is created only in moving the song lyrics. When modern editors move the song, they then must place it immediately before the women enter the stage, creating an odd stage picture in which, firstly, we hear an offstage song, for no reason, and secondly, the women wander on to the balcony for no reason. Why have the song offstage if the women are about to enter? The answer is because they do not enter just to get some fresh air but rather because someone has started yelling at them. If the song disrupts the men's conversation, and if Petronius yells back at the women above, his line becomes an impetus for the women to exit their chamber and to confront the party pooper down below.

The theatrical logic and simplicity of this sequence becomes apparent through this reading, but one that can only be seen by embracing Fletcher's theatricality and his love of interruptions that break our expectations. His plays are delightful in their defiance of decorum and in their ability to make us guess and second-guess what might or could be happening. Fletcher places his audiences in the same position as his characters, muddling through the complexities that arise in these situations. Unlike Shakespeare, who might have written a scene that the modern editors (editors perhaps more familiar with the Bard) crafted in moving the song, Fletcher does not privilege his audience with dramatic irony, nor does he give clear dramatic cues for occurrences like songs. Instead, his texts burst forth (witness B&F F1's exclamation mark 'Song!') and rupture our expectations, as do the women in *The Woman's Prize*, breaking out of their confining patriarchal expectations to find a sense of 'due equality'.[89] Interruptions then provide a form through which readers, actors, and editors must consider these texts and the dynamic conceptions of power that they present. To ignore this form, despite its seeming obviousness, is to result in editions of *The Woman's Prize* for the last 200 years. They may transmit a version of the text, but one that does a disservice to a key part of the playwright's aesthetic craft.

Conclusion

Scenes, spirits, and songs: these theatrical figurations that make up the drama of Jonson, Shakespeare, and Fletcher all engage the interruptive form, mostly through their rupturing entrances, which themselves further notions of power. Such forms then necessitate examination of early texts and question the choices that editors have made over the 400 years since these plays were first written and performed. In the way that dialogic interruptions reveal character and style, and self-interruptions expose interiority, action interruptions highlight the problematic relationship between theatrical and literary texts and underscore the choices made by those that seek to mediate between these forces: the editors. While some editorial choices make sense for clarity, such as moving Banquo's ghost closer to when he is acknowledged, they also highlight a missed opportunity to consider the formal methodologies of the texts themselves and the authors behind them. While the surviving printed and manuscript texts may be imperfect records of what was actually written or performed, the understanding of interruptive style via the previous chapters generates readings within these texts that accord with the playwrights' various aesthetics.

SECTION II

Macrointerruptions

4

Dramaturgy

This chapter transitions from the usage of interruptions within dialogues, monologues, and actions to usages of interruptions that affect forms beyond those identifiable local moments. Such interruptions influence dramaturgy and convention. These macrointerruptions break into an ongoing form and alter the continuation of that preset occurrence. An easy example is the hinge in Shakespeare's *The Winter's Tale*, when the figure of Time suddenly appears. The play seems to be continuing on a tragic course; however, one figure quickly changes the tone, 'marking the move from tragic conflict to the hope of a new beginning.'[1] This juxtaposition is a macrointerruption that Shakespeare places to disrupt the tragic premise, leading towards the hopeful continuation of romance. Unlike microinterruptions that affect audiences indirectly (through relationships that are either among characters or within a character), macrointerruptions specifically engage the relationship between a playwright and an audience. In the following two chapters, I will explore macrointerruptions: firstly, examining them in connection to dramaturgical structures, and then in connection to theatrical convention. Unlike microinterruptions that possess identifiable markers, such as grammar, acknowledgment, and punctuation, macrointerruptions are even more unstable in identification as astute audience members may identify a rupture before it occurs, removing it of its power. While such identification deflates the rupture and changes an intended effect, the author's attempt to alter the perception of the audience through potentially unexpected occurrences reflects the playwright's perceived relationship to that audience. Macrointerruptions, therefore, reveal the relationships between authors and audiences.

We might immediately ask: If interruptions hinge upon ruptured expectations, then are unknown plots always sites of macrointerruptions? So too, is there a difference between a plot in which what happens is unknown versus a plot where the end is known? Despite our own current culture's obsession with 'spoilers',[2] early modern playwrights, with their rehashing of old stories and use of revealing prologues, indicate a much lower investment in such preemptive revelations. Additionally, an audience's familiarity both locally and culturally affects their creation of expectations. Shakespeare's ubiquity in schools and theatres means that even his most obscure texts usually possess a relative familiarity as opposed to Fletcher's most lauded work. Therefore, the bias in this analysis will be, or might be, towards seeing Fletcher as the more macrointerruptive playwright simply because what he does is so different from our familiarity with 'our contemporary' Shakespeare.[3] In the ensuing analysis, I am interested in examining specifically how Shakespeare, Jonson, and Fletcher altered plots and dramaturgy to challenge the expectations of their audiences. The following plays carry particularly significant usages of the usages of macrointerruptions and reveal aspects of each playwright's overall dramaturgy.

A macrointerruption of dramaturgy is a moment when a playwright engenders an expectation in the structure of a play only to rupture that expectation. The curious outcome of macrointerruptions is that the continuation is less clear than in microinterruptions. As the premise depends upon an audience's expectations of a plot, the continuation depends on how much the rupture has altered or disrupted those expectations. While playwrights might continue the structure in a method that indicates their desires for the continuation, the audience's own continuation might be slightly or severely at odds with the one scripted. This discrepancy in the continuation becomes a central feature of macrointerruptions both of dramaturgy and, as we shall see, of theatrical conventions. This chapter will focus on three specific texts: Jonson's *Every Man Out of His Humour* (1599), Shakespeare's *The Winter's Tale* (1609), and Fletcher's *The Chances* (1617). From Jonson's use of the Grex, Shakespeare's statue of Hermione, to Fletcher's first act, these plays represent each playwright's attempts to engage macrointerruptions. Jonson crafts a particular sense of interruptive affect throughout his play, disrupting the lines between play world and real world; Shakespeare abandons his usual dramatic irony to engage in a playfully interruptive form that culminates into almost a surprise; finally, Fletcher's play presents an anomalous opening in which exposition is subsumed into action. These three plays do not represent all of the interesting ways to interrupt received notions of dramaturgy, but they do present three distinct modes of doing so. Through considering dramaturgical interruptions, we begin to understand the relationship that the playwrights developed with their audiences.

Jonson and *Every Man Out of His Humor*

Jonson's *Every Man Out of His Humor* is a beast of a play. A peripatetic, expansive consideration of what plays are, it has met with little popular acclaim and limited critical interest. Randall Martin calls it 'a challenging experiment in dramatic form and a theoretical manifesto'.[4] Any reader of the play would likely agree with Martin's assessment: it is a sprawling work with 'an eddying, circular structure designed entirely for the display of eccentricity'.[5] Indeed, the play shows eccentricity of character, as the title indicates, as well as in construction and overall design. In fact, it deploys several aspects of expected dramaturgy but uses them unconventionally. In this way, we might begin to conceptualize the whole play as a sustained macrointerruption in which Jonson disrupts any expectations of what this work might be. From the Induction with the Grex or chorus to the non-straightforward plot, to the sudden reversals, to the censored and multiple endings, Jonson's play defies what a play is. The play's ending caused controversy by using Queen Elizabeth as a deus ex machina, which has led scholars to parrot that the earliest performance was a failure.[6] Helen Ostovich, however, has defended the play, stating, 'There is no evidence that *EMO* was a popular failure', noting that subsequent performances suggest the opposite.[7] Indisputably, the printed text was a success, garnering three editions in 1600 alone.[8] Martin further notes that it was subsequently 'quoted, imitated, and burlesqued' through the rest of the century.[9] Additionally, it seems to have had multiple performances at the Globe and was revived at court for James I.[10] After the Restoration, its performances practically cease, and aside from one conference performance, there have been no contemporary ones.[11] Why this fascinating theatrical and dramatic work has not been performed is entirely unclear. Its dark humor and episodic, non-linear nature potentially have more interest for a poststructuralist audience than an eighteenth- or nineteenth-century one, but like many plays in the Fletcher canon, this play has suffered from continued neoclassical and Romantic critiques.

I lament the lack of stage history because this play is so incredibly concerned with the action of the stage and the dramaturgy of events on it. To analyze this investment and its own illustration of Jonson's macrointerruptive dramaturgy, I will focus on instances pertaining to the Grex. Jonson's Grex, a term he borrowed from Plautus, which means band or company or flock, is a choral structure that begins the play in an Induction and remains on the stage to comment on the action.[12] The general structure of an induction and even choral onlookers would not have been particularly novel for theatregoers in 1599;[13] however, Jonson uses that expectation to alter the presentation of these characters and to question the way that people attend the theatre itself. Through the Grex and particularly in episodes that distinctly comment upon aspects of the play's dramaturgy, Jonson fosters dramaturgical expectations within the audience that he ultimately ruptures, continuing on in his own path towards presenting a new type of 'Comicall Satyre'.[14]

Jonson frames the Grex within an interruptive occurrence at the very beginning. The first printing of the play starts the text with the stage direction, '*Inductio, sono secondo*' (Ind.0SD).[15] This direction first defines the opening section as an Induction, meaning an opening framing device and not part of the play proper.[16] After that classification, the text then provides a direction pertaining to the entrance of the characters: Asper, Cordatus, and Mitis are to enter after the second sounding of the trumpet that announced the beginning of the play.[17] Therefore, the audience would see three characters enter the stage and begin a scene before the play itself begins. At least fourteen plays that premiered before *Every Man Out* have inductions,[18] making such forms typical to Elizabethan audiences. What Jonson specifically adds, however, is the timing of the Induction relative to the Prologue and the other significations about the play's beginning. The typical beginning of a play would start at the sound of the third trumpet. For example, Thomas

Heywood's *The Four Prentices of London*, another play with an induction, begins with a character that declares:

> What mean you, my masters, to appear thus before your times? Do you not know that I am the Prologue? Do you not see this long black velvet cloak upon my back? Have you not sounded thrice?[19]

The protocol is that Prologues wear black velvet cloaks and appear at the third sound of the trumpet. Out of the other plays before *EMO*, only John Marston's *Antonio and Mellida*, also from 1599, has both an Induction and a Prologue. But unlike Jonson's text, it does not have any stage directions about the sound. Marston's play only provides the scene breaks of Induction, The Prologue, and then Actus Primus.[20] Alan Dessen and Leslie Thomsen in their dictionary also offer no further examples of such instructions relating to the trumpet calls.[21] Starting the Induction at the second sounding and then cueing the third sounding to introduce the Prologue is, therefore, a Jonsonian construction intended to disrupt the audience's comprehension of the play world versus the real world, in that action begins on the stage prior to the third sounding, which usually indicated the start of a play.[22] Jonson begins this play by interrupting an important dramaturgy, namely the beginning of the play. Doing so would affect the audience at first by confusing them as to what is happening on the stage, and then by softening the barriers between the fictional world and the world of the audience.[23]

Jonson's Induction comprises two distinct sections: first, the opening with Asper; second, the failure to produce a Prologue. These sections interrupt each other and are further coloured through a series of microinterruptions. Jonson melds his macrointerruptions with microinterruptions to highlight the connection between the dramaturgy and the dialogue. The opening section begins with the three characters in the middle of a conversation, similar to the opening of *The Alchemist*, and highlights Jonson's overall interruptive paradigm:

> CORDATUS: Nay, my dear Asper—
> MITIS: Stay your mind—
> ASPER: Away!
> (IND.1)[24]

Jonson invests the play from the beginning with a sense of intense interruption, as first Cordatus and then Mitis try to speak to Asper, but he ultimately ignores their pleas and delivers a lengthy speech explaining his annoyance with the world. The power dynamic is clearly illustrated as both Asper as presenter and Jonson as playwright demonstrate their control over both the characters and the audience, respectively. Even with Cordatus and Mitis later interrupting Asper's rants to once again try to calm him down, Asper launches into further explications over his disaffection for people and their vices. Through this character, Jonson demonstrates that interruptions are about control and that this play and his role in it will be one of control.

Jonson further uses dramaturgical interruptions when Asper suddenly notices the live audience surrounding him. Before Asper realizes this broader audience, Mitis calls for Asper to 'Contain [his] spirit in more stricter bounds,' and Cordatus adds before Asper can speak again:

> Unless your breath had power
> To melt the world and mould it new again,
> It is in vain to spend it in these moods

(IND.44, 46-48)

Both of these statements illustrate the problem of this play: namely, Jonson refuses to let arbitrary strictures or boundaries control him and that he intends for his language to change the world around him. The second image in particular is an apt expression of a theatre of imagination, which is the theatre of the early modern period. Furthermore, plays themselves as imaginative transformations through language are vain enterprises; however, this play, and Jonson's work in general, strives to demonstrate how such vanity may also produce utility. In rectifying the humours of the characters in the play, Jonson aims at the audience. For him to go beyond the bounds of an expected dramaturgy is to challenge the audience, and, therefore, Cordatus's hypothetical is in fact Jonson's hypothesis. He aims to rupture the expectations of the audience and thereby through language and theatre to transform the onlookers into something 'new'.

At this moment in the dialogue, Asper notices the live audience and addresses them:

I not observed this throngèd round till now.—
Gracious and kind spectators, you are welcome.
Apollo and the Muses feast your eyes
With graceful objects, and may our Minerva
Answer your hopes unto their largest strain.

(IND.49-53)

Here is, perhaps, the only moment in which the off-stage audience interrupts the action of the play, in which the observers have a moment to be in control, as they are suddenly made to be central to the goings-on. Like all scripted moments, however, that power is illusory and only transferred through the author's construction. Asper's taking them in is a power move as he turns his attentions to the audience and immediately changes his tone and tactics. Gone are his comments about whips and lashes, and now he talks of Muses and feasts. The sudden transformation in a moment when the off-stage audience suddenly becomes a character typifies the tension that Jonson imbues in the dramaturgy throughout the play. Part of this dramaturgy underscores the play's sense of 'dilation',[25] of continually opening outward towards the audience. Therefore, the moment of Asper seeing the audience typifies part of Jonson's interruptive dramaturgy—after three long speeches, Asper suddenly changes his focus. We do not expect to be taken in by the character. Nor do we expect such fawning generosity from his mouth; yet Jonson demonstrates the unpredictability of the endeavor which his audience is about to experience. This form of sudden rupture that plays upon audience expectations through the control of the playwright typifies Jonsonian macrointerruptions in *Every Man Out*.

Before the second section of the Induction begins, an exchange occurs after Asper's exit that highlights the function of the other Grex throughout the play. Mitis is doubtful of the play and inquires, 'You have seen his play, Cordatus. Pray you, how is't?' (Ind.224). Mitis lets us know that Cordatus is gifted with foreknowledge of the play; he, like a repeat theatregoer or reader, knows what will happen and so can highlight, point out, or challenge aspects of the text in this iteration. In constructing Cordatus thus, Jonson reminds the audience of the rehearsed and repetitive nature of both theatre and literary texts. They exist seemingly in the moment but always represent something that has always-already happened. Even with this aspect of the theatrical being underlined, the status of Cordatus as a character with foreknowledge privileges his point of view and his commentaries upon the action. So too, his presence forestalls the potentiality of the unexpected: any surprises are erased through his presence as a character that possesses omniscient knowledge through iteration.

In response to Mitis's query, Cordatus delivers a lecture about the play's connections to the roots of comedy, aligning it more with the Old Comedy of Aristophanes than the New Comedy of Plautus and Terence. William Blissett notes that Aristophanic comedy has 'no architecture, no stasis within bounds' but is built upon 'movement, [a] swirl of ideas, word play, [and] stylistic acrobatics'.[26] Such description works for Jonson's play as well. The Grex in particular and its problematic relationship to expectation and dramaturgy emphasize such movement beyond the bounds of strict adherence. They highlight a movement beyond Mitis's 'stricter bounds', which he asks Asper to follow. Russ McDonald sees the opening constructions, such as this section on comedic history, as ways to 'orient the audience morally and aesthetically';[27] instead, they playfully complicate our comprehension, demonstrating the processes that Jonson explores. The 'repeated intrusions', which I will discuss, do 'keep before us the problem of satiric mimesis',[28] but they also represent that problem itself. They are a part of the play and even within an on-stage Inductive framework they participate meaningfully with the work, cultivating the expanded nature of the text. Rather than exemplifying such controlling language that McDonald uses, the Grex is an expansive structure that ruptures our own sense of spectatorship and thereby complicates our relationship to the play itself. In other words, they do not orient but perhaps disorient; they do not locate but dislocate.

After the discussion of comedy history, the play tries once more to begin, this time with the trumpet sounding a third time and a Prologue entering. Before the sounding of the trumpet, Cordatus notes, 'I would they would begin once. This protraction is able to sour the best-settled patience in the theatre' (Ind.267). His comment, of course, notes that their history conversation has been somewhat tedious in its length, but it also emphasizes the actual time that has passed on the stage so far before the play proper has begun. It could also remind the audience of Asper's first call to the trumpets to 'sound, ho, and begin!', which was 120 lines earlier or roughly six minutes of stage time (Ind.151). The underscoring of time passing is yet another way in which Jonson stresses an aspect of dramatic representation only to undermine it. Theatre takes time and space. Since Jonson's odd usage of the induction and the trumpet calls already play around with the space by mediating the audience's comprehension of real world and play world, he then turns towards temporal dislocation in highlighting for the audience the literal passing of time that they are experiencing. This comment about time leads to the trumpet call and the Prologue's entrance. While the Induction in Heywood's *Four Prentices* eventually renders a conventional prologue before the play begins,[29] Jonson once more destroys such expectations:

> CORDATUS: Oh, here comes the Prologue.—Now, sir, if you had stayed a little longer, I meant to have spoke your prologue for you, i'faith.
> PROLOGUE: Marry, with all my heart, sir, you shall do it yet, and I thank you.
> *[He begins to leave.]*
> CORDATUS: Nay, nay, stay, stay, hear you?
> (IND.269-72)

Cordatus's jibe at the entering actor provokes the actor unexpectedly to leave; he thanks Cordatus for speaking the prologue and vacates the space, exiting without delivering a prologue. Cordatus, in fact, could indeed give us the prologue as he has previously seen the play. Like the rest of the Induction, Jonson gives the audience a Prologue that is not a Prologue at all; it is instead an illustration of the tension between performer and audience. Just when Cordatus begins to actually deliver the prologue, Carlo Buffone in the final dramaturgical interruption of the Induction interrupts him. Carlo cuts off Cordatus eventually giving us a prologue in the guise of a speech about drinking and about the author of the play. Once more, we are given the shape of an expected dramaturgy, but Jonson destroys it to produce a new structure, through which he tests the limits of the theatrical event and perhaps the patience of his potentially bewildered audience.

What I have tried to demonstrate in reading several key moments of the Induction is Jonson's method of rupture and expansion. In some ways, we might think that this approach differs from Jonson's typical approach to interruptions, which are usually controlled. These interruptions and expansions, however, represent Jonson's attempt to create a new type of play, one specifically of his creation. Through that authorial aim, his interruptions illustrate his manipulation of and control over the audience's expectations. He feeds the audience a sense of comfort through the guise of familiar dramaturgies, but then he ruptures them to illustrate his larger goal of breaking open dramaturgy itself.

Not counting the Induction or the ending, the Grex speaks up thirty-three times throughout the play. These intrusions usually occur at the end of scenes and most often during moments when the stage is empty of all other characters.[30] In fact, fourteen of the sixteen cleared stages feature exchanges by the Grex.[31] Another three Grex moments take place when a French scene break would occur, namely at a character's entrance or exit. Therefore, many of the Grex exchanges would not seem to be interruptions to the scene at all but rather are typical aspects of the play's dramaturgy: any time all other characters leave the stage or we are introduced to a new character, we can expect Cordatus and Mitis to comment upon the preceding actions and usually note who is about to enter. The other half of the Grex occurrences are moments in which Cordatus and Mitis speak up in ways that rupture the performed scene. While these moments are interruptions, wresting power from the other characters to deliver commentary of various tones and types, they are also oftentimes insignificant and uninteresting.[32] For example, the first such moment occurs after Macilente's speech in the first scene of the play proper:

> MACILENTE: Oh, they are thoughts that have transfixed my heart,
>   And often, i'the strength of apprehension,
>   Made my cold passion stand upon my face,
>   Like drops of sweat on a stiff cake of ice.
>   GREX
> CORDATUS: This alludes well to that of the poet,
>   *Invidus suspirat, gemit, incutitque dentes,*
>   *Sudat frigidus, intuens quod odit.*
> MITIS: Oh, peace: you break the scene.
>   (1.1.29-36)

Cordatus delivers a Latin quotation that describes what Macilente himself has just been describing; he adds a verbal footnote of classical precedent to Macilente's speech. Unlike many other moments of Latin phrases in Jonson's plays, which receive a brief translation afterward, this one remains untranslated as Mitis breaks in to tell Cordatus to be silent. Mitis disrupts the potential full explication that Cordatus's information could deliver by highlighting the structure of the interruption that the Grex embodies in its ability to speak up during the performance. Cordatus may break the scene, but Jonson has already done that. Here the information and commentary supplied, beyond highlighting the interruptive form at play itself does not deliver or produce further information or meaning for an audience, especially for a public theatre audience.[33] The use of Latin without translation may then relate to the habits of an educated critic, which means that Jonson uses this first macrointerruption to dramatize an anticipated reaction to his play thus far. As Mitis cuts off Cordatus from further explication, he then critiques the rupture, emphasizing a return to the play. The use of the two characters allows Jonson to have it both ways: he can interrupt the text with quotation to explicate, and he can undercut that explication through an emphasis on its destructiveness. As it does not engender a continuation specifically, we can consider that the following scene becomes coloured by the deployment of the theatrical footnote.[34]

Even though the Grex commentaries that occur during cleared stages do not seem interruptive, those moments actually develop a methodology for understanding Jonson's interruptive form in *Every Man Out*. This reversal then typifies a Jonsonian control in which the interruptive Grex moments are rarely insightful as to the nature of interruptive forms; however, by making potentially interruptive forms not interruptive, Jonson highlights the potentiality for interruption in the play itself. Even as the play feels like it is continually expanding outward, Jonson's crafting of these pithy scenes, namely how they function contrary to expectations, demonstrates his control over his play text. To give an example, one moment of the play that has been criticized as unsatisfactory and too sudden, and which leads to a Grex, is Sordido's attempted suicide and conversion in 3.2.[35] After the Rustici interrupt Sordido's hanging and Sordido decides to be a better man, the Grex comment on this scene. Mitis claims:

> But in good faith, signor, your author hath largely outstripped my expectation in this scene. For when I saw Sordido so desperately intended, I thought I had had a hand of him then.
>
> (3.2.114-117)

While Mitis cannot speak for all audience members, he perhaps represents what Jonson expects of an audience: that they think they understand the character not only of the play but of the individuals within it. Jonson anticipates the nature of audiences in that we create expectations of what we think will happen and how characters will act. Jonson's previous scenes have led Mitis to think that Sordido will actually hang himself, but that is not what happens. The conversion of the hoarding miser 'outstrips' Mitis's 'expectation'—or, to put it another way, it ruptures his premise. The Jonsonian twist here is that the reversal of the expectations is controlled through the deployment of the Grex. In fact, by dramatizing the questioning of the conversion itself and the sudden rupture, Jonson writes the continuation as a way to mitigate its effect. Unlike Fletcher who deploys sudden ruptures and forces audiences to consider the continuation themselves, Jonson controls the reception of the rupture by writing out what that reception should be.

As Mitis further explains his objections, he introduces the problem of genre and expectation. Mitis continues:

> I... had framed my objection to it ready, which may yet be very fitly urged, and with some necessity; for though his purposed violence lost th'effect and extended not to death, yet the intent and horror of the object was more than the nature of a comedy will in any sort allow.
>
> (3.2.119-22)

The rupture comes to the forefront as Mitis objects to his understood premise: he was prepared to reject the playwright's presentation as not suitable to Mitis's conception of the play. Therefore, his premises are already predisposed towards distrusting the author. Even once the author has ruptured those assumptions and taken the play in a new course, Mitis still objects, feeling that the closeness of the scene towards 'horror' makes the play no comedy. Here, Jonson defends his choices via classical texts when Cordatus cites Plautus as a precedent, which Mitis accepts, noting that Cordatus's 'memory is happier than [his]' (3.2.129). The use of classical texts and the acknowledgment of a profound memory are Jonsonian. What has been missed in this exchange is how close Jonson comes to defining or exploring tragicomedy. In fact, he records the problems of generic expectations and how macrointerruptions complicate those expectations. Mitis has a hard time accepting the previous scene because of its tragic sensibility; however, the comedic resolution makes it no tragedy, to loosely quote Fletcher.[36] Jonson does not call *Every Man Out* a tragicomedy; he uses the label comical satire. But Cordatus and Mitis offer that the generic mixture feels right for a tragicomedy. Furthermore, the violence at the end towards Puntarvolo's Dog and Carlo Buffone both suggest a stronger connection to a tragicomic world and not one of comedy itself. Macilente's sudden conversion, however effected, too plays into this paradigm.

Cordatus concludes this Grex with a further injunction to Mitis after his analytical response to the action. He instructs, 'Never preoccupy your imagination withal. Let your mind keep company with the scene still' (131-32). Ironically, Jonson argues for an unanalytical and uncritical response to his play. He enjoins Mitis, through Cordatus, that he should simply watch the play. He negates the importance of immediate reflection. With his later addendum of 'lose not yourself' (3.2.134), Cordatus further emphasizes that to try to guess the playwright's course and goals is to get lost within the play. Rather, the audience is to experience the play and the characters as they unfold. In this way, it anticipates Jonson's prologue to *Epicene*, where he asks that criticism should be withheld until the entirety is seen.[37] Admittedly, Jonson realizes that he cannot control the minds of his audience that will evaluate and reflect on the play as it unfolds, and so, of course, the Grex continue to occur. Neither Mitis nor Cordatus can stop from thinking about what the playwright presents, no matter the playwright's desire to control such responses. But in dramatizing that moment, in illustrating the inefficacy of keeping up with someone who has a happier memory than us, we will lose ourselves in the expanding 'centrifugal' forces of the play.[38]

In one of the final Grex exchanges, Mitis underscores their role in the interruptions that characterize this complicated play. At the end of *Act Four*, as the many plots are heading towards a conclusion and as Cordatus and Mitis discuss Macilente's character, Mitis responds:

> Ay, marry, sir, this is that on which my expectation has dwelt all this while; for I must tell you, signor, though I was loath to interrupt the scene, yet I made it a question in mine own private discourse how he should properly call it *Every Man Out of His Humour* when I saw all his actors so strongly pursue and continue their humours.
>
> (4.5.129-33)

Once more Mitis invokes his expectation and even notes that he did not want to interrupt the action of the play to question the way that it is proceeding. However, Mitis is never loath to question or interrupt the flow of the author's course, even if he says that he is, and despite the earlier injunction to consider the play in full and to cease 'private discourse', Mitis does not do so. Jonson shows that his language of containment in Cordatus's pleas is as artificial as the rest of the theatrical endeavour in front of him. He even invokes the title as seemingly counterproductive to what Mitis claims to have seen, but in the interruptive forms, Jonson does give the audience the opposite of the contained and expected 'in', as the characters and the play itself moves 'out' of their expectations.

While some critics may claim that Mitis and Cordatus represent Jonson's attempt 'to preempt a range of criticism that [he] anticipated from his spectators, as a way of keeping them in line',[39] such repetition of these exchanges between the characters, as well as this particular iteration in Mitis being 'loath to interrupt the scene', represents a playful Jonsonian construction in which the envisaged containment is never possible. In this way, Jonson admits that his ability to control reactions is an impossibility as spectators continue to think and consider the meaning and the structure of the play they watch. To argue that Mitis and Cordatus represent Jonson's attempt to contain response is to read this play as a non-literary work and to devalue Jonson's own perceptions of humanity. The recurrence of Grex moments that continuously 'interrupt the scene' demonstrates Jonson's complex negotiation and playful control over expectations. While he guides audiences towards a response, he also admits the Sisyphean task of fully controlling such responses.

Critics want to find Jonson in the mouth of Asper, Macilente, Carlo, and Cordatus, but we should not forget that he is in the mouth of all of his characters. He has crafted them for better or worse, and to pinpoint a specific mouthpiece removes Jonson of his authority over the text, ironically a potentially un-Jonsonian move. Conversely, we might find Jonson most in the mitigating and subversive Mitis, who offers almost demurely contrary opinions to the action that ensues. In this interruptive character, Jonson presents the problems of attempting to control audience responses because enjoining a person not to think about something only makes them think about it more. Therefore, Mitis's objections more likely ring louder for an audience than do Cordatus's defenses. Jonson criticizes his own work to highlight the artificial and problematic nature of the theatrical endeavor as represented by this dramatic text. In this way, we can see that Jonson struggles with his control as *auteur*, and in this 'theoretical manifesto', highlights the interruptive problem of a thinking audience.

Shakespeare and *The Winter's Tale*

While Jonson's dramaturgical macrointerruptions directly engage the audience response through the Grex, Shakespeare's approach in *The Winter's Tale* hinges on alterations of the narrative itself. *The Winter's Tale* seems like two separate plays. The structure shows a clear bifurcation between two halves, even if scholars cannot agree on the relationship between those halves.[40] The bipartite construction indicates Shakespeare's engagement with dramaturgical macrointerruption. In fact, Alison Findlay argues that the play has a tripartite structure, which further overlays itself onto the form of the interruption: tragic premise, pastoral rupture and romantic continuation.[41] Unlike Shakespeare's other plays, he here avoids dramatic irony and instead follows the plays of Jonson or Fletcher. Indeed, the influence of Fletcher here on this play is confused and uncertain: current dating research offers that three of Fletcher's plays came before *The Winter's Tale* and two more premiered the same year.[42] Rather it might be better to consider that this play participates in a grouping of influence among Shakespeare, Beaumont, and Fletcher during the years 1609–11.[43] To consider Shakespeare's dramaturgy though, I will focus instead on his relationship to another writer: Robert Greene. Shakespeare borrowed the central plot of this play from Greene's enormously popular prose romance *Pandosto*,[44] and I start this section by considering the divergent choices each writer made in opening their texts. Shakespeare's transformation of story into drama explores the usage of macrointerruption by playing with an audience's expectations: first setting them up and then rupturing them. I will then move to an examination of the statue scene, where Shakespeare, contrary to almost every other plot in his canon, avoids overly obvious dramatic irony and produces the closest he comes to the Jonsonian/Fletcherean/Middletonian surprise ending.[45] In doing so, he alters his relationship with the audience, but backs away from a totalizing surprise by embedding hints.

One of the major differences between Greene and Shakespeare is the source of Leontes's jealousy.[46] While Greene prepares his audience for the jealous passion in Pandosto, Shakespeare surprises the audience with Leontes's sudden onset of jealous rage. Instead of focusing on the direct comparison of Greene's descriptions of Pandosto's burgeoning jealousy versus Leontes in 1.2, I am rather interested in Greene's opening paragraph versus Shakespeare's opening scene. These two initial structures reveal Shakespeare's use of interruptions to transfer power both among characters and between a performance and an audience, the latter transfer becoming an important aspect of the final scene with the statue. Greene begins his prose romance with a paragraph that sets out several expectations:

> Among al the Passions wherewith human mindes are perplexed, there is not that so galleth with restlesse despight, as that infectious soare of Iealousie: for all other griefes are eyther to bee appeased with sensible perswasions, to be cured with wholesome counsel, to be relieved in want, or by tract of time to be worne out, (Iealousie only excepted) which is so sawsed with suspitious doubtes, and pinching mistrust, that whoso seekes by friendly counsail to rase out this hellish passion, it foorthwith suspectech that he geueth this aduise to couer his owne guiltinesse.[47]

Greene's first sentence, through its euphuistic prose style, enacts the insidious nature of jealous thoughts. He begins by alerting his reader to his purpose: namely, to illustrate the horrors of a jealous passion.

He sets it apart antithetically from other passions, noting how they can be relieved. Then he uses a parenthetical, an interruptive phrase, to rupture the flow of the idea bringing it back to jealousy. Through the rupture that then dominates, Greene illustrates the insidious way in which jealous thoughts never go away. They return and dominate the thinking of the person, just as the idea itself here ruptures the conversation about passions. Inga-Stina Ewbank notes that 'Greene's energies . . . have all gone into the language, so that the dominant impression is of a style in which irrational human acts are rationalized by the symmetries and antithetical balances of vocabulary and syntax'.[48] While Greene's language does illustrate his point, this moment argues against Ewbank's summary of Greene being condensed into a rationalization. In fact, this sentence performs the jealous act itself in a way that is particularly unbalanced and not clearly antithetical. In doing so, Greene's syntax produces the interruptive nature of a jealous passion.

Greene then provides a series of sentences that lead into the story, laying out Pandosto's character before even getting to the narrative itself. Greene writes:

> Yea, who so is payned with the restlesse torment doubteth all, dystrusteh him-selfe, is always frosen with feare, and fired with suspition, hauing that wherein consisteth all his ioy, to be the breeder of his miserie. Yea, it is such a heauy enemy to that holy estate of matrimony, sowing between the married couple such deadly seedes of secret hatred, as Loue being once rased out by spightful distrust, there oft ensueth bloudy reuenge, as this ensuing Hystorie manifestly prooueth:[49]

This specific list of actions and feelings that jealousy engenders becomes a shorthand for the character of Pandosto in the rest of the narrative. Greene delivers a character, almost like Jonson's descriptions in the printed version of *Every Man Out*,[50] that predisposes the audience to understand the actions of Pandosto through this lens. In laying out the problems of jealousy so specifically before the story begins, he not only illustrates the problems of the passion but also predisposes the reader to consider Pandosto through this perception. The narrator controls our point of view as we enter the story, foregrounding the passion to be explored. He ends this section with an assertion of the story's proof, claiming that the story will demonstrate the problems of such a passion as he has laid them out. Such assurances again control the reception as they insinuate that these emotions are not only to be understood but will be demonstrated within the story itself, meaning that if they seem lacking, they are assumed to be there, and when they are present, they are actively proving the point. Such an argument and control over expectations removes the ability of the jealousy to rupture the reader's expectations. Greene's later descriptions of Bellaria and Egisthus (the characters aligned with Shakespeare's Hermione and Polixenes) do not create nor do they need to create a foundation for Pandosto's jealousy. This paragraph establishes his character before the story even begins.

The final line of this introductory paragraph cements this comprehension by specifically naming Pandosto:

> wherein *Pandosto* (furiously incensed by causelesse Iealousie) procured the death of his most louing and loyall wife, and his owne endlesse sorrow and misery.[51]

Greene links his discussion of jealousy to the character that will experience it and once more solidifies the importance of the jealous passion through a parenthetical addition. Furthermore, he establishes the end of the story by clearly stating that Bellaria will die and that Pandosto will not recover from that death. This explication of the plot, like the opening chorus in *Romeo and Juliet*, establishes a reader's expectations of the plot, and while permitting questions about how these events occur, they preclude ruptures of the narrative structures, unless the opening paragraph is meant to mislead the reader. In Greene's case, this is not so: Bellaria dies and Pandosto, after being reunited with his long-lost daughter, kills himself. Greene uses his language to guide the reader's expectations and demonstrates within its syntax the constructions of the central passion that he intends to explore. Overall, this paragraph is an induction or prologue; it is set apart from the text[52] and introduces the reader to the main action and main character. In this way, Greene explains and explains away the jealousy, making it utterly predictable, by including it within the nature of Pandosto through his establishing of the theme.

For *The Winter's Tale*, Shakespeare does not use an Induction or Prologue, but rather has two courtiers begin the play discussing the actions of the court.[53] Dutifully, these lords—Camillo and

Archidamus—discuss the relationship between their kings and countries and comment positively upon the young prince Mamillius. They highlight that the two countries are well connected and that the kings are possessed of a love for each other because of their pasts. This scene acts as a counterpoint to Leontes's scenes; it is a 'still, small voice' before 'Leontes's storm perpetual'.[54] The courtiers are 'clear and direct in their outlook',[55] though some scholars have commented upon the hints towards a more negative outcome, presaging what is to come.[56] What is striking about the scene though is that Shakespeare peppers it with several dialogic interruptions between the courtiers. In doing so, he, like Greene's syntactic interruptions, highlights a desire to awaken the sense of rupture to come. After Archidamus asserts that if Camillo comes to Bohemia, he will see a 'great difference', Camillo responds:

> CAMILLO: I think this coming summer the King of
>   Sicilia means to pay Bohemia the visitation which he
>   justly owes him.[57]
> ARCHIDAMUS: Wherein our entertainment shall shame
>   us, we will be justified in our loves; for indeed—
> CAMILLO: Beseech you—
> ARCHIDAMUS: Verily, I speak it in the freedom of my
>   knowledge. We cannot with such magnificence—in so
>   rare—I know not what to say[—][58] We will give you
>   sleepy
>   drinks, that your senses, unintelligent of our
>   insufficiency, may, though they cannot praise us, as
>   little accuse us.
>   (1.1.5-16)

The series of dialogic microinterruptions and self-interruptions creates a sense of uncertain forward progression. It reflects Greene's own interruptions in highlighting the structure of jealousy. While I am not arguing that 'Greene's texts are ghosts haunting' the play in a 'shadowy presence',[59] I do posit that as Greene's interruption instigates a consideration of jealousy and its power, Shakespeare linguistically begins his play in a state of rupture. The interruptions specifically belie the fact that the conversation seems kind and generous. Camillo's rupture intends to stop Archidamus from speaking further about his home; even with an air of politeness, the move is one that attempts to control the conversation. Archidamus subsequently refuses that rupture and continues. Archidamus then controls the conversation between the courtiers, ironically exerting power by arguing for the deficiency of his own country.

The dialogic interruptions lead to self-interruptions that demonstrate Archidamus's own inability to offer what seems an adequate response to the generosity of the Sicilian court. The line ends with the aposiopesis of 'I know not what to say' and then suggests that they will drug the Sicilians when they come to visit. In trailing off, in leaving more to be said, but then in coming back to saying something, Archidamus illustrates his desire to control the conversation and therefore the perception of his country. His need for power eventually subsides into Camillo's long speech about the kings' unity, but this explication from Camillo comes after the moment of contention in which the two courtiers have vied for speaking rights. The conversation establishes the world of this play as one of competition and rupture. Expectations do not stand. Archidamus cannot hold power; the kings seem to be friends on the outside, but as Leontes quickly shows, that is not the course of the play. This dialogue 'exploits the artificiality' of exposition[60] by embedding it within interruptive forms that not only reflect Shakespeare's source specifically but also generally. Like Greene's insistence on the importance of jealousy to his narrative, Shakespeare insists upon the importance of rupture to the play that is about to unfold. While Yayoi Miyashita argues that the entire play 'pre-echoes' the surprise in the statue scene,[61] what I aim to show here is not another way in which the play prefigures what is to come but rather how it plays upon an audience's expectations by verbally highlighting the larger structures of the work. In this way, Shakespeare follows both Greene and Jonson in aligning the micro to the macro.

While you might expect me to discuss the 'hinge' as it is called between the tragedy of the first three acts and the comedy in the second two,[62] or to look at the news of Mamillius's death or the chorus of Time or the bear,[63] I leave all of these many ruptures for the reader to explore in order to turn to a singular rupture in the canon of Shakespearean dramaturgy: Hermione's statue. Arguably, the most important rupture of the play is ironically something stationary. Bertrand Evans's study of Shakespeare's use of dramatic irony (though he terms it 'discrepant awareness') explores the unexpected nature of Hermione's survival. Evans suggests that bringing Hermione back to life is the 'prospect least likely' based 'on the record of [Shakespeare's] whole career'.[64] He examines *Cymbeline* and *Pericles* as corollaries, but finds explication and ironic distance in those plays, whereas in *The Winter's Tale*, 'Shakespeare willfully serves us false information with the clear intent that we believe it'.[65] Dramaturgically then, unlike Shakespeare's other major reversals that are either foreshadowed or presented as dramatic irony, Shakespeare reverses the fate of Greene's Bellaria to provide an ending of reunion and forgiveness by rescuing Hermione. This deception may, as Charles Hieatt says, 'depart[] from previous standards of verisimilitude' and 'challenge our credulity',[66] but it also participates in a dramaturgical interruption that challenges the audience's expectations.[67] Hieatt's objections are both stipulated upon an idea that participation in the theatre engenders such naturalistic senses and that the artificial nature of the endeavor is not already present.[68] Hieatt's disparagement insinuates that while a figure personating Time is not incredulous, the idea that a woman might pretend to be dead for sixteen years because of her husband's abuse somehow is.

Despite divergent readings of Shakespeare's engagement of the interruption, what is important is that no matter how unexpected the ending is, Shakespeare does supply some hints. Evans accurately notes that Shakespeare shies away from fully rupturing expectations as he 'hurriedly provide[s] hints to give us our usual advantage in the denouement'.[69] The language discussing the statue embeds Shakespearean dramatic irony by commenting upon the lifelikeness and the ageing of the statue. Twelve pieces of dialogue indicate that the statue is alive, either through observations of its warmth and breath or through Paulina's injunctions not to touch. The only moment that actually supports seeing the statue as statue is Leontes's description:

> O, thus she stood,
> Even with such life of majesty—warm life,
> As now it coldly stands—when I first wooed her.

(5.3.34-36)

This moment illustrates Leontes's willingness to see what he is being shown. He accepts the statue-ness of the statue until thirty lines later when Paulina says that he 'may think anon it moves' (5.3.61), at which point Leontes notes, 'Would you not deem it breathed, and that those veins/Did verily bear blood?' (5.3.64-65). Again, Paulina orchestrates the finale, and Leontes is only a spectator, consuming what she sells him. After she claims that he might think it 'lives', he then sees 'an air comes from her' (5.3.70, 78). Leontes's responses are our responses to Shakespeare directing us through the scene. He leads us towards the realization that the Hermione is not dead. In doing so, he engenders expectations that defy the rupture; he, as Evans notes, allows us privilege over Leontes, who is overwhelmed with emotion, even if we too are emotionally moved. In this way, we might begin to see that Shakespeare, perhaps more so than Jonson, tries to control the audience response by giving us a sense of superiority. We are better than Leontes and think we know more, even if we initially did not.

One further complication of the statue scene is the presentation on the stage.[70] The statue is revealed on line 20 but does not descend until around line 100, an eighty-line span that would have taken roughly four minutes of stage time.[71] Additionally, the statue must be played by an actor, meaning that as soon as Hermione is revealed, the audience would begin to expect that something is different, and that the statue is not a statue. The actress Helena Faucit commented upon playing this scene:

> You may imagine how difficult it must be to stand in one position, with a full light thrown upon you, without moving an eyelid for so long a time. I never thought to have the time measured, but I should say that it must be more than ten minutes—it seemed like *ten* times ten.[72]

The length of time and the presence of a live body both indicate that the moment becomes a complex one to stage and further complicates any notion that Shakespeare intends to rupture our expectation here. In fact, the reveal of the statue itself may be considered the rupture, as at that moment the audience can begin to perceive the reversal that the play enacts.

In examining Shakespeare's dramaturgy for *The Winter's Tale*, scholars have commented that the most important reunion is that between Leontes and Hermione.[73] The reunion between Leontes and Perdita is reported second-hand in the scene before, thereby removing us from accessing what seems like an important scene.

Furthermore, the final scene itself focuses on Leontes's reactions to the statue almost entirely, with Perdita only providing two short speeches. Therefore, the expectation being built is that we will see Hermione forgive Leontes, which happens as she 'embraces him' and 'hangs about his neck' (5.3.111, 112). However, that reunion too seems not to be the important reunion; the play truly celebrates the reunion of mother and daughter as Hermione reserves her language entirely for Perdita.[74] Conceivably, Hermione agrees to come back once news of her daughter reaches her, meaning that knowledge of the oracle's assertion of Perdita's survival led Hermione to 'preserve' herself 'to see the issue' (5.3.128, 129). But this too does not fully explain the construction of the reunions, some on-stage and some off. Overall, Shakespeare seems most invested in the reunion of Hermione to the audience. We too have been without Hermione for the last half of the play, and finally we once more get to be in the presence of the Queen. Perhaps this final moment and change, this movement away from Leontes, is yet another interruption, a chance to recolour the play from its control within the confines of the jealous man and into the forgiving embraces of a wife/mother/woman. Here, Shakespeare demonstrates his departure from Greene most in that he continues to interrupt our expectations of these scenes, leading to unexpected continuations, which itself, in avoiding a totalizing dramatic irony, interrupts our conception of Shakespeare as a dramatist.[75]

Fletcher and *The Chances*

Fletcher's riotous comedy *The Chances* also participates in disrupting dramaturgical structures through its uniquely formulated and disorienting first act. Like Shakespeare, Fletcher too recreates narrative source, and like Jonson, Fletcher reframes a typical dramaturgy (namely exposition) to discombobulate the audience. In this play, then, Fletcher demonstrates the theatrical power of such disruptions. Cyrus Hoy considered *The Chances* as an example of Fletcher's 'mature comic art', which he defined as 'an art that was able to put the often creaking conventions of romantic distress and bliss at the service of contemporary images of fashion, folly and pleasure'.[76] Despite such high praise, this play, like most of the Fletcher canon, has received scant critical attention, even being called a 'slight play' or a 'more than passable entertainment'.[77] Most criticism has centred on the play's indebtedness to its prose source, Cervantes's *La señora Cornelia*, especially in connection to the play's depiction of women.[78] However, no one considers the play's unique opening. To consider this structure, I will refer to Cervantes's novella, but despite that work's own structural preoccupations, especially with deferrals,[79] I will focus more on Fletcher's own interruptive dramaturgy in presenting his audience with a quick succession of scenes, almost in media res, with little to no identifying information for the characters and their conflicts. In this way, I disagree with Mary Bjork's conclusion that 'Viewed in isolation from its source, Fletcher's play is an amusing comedy that . . . doesn't seem to have anything profound to say'.[80] As with most Fletcherean criticism, Bjork finds that the work only offers interest in relation to something outside of it, often something more canonical, like Cervantes. However, the play's dramaturgy presents something more interesting than a simple source study might indicate. Fletcher disrupts our expectations of how a drama should begin. Unlike Jonson's disruption of the theatrical opening at the second sounding, Fletcher more subtly crafts expository material into an engaging first act, thereby interrupting typical dramaturgy. This interruptive methodology transports a distinctly prose narrative into a novel theatrical deployment that engages spectators through confusion and happenstance occurrences; hence the vague title itself.

The play explores the chance encounters between Don John and Don Frederick, two young gentlemen, and Constantia, a young woman who has just given birth to the Duke's child. Constantia's brother Petruchio and the Duke prowl the streets looking to fight each other. A confusion over identities occurs, and competing stories vie for truth, which leads to a final encounter in the house of a conjuror who has a disguised Constantia confront her lover the Duke.[81] The story of the play closely follows that of Cervantes's novella; however, the power of narrative overcomes that work. The Spanish text possesses a 'crystal-clear expositional beginning', which moves into 'opacity and confusion and relentless action at a breakneck speed'.[82] Even with such action, the novella repeatedly insists upon the power of narrative, as exemplified when the narrator states, 'And he then narrated all that had happened to him', followed by a list of the events.[83] As this line demonstrates, Cervantes's story focuses upon narrated stories. This twice-told information produces a repetitive structure that highlights the repeated nature of prose narratives themselves, which is at odds with the perceived 'present' in the theatre (even though it too is an always-already iterated structure through rehearsal and repeat performances). With Cervantes choosing to highlight these narrations as methods for exploring the characters' stories, he, therefore, does not give Fletcher the basis for Fletcher's dramaturgy in the first act.

Fletcher's first act contains more separate scenes than any other first act in his entire canon, with eleven distinctly cleared stages—and all eleven are marked in the B&F 1647 Folio.[84] In fact, other than Shakespeare's *Coriolanus*, this play has the most scenes in *Act One* out of all plays by Shakespeare, Jonson, or Fletcher.[85] The scenes that comprise the act are themselves short: the longest scene is ninety-eight lines and the two shortest are each only nine. As the longest scene would only take roughly around five minutes to perform, the transition from scene to scene would feel quick and rapid as no scene lasts for long. This entire play, totaling only 1,827 spoken lines, is not lengthy, but the longest act is in fact the first one.[86] However, the average number of lines per scene in the first act is forty-four, which makes it half the size of the closest other average lines per scene by act (which is *Act Four*, with an average of eighty-four lines per scene) and significantly shorter than the average for the entire play (seventy lines per scene). These numbers mean that despite its relative length on the stage, the act comprises short bursts of scenes. As this occurs at the beginning of the play, these snippets happen as the audience attempts to understand what is happening and to figure out who the characters are. Doing so amidst rapid-fire changes of personnel on the stage makes clarifying the exposition much more difficult.[87] Therefore, Fletcher purposefully makes the audience seemingly lost as they have very little on which to ground their expectations or understandings. Even the title would give audiences no indication of which characters to follow. The only hint in the title is that the play is about 'a happening or occurrence of things in a particular way',[88] or a group of scenes in a play. Even the vague titles of *As You Like It* or *Much Ado About Nothing* provide the audience with an aphoristic sense of playfulness.[89] Fletcher might as well have titled the play *Play*.[90] Through the openness of this title, Fletcher deliberately plays with his audience in ultimately disrupting their ability to create expectations.

The first scene, while almost a typical exposition scene, defies such usual dramaturgy in that it insists on being specific about unimportant information while neglecting to inform the audience about important information. Like *The Winter's Tale*, the play begins with two men discussing their master's behaviours, but here we are lowered a social class as these are 'serving-men' not courtiers. While we learn that their masters are ignoring their studies and have been trying to catch a glimpse of a reportedly beautiful woman, we do not learn anyone's name: anyone except one of the serving men. The first line of the play is, 'I would we were remov'd from this Town, *Anthony*' (1.1.1),[91] indicating the servant's desire to leave and the name of the other servant. While the line serves as a usual piece of exposition, we continue to hear Anthony's name repeated:

> PETER: Why good tame *Anthony*?
>   Tell me but this: to what end came we hither?
> ANTHONY: To wait upon our Masters.
> PETER: But how *Anthony*?
>   Answer me that; resolve me there good *Anthony*?
> ANTHONY: To serve their uses.
> PETER: Shew your uses *Anthony*.
> ANTHONY: To be imploy'd in any thing.
> PETER: No *Anthony*,
>   Not any thing I take it . . .
>
>   (1.1.8-14)

The italic emphasis on the name is replicated from the Folio, and it underscores the excessive repetition of Anthony's name. [Peter][92] uses it again five lines later and then once more before both servants exit. Therefore, in the fifty-three lines that open the play, we hear the name of Anthony eight times. We do not learn the name of the other conversant outside of the speech prefixes that identify him for readers but not spectators. Furthermore, we are not given the names of their masters, and probably most importantly to the plot, we are not given the name of the beautiful woman that both masters desire to see.[93] Fletcher opens the play by providing excessive amounts of not useful, peripheral, distracting information for the audience while depriving us of pertinent facts. This willingness to counter an audience's expectation of an expositional scene highlights Fletcher's interruptive dramaturgy. He begins the work not with necessary information but with the lack of information, or rather with the provision of unimportant information. This tension between knowing and not knowing drives the rest of the play up to the final scene with its performance of conjured identity. The dramaturgical form, therefore, emphasizes the larger issues at stake about knowledge of one's identity, showing how the interruption of delivering important information calls into question the audience's ability to know a character, which is a recurrent idea in the play.

The scene continues as the servant's masters enter. They reiterate their desire to see the beautiful lady, and then they set off on their accustomed walks. We do not learn their names, nor much more about them before they leave the stage. In fact, the next name we learn is for a more important character than Anthony, namely Antonio. At the beginning of the second scene, a nameless gentleman identifies another character by exclaiming, 'Fie Antonio' (1.2.1). We may now perceive Fletcher's playful construction fully coming to bear. As Fletcher introduces the next problem, Antonio enters with the line 'Cut his winde-pipe, I say' (1.2.1); the playwright gives us an almost-worse-than-unhelpful nomenclature because it resembles the only name we know so far. This play is a play about Anthonies. The scene briefly drops the name problem, as it eventually identifies Petruchio—though in an awkward self-reference:

> no 'tis honour,
> Honour, my noble friends, that idoll honour,
> That all the world now worships, not *Petruchio*
> Must doe this justice.
>
> (1.2.28-31)

While this might create some confusion, an actor could deliver the line to make sense for an audience. These playful identifications perhaps confuse but also highlight the lack of clarity over the possessive pronoun in Antonio's first line. The 'his' who is threatened is obviously an important aspect of the scene; however, we get no indication that that personage is the Duke, and while we will meet the man in Folio Scene Five, we will not know he is the Duke until [Constantia] mistakes [John] for him in *Act Two*. Therefore, this line, as well as Antonio's further lines of violence, are rendered less powerful for the audience as they cannot yet perceive the political sedition involved in them. What Fletcher rather presents (on stage and not in speech prefixes) are two men fighting each other over a vague issue of honour. Like the unidentified antecedent to 'his' above, the antecedent cause for their quarrel is not defined until the end of the act when [Constantia] identifies herself as that cause.

The play continues its delightful confusion of names in the next scene where [John] unknowingly receives [Constantia]'s child. The moment occurs almost identically in Cervantes's story, and Bjork offers that one central but overlooked aspect of the moment is that it 'stems from a lie'.[94] The Juan/John character lies about his identity to the voice that he hears and, therefore, insinuates himself into the action in an unnecessary way. While Bjork uses this observation to bolster her overall argument that Fletcher 'amplifies the darker qualities of Cervantes' character',[95] she misses that on stage in this moment [John] does not necessarily lie. At the moment when the Woman offstage asks for 'Signieur Fabritio' (1.3.17), the audience does not know [John]'s name. In fact, he could be Fabritio. His responses to the name further indicate the playful deferral of his identity:

> WOMAN: (*within*)
>   Signieur *Fabritio*?
> JOHN: Ile goe nearer.
> WOMAN: (*within*)   *Fabritio*?
> JOHN: This is a womans tongue, here may be good done.
> WOMAN: (*within*)
>   Who's there? *Fabritio*?
> JOHN: I.
>
>   (1.3.17-19)

Like [Peter]'s repetition of Anthony in the first scene, the offstage voice calls again and again for Fabritio, and eventually [John] replies that he is this person. The audience might perceive that he is not Fabritio as he responds, 'here may be good done', and the actor could (but may not) use non-verbal cues to indicate his lie. Indeed, just after this moment of confusion, literally after he exits [Frederick] finally gives us John's name. Before that revelation, Fletcher continues his playful name game in the opening of the play by offering a name for a character, which is in fact not his name, but also suggesting or allowing that it may be his name. Like the repeated Anthony/Antonio, we receive a useless name, a character that eventually appears in Cervantes *but not in Fletcher*. Unlike the Spanish novella, the English play contains only one character to whom the name 'Fabritio' is attached; the audience only sees one

'Fabritio', whose name is actually John. [John]'s response of 'I' becomes even more powerful in this reading because of the pun on the first-person pronoun. While that playfulness would be readily available for a reading audience, they also have speech prefixes that preset character names in a way that destroys the theatrical playfulness over identity. This consideration of Fletcher's dramaturgy of naming in the first few scenes of the play highlights one of his theatrical interruptions. The availability of the rupture to take place, the confusion necessary to generate the chaotic power of the scenes, only lives on the stage where dramatic textual apparati like speech prefixes do not predispose his audience to seeing the playful game at work.[96]

Another key example of how his theatrical dramaturgy disrupts our typical expectations of exposition is the entirety of Folio scene 5. Below are the nine lines/seventy-eight words that comprise the scene:

> *Enter* DUKE, *and three Gentlemen.*
> DUKE: Welcome to Towne, are ye all fit?
> 1. GENTLEMAN: To point Sir.
> DUKE: Where are the horses?
> 2. GENTLEMAN: Where they were appointed.
> DUKE: Be private, and whatsoever fortune
>   Offer it selfe, let's stand sure.
> 3. GENTLEMAN: Feare not us,
>   'Ere ye shall be endangered, or deluded,
>   Wee'll make a black night on't.
> DUKE: No more, I know it;
>   You know your Quarters?
> 1. GENTLEMAN: Will you goe alone sir?
> DUKE: Ye shall not be farre from me, the least noise
>   Shall bring ye to my rescue.
> 2. GENTLEMAN: We are counsell'd.
>   *Exeunt*
>   (1.5[4])

For a reader, this scene provides an antithesis to the second scene when Antonio offers threats of serious violence. We can see that the Duke is probably the 'his' referred to in the second scene, and we may begin to assess the gravity of the situation. A theatre audience, however, has little context for anything that occurs here.

We can identify a man in charge, we might tell rank or social station, and we can figure out that he has set up some protections for himself as he expects a quarrel. We might further connect this short scene to the longer one before. However, this scene in the theatre provides little information on its own in the dialogue beyond the fact that the men are ready to serve the man in charge. The most important piece of information is the final comment that the men are to come if they hear any noise. That direction creates an expectation that when we next see this character if he is in a confrontation, we should expect that these other men will aid him. This expectation, however, is ruptured in the second act, when it is [John] and not these gentlemen who come to the Duke's aid. Therefore, even the most significant aspect of the scene is eventually undermined as Fletcher ruptures the audience's expectations of events that unfold.

This short, almost unimportant scene nevertheless demonstrates two important aspects of Fletcher's dramaturgy. First, it highlights the ruptured expectation of exposition by offering little in the way of usual exposition. We would understand this scene in the middle of the play or at the climactic final battle when we are familiar with the characters and the conflict. Here, however, we are ignorant of the context, making the scene potentially more confusing than enlightening. Second, its speed participates in the overall speed of the first act that rushes through the introduction of characters and conflict in its own vague way. By subsuming traditional expositional structures within the hurried and chaotic environment of this first act, Fletcher displays an attempt to question the need for exposition itself. He highlights the audience's abilities to follow the theatrically vital short scenes. Finally, reading this short scene gives us more information, via speech prefixes, than seeing it, but a reading of this scene makes it look unimportant. The language is not particularly insightful to character, tone, or theme. However, when the pithy exchange is placed into the larger context on stage of these other pithy and strange encounters that surround it, it highlights a distillation of what a theatrical scenario might be. This scene then plays with exposition as exposition: the scene's demanding series of questions is about the desire for knowledge, but only the characters who themselves have context can follow this exposition, while the play deprives the audience of the usual delivery of expositional material.

The two most important surprises within the first act are, of course, the baby and [Constantia] herself. While both of these encounters are taken from Cervantes, Fletcher uses his medium—verse and the theatre—to playfully disrupt our knowledge of events, thereby illustrating the dynamics between playwright, dramaturgy, and audience. As stated before, the scene with the baby hand-off begins with [John]'s lie/confusion over his identity, but after stating that he is Fabritio, he is handed a bundle:

> WOMAN: I have stay'd this long houre for you, make no noise,
>   For things are in strange trouble: here, be secret,
>   'Tis worth your care; begone now; more eyes watch us,
>   Then may be for our safeties.
> JOHN: Harke ye?
> WOMAN: Peace: good night.
> JOHN: She is gone, and I am loaden; fortune for me;
>   It weighes well, and it feeles well; it may chance
>   To be some pack of worth: by th'masse tis heavie;
>   It if be Coyne or Jewels, 'tis worth welcome:
>   Ile ne're refuse a fortune: I am confident
>   'Tis of no common price: now to my lodging:
>   If it hit right, Ile blesse this night.
>   (1.3.21-31)

I quote this exchange in its entirety but without two important notes given to the reader. In both the Folio and Williams's edition, the Woman's entrance is '*with a childe*', and Williams during the Woman's speech adds the editorial stage direction '*Gives childe*'. Therefore, like the speech prefixes, the stage directions clarify what is occurring in this moment, but that runs counter to Fletcher's crafting of the scene. The Woman gives absolutely no indication of what is in the bundle she delivers other than that it is 'worth your care'. [John] too does not examine the bundle closely but immediately assumes that by its weight and because of her comment, that it must be 'Coyne or Jewels', but his language that emphasizes the play's title further indicates that the bundle is probably not what is expected. While he uses 'chance' to indicate that fortuitous meeting with the woman, which includes the lie about his identity, an audience may (or may not) perceive that the vague language about the package shows the openness of the true contents. [John] then exits without further inspection.

Two more scenes intervene, until John enters for a solo scene in which he finally reveals what was in the bundle, but as in the previous scene, he does not immediately tell the audience what it is. He begins:

> Was ever man so paid for being curious?
> Ever so bob'd for searching out adventures,
> As I am? did the devill lead me? must I needs be peeping
> Into mens houses where I had no businesse,
> And make my selfe a mischiefe? 'Tis well carried;
> I must take other mens occasions on me,
> And be I know not whome: most finely handeld:
> What have I got by this now? what's the purchase?
>
> (1.6[5].1-8)

His reaction clarifies that the bundle does not contain the riches he expected. In this way, John's own premise is ruptured by the contents of this bundle. Instead of declaring the contents or showing them to the audience immediately, as the stage directions do, John toys with us and makes us guess the contents of the package. He hints at the contents as payment for his curiosity, a 'mischiefe' and a 'purchase'. He gets closest to the truth when he says that it is 'other mens occasions', but in context this does not clearly signify that the bundle includes a baby. The playful delay of information is part of Fletcher's dramaturgy.[97] He delays giving character names, he delays clarifying conflict, and he delays exposition. Instead, he emphasizes happenings, occurrences, meetings, actions, entrances, and exits. The first act is a frenzy of movement with little expository information. It moves beyond the dramatic and into the theatrical.

John does of course eventually tell the audience that the contents of the bundle are 'A piece of evening Arras worke, a childe' (1.6[5].9). Even the reveal delays the specific information by placing the identification at the end of the verse line. It follows a synecdoche that in hindsight colours an almost-lewd description, but in the moment presents the audience with yet another piece of information that is unclear. What might one do behind an Arras? Polonius eavesdrops and is killed, but here John imagines that people sneak off to have illicit sexual encounters. The substitution of a child for the action of its production and the setting of that action emphasize

John's own sexual obsessions. These images among others lead Boro to criticize the play and its presentation of motherhood,[98] but in equating Fletcher's voice with John's we lose Fletcher's ability to replicate a young man's discovery of what does indeed seem to be a bastard child. As Fletcher himself was once a young man, it seems overly unkind to discredit his ability to tap into the sexual world of a twenty-something male, one who has journeyed to a city specifically to see a beautiful woman. Fletcher contrasts John with [Frederick] to illustrate that the world is not full of depraved, sexually starved young men, and has John decide after a brief consideration of leaving the baby to 'keep it' (1.6[5].39), even though it will be more trouble to him than to the man who sired it. Furthermore, in delaying the reveal of the baby, Fletcher taps back into a previous dramaturgy that he deployed in another solo scene: in *The Two Noble Kinsmen*, he delays identifying the kinsmen that the Jailer's Daughter loves in her first solo scene.[99] Here Fletcher reuses a structure that plays with audience expectations. In not telling us the contents but only allowing us first John's excitement and then his extreme disappointment, we are left with an open field of expectations that our imaginations fill. Fletcher provokes his audiences to actively engage the situation through withholding pieces of information. He presents us with what seems to be one thing and shows it another; he provokes expectations and then ruptures them.

Another significant aspect of this speech is its length: it is overlong, especially for the speedy first act. John speaks for forty-eight lines, which is almost thirty lines longer than the next longest speech in the Act.[100] Therefore, in the middle of the act, we stop with John to ruminate on the unexpected outcome of his night walk. In continuing the speech for so long, Fletcher once more seems to be toying with an audience by creating the expectation of fast changes and chaotic movements only to give us a scene of almost excessive rumination. In fact, compared to Fletcher's other solo scenes or even Shakespeare's, this one is the longest by almost ten lines.[101] Therefore, this structure, that James Hirsh critiques as having a 'potential for being undramatic',[102] disrupts the middle of the act that so far has been highly theatrical and full of movement. This speech stops and focuses us upon John as character and his plight with his bundle. It gives him the space to rant against his fortune, to make several lewd jokes, and to complicate our understanding of this play. Just as we may be settling into the speed with which Fletcher bombards us at the opening, suddenly we halt; he ruptures our expectations and diverts our consideration of his dramaturgy. He alters the relationship between him and the audience by reminding us that we cannot predict what he is going to do next. In comparison, [Frederick]'s earlier solo scene as he looks for John is a brief nine lines. If this scene created an expectation, then this lengthy speech of John's solo scene might possess the expectation that someone, namely [Frederick], might interrupt him at any moment. As no one does, Fletcher playfully offers an expectation that he ruptures in not interrupting.

The final important structural facet of this scene is the baby itself and even more so its crying. Shakespeare used infants in *Titus Andronicus*, *3 Henry VI*, *Pericles*, and *The Winter's Tale*, while Jonson only used one in *The Magnetic Lady*; Fletcher only used them twice: in the ending of the collaborative *All is True*, and here.[103] While Victorian theatre readily used infants on the stage, early modern theatres seem to have avoided such an incumbrance.[104] Even so, Andrew Sofer offers that Elizabeth in *All is True* could be an actual baby.[105] He, as is usual with Shakespearean scholars, notes that *All is True* is collaborative, but does not note that Fletcher wrote the scene with the infant Elizabeth; therefore, Fletcher is responsible for the scene that focuses upon the baby that is almost 'fetishized as a sacred icon'.[106] The major difference is that, unlike the babies in *The Winter's Tale* or *Titus* or *All is True*, the baby in *The Chances* seems to cry. Just after identifying that the bundle is in fact a baby, [John] is interrupted:

>   this comes of peeping:
> A lumpe got out of lazinesse:—good white bread,
> Let's have no bawling with yee:—'sdeath,
>
>   (1.6[5].10-12)

Williams supplies dashes for the reader to note the change in address as [John] shifts his focus to the baby, ostensibly because the baby has begun crying. The sudden rupture of noise from the bundle after the delay of the reveal itself would only heighten the comedy of the moment as the baby picks up its cue. The line could also be read as him trying to calm the baby to ensure that the baby does not in fact cry, enjoining it to not do what he perceives babies do. The speech ends with another such address:

> Come good wonder,
> Let you and I be jogging: your starv'd trebble
> Will waken the rude watch else:
>
> (1.6[5].45-47)

His comment that the baby's high-pitched voice will alert the watch indicates that part of the aural landscape of this scene is the crying of the baby. One might argue that this line too only suggests [John]'s worry about the baby starting to cry, but I see in his repeated concern either the chance to have the doll cry through some sound effect or at least John's playing up of an anticipated reaction. The crying, or even expectation of it, disrupts our consideration of the scene as a solo scene itself because, even if an inanimate doll, the sound effect gives a perceived presence to the other character on the stage at the time. This does not efface its status as a solo scene; rather, it demonstrates Fletcher's playful engagement with characters who soliloquize on the stage. Furthermore, we might consider this scene in light of one of Shakespeare's earliest explorations of interruptions: Launce's monologues with Crab, the dog in *The Two Gentlemen of Verona*. These comedic set pieces are predicated upon an unpredictable scene partner that creates uncertain interruptions. Jonson too explores this potentiality in *Every Man Out* through the continued presence of Puntarvolo's dog.[107] Here, however, the stage partner is more controlled, as long as it is a doll with sound effects.[108] Were the company to use an actual baby, then the effect would be more akin to the scenes in Shakespeare and Jonson with the dogs.[109] Furthermore, the first nine lines leading up to the reveal would potentially be ruptured themselves as the baby might cry out before the cue and destroy Fletcher's surprise. If that were the case, which again is highly unlikely, Fletcher would as playwright be putting into play an element outside of his control that could rupture his own crafted rupture. There seems to be hardly any clearer investment in the power and dramaturgical significance of interruption than using a live baby.[110]

Act One of *The Chances*—chaotic, rupturous, and full of revelations—ends on the most important revelation for the course of the play, and sets us, even briefly, back on more stable dramaturgical grounding. Like John's mistake with the baby, [Constantia] also makes a mistake in thinking that [Frederick] is

the person sent to help her escape. Unlike the previous mistake that
Fletcher uses to build a comedic revelation, [Constantia] hears one
line from [Frederick] and immediately responds:

> Alas I am mistaken, lost, undone.
> For ever perish'd. Sir, for heaven sake tell me,
> Are ye a Gentleman?
>
> (1.7[6].10-12)[111]

In a more typical Fletcherean vein, the woman immediately realizes
the error of the encounter. She recovers quickly and insists upon aid
from the person in front of her. This contrasts with John's whining
complaint that precedes the scene, when he does not realize his
mistake and then ruminates on how it affects him. In this brief
exchange, we can further see Fletcher's rupturing the dramaturgy as
well as his 'proto-feminism'.[112]

This encounter leads to the end of the act where Frederick[113]
invites [Constantia] into his room and vows to protect her, refuses
her payment, but asks to see who she is. This final request is
perhaps the only surprise for a reading audience, because it is not
until this exchange that we realize that she wears a veil, concealing
her identity. Frederick asks, 'If ye will force a favour to oblige me,/
Draw but that cloud aside', to which she responds, 'It shall be./
For I am truly confident yee are honest:/The Piece is scarce worth
looking on'. (1.11[10].21-22, 23-25). Showing her face should be
the revelation of her identity as Constantia. This should be the
moment, like the end of *Much Ado*, where we realize the heroine
is in disguise. However, Fletcher's rapid and purposefully confused
dramaturgy means that we do not know who this woman is. The
rest of the scene furthers this lack of identity as it only focuses upon
Frederick's admiration of her beauty. The dumbfounded reaction
that Frederick gives upon seeing her may help an audience to realize
that this is the woman 'Of infinite report for shape and vertue' that
has drawn the two men to Bologna (1.1.21). Frederick, however,
does not make the connection and only perceives that he has done
a good deed for a beautiful woman. In fact, he never makes the
connection; John later figures it out after talking to her brother
Petruchio—but that does not occur until the end of *Act Two*. By
closing out the first act with a literal reveal that reveals almost
nothing, but that also closes the circle and brings the audience back

to the first scene, Fletcher cleverly concludes the opening movement in a play that will continue to playfully engage expectations only to disrupt them.

The first act of Fletcher's *The Chances* illustrates his approach to an interruptive dramaturgy as he alters an audience's expectations of what exposition should be. Like Jonson's alteration of the framing device or Shakespeare's appropriation of narrative source, Fletcher's twist on exposition provokes expectation within an audience member only to rupture it through unexpected occurrences. As with all interruptions, though, we should consider the continuation to clarify the playwright's ultimate presentation of such ruptures. As has become clear by now, Jonson's approach is to control these ruptures, even if in *Every Man Out* he ultimately offers his own inability to do so. Shakespeare tries to embrace a Fletcherean rupture but backs away and embeds his adaptation with dramatic irony, which he found in his source. Fletcher continues to playfully disrupt expectations. Later in this play, we encounter a whore also named Constantia, and the final scene presents a supposedly magical summoning evocative of the Hermione reunion. Perhaps his ultimate disruption is the fact that nothing new occurs; no new relationships are made; there are no marriages here. Those that were together before the play are together at the end. The almost triteness of this reductive view, I offer, further emphasizes Fletcher's delight in the play of the theatre. This play then is about theatre for theatre's sake, offering a sustained engagement and investment into the truly playful nature of the theatrical endeavor. Therefore, as Jonson strives to create a new type of theatre through *Every Man Out*'s disruptions and as Shakespeare reworks his source into a staged disruption of expectation, Fletcher too uses dramaturgical macrointerruptions to highlight the power of the stage itself, but in a way that forces the audience into the present of the theatrical endeavor. The theatre is a space of artifice that provokes unrealistic expectations of events that both do and do not occur. That is a space that Fletcher inhabits.

5

Convention

When playwrights rupture received theatrical types, images, and set-ups, they engage in macrointerruptions that have profound effects upon the audience. The following chapter grapples with interruptions of theatrical conventions. Conventions are fundamental, as they govern audience expectations of the entire performance. For example, current audiences expect performances to begin when the house lights dim, but the early modern period, of course, had no such technology and, therefore, no such convention. As discussed in the previous chapter, the early modern period used trumpet calls to start the play, a convention that Jonson ruptured in exploring his interruptive dramaturgies in *Every Man Out*.[1] Conventions typically emerge in the course of theatre history as ruptures to older conventions. Bert States explains that theatrical conventions are like 'efficient and invisible chips' that initially enter the informational circuitry through 'attempt[s] to *break into* the circuit, to pester the circuit with nuance, to *wound* it with the resistance of its presence'.[2] States's language describes the system of convention origin as one of interruption that leads into a continuation that is initially unnoticeable. Jeremy Lopez builds on States's observation by adding that 'the residual power of this eruption always lies, only half-dormant, beneath the surface, ready to turn a familiar convention into a new one'.[3] While States describes the birth of conventions as a process that breaks through but then becomes solidified, Lopez notes that the convention is always ripe for rupture once again. Conventions explicitly engage the audience's expectations, which is the foundation of all macrointerruptions. They, however, do not possess a structure that can always be easily discerned as ruptured, but they are built of expectations, and as expectations are premises, the potential for interruption exists. Importantly, these interruptions both begin and end with an audience, as that is the power dynamic at play here: between writer/performer and reader/audience.

To investigate these macrointerruptions, this chapter uses moments of male-to-female (MTF) cross-dressing as exemplary sites because these disguises rupture expectations of a foundational convention of early modern theatre. Not only does such cross-dressing rely upon the conventions of disguise, they also touch on the larger convention of the all-male stage. MTF cross-dressing was the everyday business of the boy actor. Therefore, using MTF cross-dressing in a plot blurs the lines between reality and the theatre for early modern audiences. So too, each playwright of this study uses MTF cross-dressing specifically, allowing for cross comparison. Interrupting conventions means interrupting one's relationship to previous playwrights. Therefore, this line of inquiry further explores the triangulation among the playwrights of this study.

The fact that the early modern English commercial theatre used boy actors to play female characters need hardly be noted. This curious arrangement that reflects neither law nor European custom has inspired several studies.[4] When Shakespeare, Jonson, and Fletcher crafted female roles, they did so for a transvestite theatre. The actors for whom they wrote those roles were young men.[5] Therefore, when Rosalind in *As You Like It* dresses as Ganymede and pretends to be Rosalind for Orlando, the audience watches a young man play a woman dressed as a young man who is then pretending to be a woman. This delightful friction between these layers draws scholars and readers and theatregoers back to these texts. Despite Stephen Orgel's insistence that the moments in which 'Shakespeare makes the practice of his theatre . . . into the subject of his drama' have been 'rendered invisible',[6] his own critical work as well as others since have enlivened an interest in this complex negotiation between gender, performance, and play. As in the example of Rosalind, the most typical way for playwrights to exploit and explore the boy actor as female character was to have the boy dress as male, thereby layering a played gender on top of his theatrical gender that aligned to his personal gender.[7] The less typical usage, though perhaps the more intriguing and productive in light of the all-male stage, was to have a male character dress as a female one. While the female-to-male (FTM) cross-dressing has received much attention, male-to-female (MTF) has received very little.⁸ MTF cross-dressing was a standard convention for plotlines such as the boy bride and for general disguises, but it was never as popular as FTM cross-dressing.⁹ Michael Shapiro disallows the efficacy of this convention by dismissing it as part of 'traditional forms of revelry' and 'practical joking'.¹⁰ However, Simone Chess explores MTF cross-dressing episodes as:

> especially rich sources for relationally and socially oriented readings of gender, and that [. . .] might therefore suggest that relational queer gender could have a positive or beneficial association in early modern literary representations.¹¹

Chess notes how important these rare moments are in considering a positive aspect of queer representation. As drama is only part of her examination, she misses the theatrical power that employing these occurrences entail, namely in examining the relationship of these characters to an audience's reception. This chapter then builds on her work to consider how the MTF cross-dressing plots on the stage create tension with a foundational convention of early modern drama itself.

Shakespeare, Jonson, and Fletcher all used MTF cross-dressing in their plays, but examining how they interrupt the convention demonstrates how they approached engendering audience expectations and rupturing them. Shakespeare interrupts the convention by leaving the audience's expectations unfulfilled in an almost-paradoxically uninterrupted interruption. Conversely, Jonson and Fletcher reinvest the convention with a sense of playful authority that twists the received notions of delineated genders. In doing so, Jonson and Fletcher specifically rupture their relationships with their audiences and with Shakespeare by reinventing old schemes. This chapter then engages the relationship not only between audience and text/writer but also from writer to writer.

When Shakespeare first engages MTF cross-dressing in *The Taming of the Shrew* (1591), he revives it by rupturing several expectations that he creates within the Induction. Importantly, he does so with the audience's full awareness of the disguise, and therefore, plays upon expectations connected to the convention of disguise, which he ultimately ruptures through not offering a reveal. Jonson explodes MTF cross-dressing by assaulting it and the convention of the boy actor in *Epicene* (1609). He interrupts the assumptions of the audience through not revealing the cross-dressing until the very end. He carefully crafts this interruption through subtle deployment of other interruptive structures before the ending, leading up to Epicene's silence. Finally, Fletcher, as inheritor of both playwrights, reinvigorates MTF cross-dressing in *The Loyal Subject* (1618). In this rarely studied play, he follows Jonson's usage but interrupts the expectation by opening up the potentiality within such a rupture of a convention. Fletcher asserts a playful invocation of gender, which underscores and opens up theatrical possibilities. Studying this type of interruption reveals the intricate relationship among audience, playwright and convention, as well as explores the genealogical connections between playwrights.

Bartholomew/Lady

Shakespeare uses MTF cross-dressing in only two of his plays. In *The Merry Wives of Windsor*, Falstaff escapes dressed as an old woman (4.2) and two boys dressed as fairies are married off to Slender and Caius (5.5). Both of these instances are highly conventional farce.[12] *The Taming of the Shrew*, however, offers a more interesting usage not only rooted in the conventions of such cross-dressing, but rife with unfulfilled expectations. In the induction to the play, the Lord decides to have his page Bartholomew dress as a woman and pretend to be Sly's wife. We see the Lady interact with Sly, and, in fact, she remains with him for the remainder of their stage time. As Bartholomew is a young man dressed as a woman, he is indistinguishable from other female characters on the early modern stage. This tension between representation and reality exposes the complicated connection between audience expectation, convention, and interruption: a tension that Shakespeare exploits specifically by framing the presentation of the page in a sexualized and feminized manner. This frame constructed within a frame highlights the theatrical nature of the dramatic endeavour and, therefore, interrupts the expectation of the play's course. As the play becomes the play-within-the-play, the Bartholomew/Lady and Sly/Lord ostensibly remain on the stage, though fully subsumed into the audience. The transformation of page to Lady (off-stage) and Lady to audience (during the course of the play) ruptures our expectations of the play's return to the induction frame itself. In *The Taming of the Shrew*, Shakespeare presents an MTF cross-dressing with a reveal that never occurs, but in doing so the text of the play underscores the constructed nature of such cross-dressing. In this way, Shakespeare disrupts the comedy of the convention by underscoring the theatrical reality of it and lays the way for the later disruptions by both Jonson and Fletcher.

Few English iterations of the MTF cross-dressing theatregram exist prior to Shakespeare's Induction. In fact, only six plays use an MTF cross-dresser before *The Shrew* (see Table 5.1). They are *Gallathea* (1584), *Philotus* (1585), *The Wars of Cyrus* (1588), *The Woman in the Moon* (1588), *Orlando Furioso* (1591), and *George a Greene* (1591).[13] One of the central distinctions in the MTF cross-dressing that takes place in these six plays is the question of agency on behalf of the male dressing up as a female. In *Gallathea*, *The Woman in the Moon*, and *Philotus*, the cross-dressed male willingly adopts the disguise for personal advancement.[14] However, in *The Wars of Cyrus*, *Orlando Furioso*, and *George a Greene*, the cross-dresser has been coerced into the situation and acts the part on behalf of another character. In *The Wars*, the page Libanio pretends to be his mistress to let her escape. He does so out of 'dutie that doth bind [him] to [her] selfe';[15] therefore, his status as servant and sense of duty compel him to undertake the disguise, even if it means his death.[16] In *Orlando Furioso*, Orlando's page pays a Clown to pretend to be Angelica in a scene of comedic violence.[17] Especially with the Clown's reference to his beard and the comic beating that ensues, this moment is more alike Falstaff in *Merry Wives* than it is to Bartholomew in *The Shrew*. Finally, in *George a Greene*, as in *The Wars*, George's boy Wily dresses up as a woman to help free George's love from her father. Like Libanio, he acts upon his duty despite knowing that 'tis but a beating' if he is found out.[18] Therefore, the most direct antecedents for Shakespeare were *The Wars of Cyrus* and *George a Greene*. Notably, in both, the boy in disguise is in disguise for their entire appearance in the play. Libanio's three scenes and Wily's two are both with the boy in the apparel of the woman that they imitate, further aligning them to Shakespeare's Bartholomew. Importantly though, in all iterations of this disguise, the disguise is ultimately revealed to

Table 5.1 Plays with MTF Cross-dressing (1584–1636)

Title	Author	Year	Wiggins #	Company
Gallathea	Lyly	1584	754	Children of Paul's
Philotus	Montgomerie?	1585	766	-
The Wars of Cyrus	Anonymous	1588	813	Children of the Chapel Royal
Woman in the Moon	Lyly	1588	819	Children of Paul's
Orlando Furioso	Greene	1591	876	Queen's/Admiral's Men
George a Greene	Anonymous	1591	893	Sussex's Men
The Taming of the Shrew	Shakespeare	1591	916	Pembroke's Men?
The Taming of a Shrew	Anonymous	1594	955	Pembroke's Men?
Downfall of Robert Earl of Huntington	Munday	1598	1106	Admiral's Men
Englishman for my Money	Haughton	1598	1120	Admiral's Men
Look About You	Anonymous	1599	1184	Admiral's Men
Antonio and Mellida	Marston	1599	1218	Children of Paul's

(*Continue*)

Table 5.1 (Continued)

Title	Author	Year	Wiggins #	Company
Merry Wives of Windsor	Shakespeare	1600	1079	Lord Chamberlain's Men
What You Will	Marston	1601	1283	Children of Paul's
Labyrinthus	Hawkesworth	1603	1395	Cambridge University
Law Tricks	Day	1604	1436	Children of the Queen's Revels
May Day	Chapman	1604	1439	Children of the Queen's Revels
Westward Ho!	Dekker and Webster	1604	1450	Children of Paul's
Mad World My Masters	Middleton	1605	1479	Children of Paul's
Isle of Gulls	Day	1606	1491	Children of the Queen's Revels
Dumb Knight	Markham and Machin	1607	1563	Children of the King's Revels
Two Maids of More-Clacke	Armin	1608	1577	Children of the King's Revels
Epicene	Jonson	1610	1603	Children of the Queen's Revels
Amends for Ladies	Field	1610	1615	Children of the Queen's Revels
The Scornful Lady	Beaumont and Fletcher	1610	1626	Children of the Queen's Revels

Title	Author	Year	Lines	Company
Brazen Age	Heywood	1611	1653	Queen Anne's Men
Hector of Germany	Smith	1613	1707	Young London Tradesmen
Honest Man's Fortune	Field, Fletcher and Massinger	1615	1719	Lady Elizabeth's
Love's Cure	Fletcher and Massinger	1615	1779	King's Men
Monsieur Thomas	Fletcher	1615	1788	Queen's Revels [?]
Devil is an Ass	Jonson	1616	1810	King's Men
Swetnam the Woman Hater	Anon	1618	1855	Queen Anne's Men
Loyal Subject	Fletcher	1618	1874	King's Men
Little French Lawyer	Fletcher and Massinger	1620	1941	King's Men
School of Compliment	Shirley	1625	2158	Lady Elizabeth's
Noble Gentleman	Fletcher (and collab?)	1626	2172	King's Men
New Inn	Jonson	1629	2263	King's Men
Byrsa Basilica	Ricketts	1635	2511	University
Hollander	Glapthorne	1636	2536	Queen Henrietta's

the other characters on the stage, even if the MTF cross-dresser never appears in male attire, an aspect that Shakespeare ruptures.

At the beginning of *The Taming of the Shrew*, Shakespeare plays upon an audience's expectations of female characters by subtly referring to the convention of the boy actor. The play starts with a beggar Christopher Sly being ejected from a tavern by an irate Hostess. What is remarkable in this exchange is Sly's rejoinder: 'I'll not budge an inch, boy' (Ind.1.13). Michael Shapiro argues that this usage is an 'exposure of artifice . . . reveal[ing] the Hostess to be a theatrical construct'.[19] For a play that is about to use a cross-dressed boy as a joke and that offers complicated points of view about women in society and their social construction, this word then has a powerful resonance. However, what Shapiro misses in connecting it back to a social construct is the way that such a theatrical moment engenders expectations and alters the presentation of the women that follow. At the beginning of the play, Shakespeare disrupts the convention of the boy actor by calling out the theatricality of the convention itself. The text here offers that the play, which will soon centre on a play-within-a-play, is all about theatrical construction. Shakespeare allows his audience to see the layer of dramatic irony.[20] The drunk beggar then perceives the truth of the situation as well as the off-stage audience does, perceiving a 'reality' beneath the conventional cross-dressed boy. By disrupting our comfort with the convention, he then leads us towards a central joke of the Induction scenes, where the Lord has Bartholomew play Sly's Lady.

At the end of the first Induction scene, the Lord in *The Shrew* devises his plan to send in his page as Sly's wife and, therefore, sets up the premise for the MTF cross-dressing in the subsequent scene. His speech outlining Bartholomew's actions is his longest in the play, with thirty-one lines devoted to describing the cross-dressed boy. His instruction is unnecessary for an audience that is about to see the action itself. This tension between excessive narration and the about-to-ensue action allows for the audience to have mastery of things off-stage while also making us 'want to see action'.[21] Furthermore, Jeremy Lopez argues that exposition speeches also provide 'a definite sense of beginning'.[22] In context of the Lord and Bartholomew, this speech provides the audience with a moment to see the boy transform into the Lady. As we never view Bartholomew as himself, this speech is the chance for us to peek off-stage and watch as the Lord transforms the boy into a Lady, a transformation *literally* happening in the tiring house of all early modern theatres. The beginning of the speech plays around by delivering unnecessary information. After dismissing the players, the Lord orders, 'Sirrah, go you to Barthol'mew my page/ And see him dressed in all suits like a lady' (Ind.1.104-05). The lines effect the transformation for the audience in a moment of excessive information.[23] The nameless Lord gives us the name of his page before subsuming the identity of the page into another character. The Lord's one-line erases Bartholomew and creates the Lady, who, like the Lord, remains nameless, a functional character. Notably, the only two characters given specific named identities in the induction are Christopher Sly (though given the speech prefix 'Beggar' in the Folio) and Bartholomew the Page (given the speech prefix 'Lady').[24] The audience learns Sly's name through his own self-identification; while the text reduces him to type, the character insists upon individualization, even giving himself a genealogy.[25] In performance, this would be more pronounced because the audience would be relying on such clues as to the characters' identities (clothing, accent, actions, etc.),[26] but they are never given, aside from Sly, a name to accumulate such information onto or into.[27] Shakespeare also names the boy page. In giving us this specific identifier, Shakespeare asserts a premise that he will rupture. He gives the audience the image of a specific page, one with a specific name, but then transforms that image into the Lady who will enter in the next scene. This Lady is the only character the audience sees.

So too, the Lord's choice of Bartholomew and his reassurances thereof further underscore the convention at stake. The Lord chooses to use Bartholomew after a troupe of actors have entered, meaning that the need to use his page as a cross-dressed woman is completely unnecessary. The similar text of *The Taming of a Shrew*, in fact, has the Lord use the Boy from the acting company play the wife.[28] That Lord chooses to use a professional, which is a logical choice that derives from the convention of the all-male stage. In *The Shrew*, however, the Lord's choice to use his own page becomes as odd as the choice to surround Sly with pornography.[29] In fact, his choice not to use the professional actor and instead to entrust this action to his page indicates what he later asserts: 'I know the boy will well usurp the grace,/Voice, gait and action of a gentlewoman' (Ind.1.130-31). His certainty in the boy's ability to transform himself into a woman emphasizes a reality within the convention, meaning that the character is certain that a boy can play a woman because in the material reality of that era, the theatre had boys play women. Therefore, *The Shrew* suggests a logical assumption from the early modern theatre: that all boys could personate women. In doing so, the play oversteps the convention as convention and attempts to make the convention underlay reality itself.

While the majority of the Lord's speech describes actions and language that the page should employ, he ends the description with an action that highlights the theatrical nature of this situation. The Lord culminates the speech with a description of the page's crying, which is the only moment that admits the situation's artificiality. In offering that the boy can use 'an onion . . . in a napkin . . . close conveyed' if he 'have not a woman's gift' (Ind.1.125-26, 123), the Lord acknowledges the artifice within the production of Sly's Lady. In this admission, he offers that however close the boy is to mimicking or portraying a woman, he will never *be* a woman. The moment almost denies theatrical transformation as it suggests that Bartholomew can substitute but not become. This differentiation highlights that even if the boy can 'usurp the grace,/Voice, gait, and action' of a woman (Ind.1.130-31), that there will always be a difference between that which he plays and that which he is. These descriptions all engender expectations for an audience while emphasizing the pervasive convention of the boy actor itself.

In the ensuing scene before Bartholomew finally enters, the Lord and the servants can only convince Sly of his transformation through emphasizing the existence of the Lady. After describing the pictures that they might show him and the activities they might engage, they finally convince Sly of his transformation by talking about his lady:

> LORD: Thou art a lord, and nothing but a lord.
> Thou hast a lady far more beautiful
> Than any woman in this waning age.
> 1 SERVANT: And till the tears that she hath shed for thee
> Like envious floods o'er-ran her lovely face
> She was the fairest creature in the world–
> And yet she is inferior to none.
> SLY: Am I a lord, and have I such a lady?
>
> (IND.2.61-68)

To culminate the argument, the Lord hits hard upon not only the existence of Sly's Lady but also upon her beauty. Once more, the specific and exemplary description provided reminds the audience not only that the Lady is actually a boy but also that we have not yet seen her on stage.[30] The servant takes up the theme, elaborating on her beauty. This moment is Sly's shift from being the beggar to the pretended lord, accompanied by a shift from prose to verse. His first thought that cements his understanding of his new identity is that he has 'such a lady'. Establishing his identity upon the existence and identity of another, especially one whose identity is playfully unstable, highlights the playful instability of his adopted persona. Furthermore, it illustrates a connection between the Lord and Sly as Sly becomes subsumed within the Lord's game through the sexual game of the cross-dressed Lady. In fact, Sly's first demand as lord is to 'bring [his] lady hither to [his] sight', which even comes before his demand for 'a pot o'th' smallest ale' (Ind.2.74-75). As this iteration and those before indicate, the game that the Lord plays on Sly does not simply include a sexualized encounter with an MTF cross-dresser as part of the joke, which is how *A Shrew* presents the same moment; rather, it makes that encounter the defining aspect within an overwrought illustration of power dynamics among people: a fitting concept for the rest of this play.

When Bartholomew enters, it is not as a Boy or a Page but as a 'Lady with Attendants' (Ind.2.99SD). Even after the stage direction, her speech prefixes retain the epithet 'Lady'.[31] Unlike most modern editions that choose to use 'Page' or 'Bartholomew', the Folio only uses the speech prefix of 'Lady' to designate the cross-dressed page. Such retention illustrates the printed text's attempt to highlight the thoroughness within the convention. Here, like *George a Greene* or *The Wars of Cyrus*, a boy is made to cross-dress by a superior to fulfil a need or desire for that superior. Unlike either of those earlier iterations, Bartholomew's entrance is not only constrained through intensified expectation but also restricted into the performance of the Lady as Lady, which the prefixes demonstrate.[32] In this way, Bartholomew, even with his specific nomenclature, never exists in the world of the play: he is only ever 'Lady'.

. . . or Madam. The conversation upon her entrance focuses on her name. Sly asks, 'What must I call her? . . . "Al'ce Madam"? Or "Joan Madam"?' (Ind.2.107, 109) to which the Lord responds, '"Madam", and nothing else' (Ind.2.110). Unlike the Lord's use of the page's first name in the previous scene, here the jest eliminates specific identities in favour of functional titles, aligning the cast of the jest with the nameless Lord himself. So, Bartholomew becomes a functionary, but one whose function is specifically female, as the speech prefixes indicate. This system of naming, as Peter Stallybrass explores, is a theatrical one that emphasizes the disguise as the identity itself, which is an approach that both Jonson and Fletcher will follow, but is in contrast to *A Shrew*.[33] After this discussion of naming, Bartholomew or Lady or Madam actually makes the first move on Sly by responding to him, 'Ay, and the time seems thirty unto me,/Being all this time abandoned from your bed' (Ind.2.113-14). The play hints at the sexual interaction between the two, and Sly immediately responds, ''Tis much. Servants, leave me and her alone./ Madam, undress you and come now to bed' (Ind.2.115-16).[34] On being reminded of the conjugal opportunities of the bed, Sly directly takes her up on such a suggestion, ordering his servants to leave before demanding her to unclothe herself. The immediate danger of homosexual activity on stage becomes imminent in this moment as the Lord even leaves the Lady to defend herself.[35] Here, Shakespeare most fully plays with and also interrupts the typical MTF cross-dressing convention. He places the MTF cross-dresser within the potential for homosexual activity, but he has done so in a way that has pushed for this expectation all along. As opposed to allowing us to assume the comedic outcome, he has intensified that potentiality through emphasizing the sexual nature and the central importance of the boy/Lady within this entire jesting scenario. The arrival of a messenger ruptures the potential encounter—even if Sly states that he will 'tarry in despite of flesh and the blood' (Ind.2.126)—and brings on the play-within-a-play to overtake the Induction entirely and move the story away from one about a sexualized boy page and to one about a boy playing a sexualized woman. Importantly, the Lady stays with Sly for the duration of their appearance. This again contrasts with *A Shrew* where the Lord is the character who remains with the beggar.[36] Once again, Shakespeare places emphasis upon us seeing and watching the MTF cross-dressed boy.

The Shrew's complicated set-up for a boy/Page dressed as a woman being thrust into a sexual situation with another cross-identified character develops Shakespeare's methodology for macrointerruptions of conventions. He follows previous plays—*George a Greene* and *The Wars of Cyrus* specifically—that deploy a similar disguise motif in which a boy dresses up as a lady. However, his premise here, to use the language of interruptions, is the prolonged build-up before Bartholomew/Lady's entrance. The sexualized power dynamic that the Lord engenders in the first scene and that carries over into the expectational arousal in the second scene establishes a place of heightened sexuality and an expectation that the façade cannot last. Shakespeare ruptures this expectation not only by focusing us on the Lady after her entrance but also by not allowing Sly to realize anything odd about the encounter. The disguise is complete. The conventions hold, with no hope of reveal. Unlike Sly's initial interaction with the Hostess, who he sees doubly as both 'baggage' and 'boy', he only sees Bartholomew as the Lady. The stability of the theatrical illusion makes us take account of the larger convention at stake. In presenting a specific boy 'Bartholomew' as a generic Lady, but doing so enmeshed in a sexualized economy, Shakespeare reminds us of the specific boy actors who play generic types on the stage inside a sexualized economy based upon spectatorship. The artifice of the theatre becomes a rupture, as he neither allows Sly to see beneath the Lady nor allows her jest to end. The audience at an early modern theatre too would be expected to not see beneath the character to the boy, and a boy actor would be expected to remain thoroughly in character while on stage. Gender, like social status, becomes a playable layer, but through the deployment of the convention, it is erased and made invisible.

The status of the text of *The Shrew* is complex; therefore, we cannot be certain whether Shakespeare intended to return to the Induction at the end of the play, like the Anonymous author of *A Shrew* does. If the non-concluded Induction is a purposefully open frame, the MTF cross-dressing in the Induction would be a continued site of theatrical friction were the Lady to stay on stage. If Sly and his Lady watch the entire play to the end, a reading that the Folio text permits, then the audience is constantly made aware of the jest and would also be potentially waiting on the reveal of the cross-dressing. Instead of a break in that disguise, we instead encounter the taming plot, which concludes the play with Katherine's speech of female obedience. While that speech begins with her talking about women in third person, it shifts to first-person plural specifically when she describes female bodies: 'Why are our bodies soft, and weak, and smooth' (5.2.171). This alteration in pronoun usage, which encompasses not only Katherine as character but all women, becomes about the construction of female identity within the body of the young boy. Such a reading becomes more forceful through

Bartholomew/Lady's presence if Katherine specifically acknowledges him/her. This hypothesized moment of audience contact that would continue the ruptured expectation of reveal reminds us of the gendered tensions at play here and embodied by all-boy actors.

Shakespeare's engagement with the MTF cross-dresser ruptures the convention through toying with the audience's expectation. The continuation here is hard to determine. It could be the ending I have just proposed where the Lady remains and becomes implicated in Kate's final speech. Or, if parts of the text are missing, it could be a return to the framing device. As it stands, what early modern audiences experienced was already ruptured in the first two scenes because no reveal occurs and the joke never ends; for modern audiences and readers, we have those scenes coupled with the potential to read the end as open. For modern audiences too, we no longer employ boy actors, so Shakespeare's interruption of the convention becomes lost or at least transmuted within a different framing conception of what MTF cross-dressing means in our society today.

Epicene

Just as Shakespeare built upon previous iterations to disrupt expectations, Jonson combined the precedents of George Chapman's *May Day* (1604) to completely change the understanding of the conventions at stake. Jonson ruptured Chapman's own rupture of the conventions by combining the MTF cross-dresser with the surprise at the end.[37] The importance of *Epicene* to the discussion of macrointerruptions and conventions is that it completely disrupts the audience's expectations when Dauphine reveals that Mistress Epicene is not a woman but a boy. Jonson's coup de théâtre has become a defining hallmark of the play itself and, therefore, a critical cliché.[38] While the ending rewrites the rest of the play and provides ample room for discussion of gender,[39] the central problem that the ending evokes is Jonson's connection to his audience, or how he comments upon convention. John Sweeney offers:

> Questions of dramatic form and meaning were for [Jonson] always questions of his approach to his audience. He used the stage to formulate propositions about his spectators and thought their response as much a part of the theatrical event as the stage action.[40]

Both Katharine Maus and Richard Dutton, however, see *Epicene* as anomalous to Jonson's typical behaviour. Dutton states, 'Jonson breaks one of the supposed cardinal rules, that the audience should be kept in the know all the time';[41] Maus rewrites this as *Epicene* 'strikingly defies that normal principle of drama: keep the audience informed'.[42] Despite the use of 'breaks' and 'strikingly' to critique the ending through a violent rendering, both scholars alert a reader to the importance of Jonson's agenda. They identify that the ending is a significant rupture on Jonson's part as playwright in which he alters the relationship among audience and theatre and author. Importantly, their assumption of a 'cardinal rule' or 'normal principle' of dramatic irony stems from a biased and overemphasized examination of Shakespeare, who more often than other early modern dramatists delights in that aspect of drama. As the Induction to *The Shrew* shows, Shakespeare wants us to know what is happening, even if the characters do not.

Jonson's usage of interruptions aligns with Sweeney's idea that Jonson specifically considers his audience. Furthermore, William Slights proposes that such moments are 'theatrical irony' in which 'the audience does not share a superior position with the author but is instead duped by the same trick'.[43] Regardless of what we might want to call this move, its form is interruptive; however, the interruption of the plot, which most critics focus on, is a matter for the previous chapter. Here, I want to reconsider and reassess the import of this interruption to the conventions that it engages. Many critics assert that the ending forces the audience suddenly to reconsider the boy actor. One must remember, however, that this reconsideration participates in a rich foundation of MTF cross-dressing disguises on the early modern stage. In fact, Lucy Munro's section about the Queen's Revels' interest in MTF cross-dressing states that *Epicene*'s usage marks the convention as 'already overdetermined'.[44] My examination seeks to establish and consider the relationship of an audience to that rupture and understand how Jonson crafts that as part of his text.

To consider the play's framing of Epicene as a character and the complex expectations that Jonson engenders for his audience, we should not begin at the ending with the reveal, but at the beginning. Nothing is more anterior to a drama than is its title. Tiffany Stern in her examination of playbills argues that the information disseminated about a play beforehand significantly created expectations for an audience member. She concludes, 'The specific information bills and title-pages provided, and the language in which they did so, had to be carefully chosen.'[45] Therefore, if the title of the play in performance was *Epicene*, then an audience did have the beginning clue to consider the theatrical interruption in store for them. Furthermore, Stern notes that no matter what information else was included, the most important would be the title, but the title of *Epicene* for early performances is contested. The three early witnesses to the title are the entry in the Stationer's Register, the first print publication, and a brief anecdote by William Drummond. The Stationer's Register records the play as 'A booke called, Epicoene or the silent woman by Ben: Johnson', and two years later the rights are transferred under the name 'the Commodye of the silent Woman'.[46] The first printed publication of the play presents it as *EPICOENE, or The silent VVoman. A Comœdie*, with a running title reading *The Silent Woman*. Finally, William Drummond writes that when Jonson's 'Play of a Silent woman was first acted, ther was found Verses after on the stage against him, concluding that, that play was well named the Silent Woman. ther was never one man to say plaudite to it'.[47] So which is it? *Epicoene* or *The Silent Woman* or both? Like many early modern plays, the titles are both ambiguous and compounded.[48] Wiggins offers a compendium of data on the title for this play. He catalogues the play as 'The Silent Woman' and then lists the performed title as 'The Silent Woman', the printed title as 'Epicoene, or The Silent Woman', a contemporary usage of 'The Silent Lady', and finally an alternative modernization of 'Epicene'.[49] He provides no explication for this information but follows it with an addendum:

> I record the proposed alternative modernization primarily for the benefit of those who might use it in a search;[50] if it is not quite a false modernization, it is certainly an unhelpful one. The case turns on how obvious it should be that the silent woman is not really a woman at all. The proper name Epicoene operates in its four-syllable form by both emphasizing a Greek feminine ending and slightly obscuring the English word *epicene*, which gives the game away. The name's modernization should allow it to work that way in print, too: Epicoene, not Epicene.[51]

For Wiggins, the most important aspect of the drama and its title lie in the surprise of the ending; therefore, he opts for the use of *The Silent Woman* as the title for his catalogue entry and privileges it as the performed title, deriving most likely from Drummond's comment. However, Wiggins's commentary here is confusing as to who his audience is both in print or otherwise. The slight variation in spelling, as the examples in the *OED* demonstrate, would not have mattered for an early modern audience where the spelling was acceptable either with or without an 'o'.[52] Furthermore, he ignores the evidence within Jonson's own texts for the spellings epicoene versus epicene. In Jonson's *English Grammar*, the text prints 'epicene', while in *Neptune's Triumph* it reads 'epicoene'—the latter specifically not in a moment where the idea should be obscured. Therefore, if Wiggins means that such a spelling should be retained through Jonson's desire to obfuscate the clue, his evidence is unclear and unconvincing.

I am therefore inclined to think that the title included *Epicoene*, through which Jonson would be winking towards the educated members of his audience.[53] The word 'epicene', as derived from Greek and Latin grammar, refers to a noun that is either masculine or feminine in gender.[54] Therefore, the classically derived word as the title of the play points towards the surprise ending. Slights calls the title 'curious', and Bevington tries to explain it in light of the finale: 'We were warned ... yet we may have assumed ... that "epicene" refers to the sexual ambiguity of an all-boy acting company.'[55] I, however, agree with Reuben Sanchez: 'Jonson intended, even expected, the theatre audience to get it, to understand the secret of Epicoene's sex well before the onstage audience does.'[56] Indeed the title and character name indicate some complication, and the construction of the ending further implies the playful control in Jonson's text.[57] If the title were *Epicoene* at the first performances, then Jonson expected at least some of his audiences to get the grammatical reference. If that is the case, then the play's import cannot solely be predicated upon the reveal at the end, as Wiggins insists.[58]

The title along with the beginning of the text both prepares and does not prepare a reader or an audience member for this eventual interruption of the convention. If audiences were given the title *Epicoene, or The Silent Woman*, the play already presents them with a bit of a confusing issue. Knowledge about the meaning of epicene means that an audience member would be looking for issues of mixed or indeterminate gender within the play. This gender occlusion would contrast to the stereotypical misogynistic ideal of a 'silent woman'. So, an audience member would be looking for a supposedly silent woman who also is connected to or represents issues of indeterminate or mixed gender. The play introduces the silent woman as soon as Dauphine enters and Clerimont comments that Morose has found 'one that's lodged i'the next street to him, who is exceedingly soft-spoken, thrifty of her speech, that spends but six words a day' (1.2.24-26).[59] This is the first mention of Epicene in the play, but not by name; instead, the emphasis is on her almost complete silence. In this manner, Jonson establishes the expectation through exposition not only that we will meet this silent woman but also that she will probably fail in Morose's expectations, just as Truewit avers that he surely 'has found none' (1.2.23). Shortly thereafter, La Foole not only further highlights Epicene's silence but also provides her name. In enjoining Dauphine to dinner, he lists the guests and notes 'they come o'purpose to see the silent gentlewoman, Mistress Epicene, that honest Sir John Daw has promised to bring thither—' (1.4.39-40). This line provides the title, though inverted: the silent woman before Epicene. Perhaps this verbal indication would remind a playgoer of the title as they think back to 'Epicene or The Silent Woman'. If an audience member has no idea of the grammatical root of epicene, then they will take this moment and all subsequent ones as simply an iteration of a character's name. However, if an audience member knows the usage, then Epicene's gender must be in question. I cannot agree with Bevington that someone who knows the meaning of epicene would consider that it simply 'refers to the sexual ambiguity of an all-boy acting company in which the part of a woman has to be played by a pre-adolescent male'.[60] That is like arguing that because the play and one character is named Volpone, we should also assume that the play is full of foxlike characters. The extension of one character's name and attributes to the entire endeavour seems fallacious in considering how Jonson handles onomastics. The evocative names used in this play highlight aspects of specific characters, not of the entire play in general. Therefore, even with her name only being mentioned six times in the dialogue, those iterations are enough to remind a knowledgeable audience member either that she has aspects of her gender presentation that are more complicated than we might yet know or that she will complicate notions of gender presentation in the course of the play, which indeed she has and she does.

Even the Dramatis Personae in the first printing in the 1616 *Works* is cleverly ambiguous, further reifying the complex presentation of Epicene's gender and the complex knowledge about it. In that list, Jonson calls Epicene 'A yong Gent. suppos'd the silent Woman'.[61] While this might seem like a moment of reveal, displaying Epicene as a gentleman before the play even begins (which arguably he is, both character and actor-wise), the subsequent description of Sir John Daw as 'her servant' confuses this assumption. Thereafter, the shortened 'Gent.' after Epicoene becomes unlike the 'Gent.'s that preceded it, now being reread as Gentlewoman. So too any hints that 'suppos'd' suggested as far as gender identity is concerned become about the other half of her indicator—her silence. The indeterminacy is the key. In fact, the whole usage of Epicene hinges upon the idea of both/and gender-wise. Jonson permits clues to his design while emphasizing the confusing admixture present in the characterization. Admittedly, the audience member I offer is knowledgeable. One must have a familiarity with grammar to know what epicene is and realize the issue of gender indeterminism at stake. Jonson permits this type of a playgoer or reader, to guess at his design. In crafting an interruption that reaches into the heart of a convention, Jonson questions that convention both to control his audience and to allow us to see through the theatricality as well. Jonson's game is not much fun if the audience is not playing along. Therefore, to conceive of the final reveal as a complete surprise seems to undervalue the way in which Jonson has crafted the reveal itself. This is not a rupture that derives happenstance from circumstances, but rather, like Dauphine's plot from the beginning, it represents a preconceived design.

The original Prologue also references this design through its use of a food metaphor. At the end of the speech, the writer asks:

The poet prays you, then, with better thought
To sit, and, when his cates are all in brought,
Though there be none far-fet, there will dear-bought
Be fit for ladies: some for lords, knights, squires . . .

(PROLOGUE.18-22)

The entreaty here sets up two opposing issues in light of this play's surprise ending. First, Jonson begs that the audience wait through the entire play for 'all' of 'his cates' to be 'in brought', meaning that he desires the audience to consider the work as a whole, and not simply as pieces to be taken apart. He suggests that the play takes part in an overarching design, which cannot be appreciated piecemeal. Therefore, the audience must learn at the end with Morose that Epicene is not a woman in order to then judge and consider the rest of the play. This need for consideration is continued as Jonson concludes:

> Nor is it only while you keep your seat
> Here that his feast will last; but you shall eat
> A week at ord'naries on his broken meat,
>   If his muse be true,
>   Who commends her to you.
>
> (PROLOGUE.25-29)

Jonson offers that the significance and impact of this play is not that which passes ephemerally away, but is rather one that stays with the audience after the play is completed. The rupture at the end in which he disrupts the entire preceding plot through revealing what was only hinted at before does such a feat in that it begs an audience to reassess the entire play in light of the new information and 'raises some disquieting retrospective questions'.[62] Our thoughts that occurred during the performance, our half-formed thoughts before the 'cates' were 'all in brought', are only the initial impulses but not the refined reflections that the play demands. Importantly, this play, unlike so many others, makes the questions about who knows what important not only for the characters within the drama but also for those 'beyond the characters to involve the auditors and the author as well'.[63] In learning of Dauphine's ruse with Epicene, we have a chance to re-evaluate the play and consider how the moments with Epicene change with the knowledge of an unacknowledged character lurking beneath the dress, a character much more similar to the boy actor who personates Epicene than to Mistress Epicene herself.[64]

Jonson takes what Shakespeare toys with in *The Shrew* and what Chapman complicates in *May Day* and adds it together into the theatrical surprise of Epicene's gender. As I have illustrated, a learned audience member or reader would have an idea of Epicene's identity, but not until the final scene does Jonson let the audience into

Dauphine's secret plot. Structurally, he layers his macrointerruption through a build-up of microinterruptions in the dialogue of the final scene (5.4). After Morose cuts off Epicene's speech, the subsequent interruptions cluster around the three attempts that Morose makes to rid himself of his wife: first by claiming impotence, second through exposure of her premarital sex, and finally through Dauphine's revelation of Epicene's gender.

The first attempt and its interruptions function in a manner that is commensurate with typical dramatic irony. Jonson leads up to Morose's revelation of his lack of gendered identity through his impotence using repeated microinterruptions:

MOROSE: Ladies, I must crave all your pardons—
TRUEWIT: Silence, ladies.
MOROSE: For a wrong I have done to your whole sex in marrying this fair and virtuous gentlewoman—
CLERIMONT: Hear him, good ladies.
MOROSE: Being guilty of an infirmity which, before I conferred with these learned men, I thought I might have concealed—
TRUEWIT: But now being better informed in his conscience by them, he is to declare it and give satisfaction by asking your public forgiveness.
MOROSE: I am no man, ladies.
ALL: How!

(5.4.26-36)

Morose is interrupted three times as he attempts to admit that he is impotent. The first two interruptions indicate two possibilities as they might suggest that the ladies continue to chatter and need to be quieted to hear Morose's confession or they offer a comedic highlighting of Morose's confession as both Truewit and Clerimont ask for already-established silence. The young men's interruptive support in this moment illustrates the power they wield over both Morose and the ladies. They craft the end of the drama through control of what information is revealed or not revealed. While this information is not a surprise to us, their control participates in dramatic irony as the ladies do not know what is about to be uncovered.

The final interruption in this passage and Morose's revelation itself develop a climax and almost an ending for the play. Truewit wrests power from Morose's story by building it up and making it more significant than Morose seems to be playing. Truewit demonstrates his sense of control as he elaborates on Morose's desire to 'declare it' and 'give satisfaction'. This interruption is continued by Morose as he offers the simple statement: 'I am no man, ladies'. While his confession is meant to explain that he is impotent, the choice of language resonates with a play that is about confused gendered identities. This moment builds on how the name itself may have led audience members or readers to think about the complications of gender, a fact that a stage full of boys would also foreground. His confession of not being a man does highlight that he is in fact a boy, but also potentially creates a moment in the drama where a disguise plot can be revealed for the on-stage audience, which provokes the excited response of 'How!'. While Morose goes on to explain his problem of 'frigidity' (5.4.37), for a brief moment we see him as 'no man', that is, as a boy actor, we might even see him as not male, and our sense of convention, if not interrupted, fluctuates and softens. In establishing this structure in the final scene, Jonson gives further hints to the audience and the readers and prepares us for the larger macrointerruption to come.

Epicene dismisses Morose's explanation, and short of a physical examination, he is forced to discover another reason to divorce her, which leads to the next three interruptions and the second climatic moment. This attempt begins with an interruption of Otter by Morose as he excitedly hopes to learn of another way out of the marriage (5.4.65-66), which soon leads to La Foole and Daw attempting to reveal their own relations with Epicene:

MOROSE: What is true, gentlemen? What do you assure me?
DAW: That we have known your bride, sir—
LA FOOLE: In good fashion. She was our mistress, or so—
CLERIMONT: Nay, you must be plain, knights, as you were to me.
OTTER: Ay, the question is, if you have *carnaliter* or no.
LA FOOLE: *Carnaliter*? What else, sir?
OTTER: It is enough: a plain nullity.
EPICENE: I am undone, I am undone!
MOROSE: Oh, let me worship and adore you, gentlemen!
EPICENE: I am undone!

(5.4.89-98)

Here, the interruptions are quick and lively as Daw and then La Foole attempt to avoid being too explicit, whether for reputation's sake as they claim or because they are lying, the text never clarifies. However, it ends with a potentially overlooked interruption because of Epicene's repeated cue. As Simon Palfrey and Tiffany Stern demonstrate, a repeated cue, like Epicene's 'I am undone', could cause an interruption and disrupt the text as Morose tries to speak but cannot.[65] Here Morose might begin his line's 'Oh' before the second 'undone', creating a brief interruption that is unsuccessful. The control of the repeated cue then lies within the cuer who asserts his premise back over the interrupter who has begun speaking, especially in this case, when Epicene reiterates her line. Epicene, despite her protestations, is not actually undone as she knows that her marriage is not real to begin with. Her playful solicitation of sympathy illustrates her wiles as an actor. Furthermore, before the beginning of this attempt, Truewit tells Dauphine, 'Dauphine, whisper the bride that she carry it as if she were guilty and ashamed' (5.4.61-2). This aside establishes that Epicene is knowingly out to gull and play with Morose and that Truewit realizes this about her. Epicene, therefore, in her 'undone's gives us a moment of seeing her as an actor, manipulating Morose, but through this interruption the audience can further see through the complicated relationships on stage. Seeing her as an actor within the gulling of her husband (before we fully realize the sham of her marriage) makes the audience further prepared for the theatrical rupture to come.

The third and final attempt to divorce Morose and Epicene is not only effective but also delivers the significant rupture of the drama. Like the other attempts, it is characterized through microinterruptions, in which Morose interrupts Dauphine (5.4.134, 148). Morose, in his least powerful moment, attempts to grab the power that Dauphine clearly possesses as he promises a solution to Morose's problem. In attempting to gain the power of the moment, Morose reveals his own weakness as Dauphine reasserts his final plan only after getting Morose's signature. Morose becomes the least potent character as he vies for a last semblance of authority, though in signing the document he gives all authority away.[66] The rupture that critics have continued to discuss is the moment when Dauphine reveals the ploy:

DAUPHINE: Then here is your release, sir.
                (*He takes off Epicene's peruke.*)

> You have married a boy, a gentleman's son that I have brought up this half year at my great charges, and for this composition which I have now made with you.
>
> (5.4.165-68)

This simple action, the removal of a wig, has generated much critical discussion. Phyllis Rackin notes, 'Thus in *Epicoene*, where reality is social, gender is an ineluctable reality; instead of celebrating androgyny, the play indulges in homophobic satires, and sex roles are rigidly enforced.'[67] Richmond Barbour explains, 'The removal of Epicoene's wig demonstrates forcefully that collective imagination, quickened by dress and expectation, constructs gender.'[68] Jean Howard argues, 'In this instance, male cross-dressing becomes a way to appropriate and then erase the troubling figure of wife.'[69] And Simone Chess offers, 'Epicoene stands on stage, unwigged but still in his dress, no longer needed for Dauphine's success or Morose's investments, a trafficked object now stripped of trade value.'[70] These varying reactions to the same action demonstrate the productive and powerful move. So, is the final action one of constructed gender or enforced sex roles? Does it eliminate the wife or devalue the trafficked child?

With the removal of the wig and revelation of Epicene's epicene nature, Dauphine ruptures our expectations of MTF cross-dressing through revealing that we have been watching such conventions all along. Significantly, the layered conventions of the all-male stage and disguise allow Jonson to masquerade the character in front of us, dropping hints, but never revealing the truth until the final moment. In this rupture, we come to re-evaluate the premise in order to continue our spectatorship. As both Chess and Barbour highlight, the boy on stage is still in dress though no longer wigged. This stage picture complicates the reductive reading of the end's theatricality because the revelation is not directly of the boy actor underneath as many read it, but rather of *another* character. This reveal provides what Shakespeare does not, as we see the young page dressed up and playing at his master's game. Like Bartholomew, Epicene is made to play this game. However, Dauphine explains that he has trained him, unlike *The Shrew*'s Lord. The training leads to Dauphine's complicated attempt to secure his inheritance, which is ultimately successful. While Shakespeare provides the subjective identity of the boy underneath, but presents the Lady/Madam, Jonson provides only the female character even when we are confronted with the boy at the end. The creation of the new character adds to the complicated process of character creation already at work in a play where boys play women. To leap to the underlying boy actor is to ignore Jonson's clever construction of the intermediate character, a character that we have been watching, even without realizing it, for the entire play.

Importantly, once the 'gentleman's son' has been revealed, he speaks no more. The boy, and not the woman, is silent. While Chess reads this as a sign of his final power as a 'trafficked object' who has 'access to locked-away resources',[71] I find this silence to be the most indicative of his lack of control. In this silence, emphasized in the Folio text with a printed space (see Figure 5.1), the character is seemingly offered the chance to speak but does not as she/he is cut off by Truewit. The theatrical possibility dramatically rendered in that space demonstrates a possibility for Epicene's power, but then removes it. Just as Shakespeare's Bartholomew is kept under control by the Lord, so too Epicene is controlled by the men around her, even after she becomes male. In this transformation then, we see a more exacting exposure of power than a simply gendered one. Gender may be constructed, but power is controlled, and in this text it is controlled by the three young men.

> some new matter to be laught at: you deserue to liue in an aire as corrupted, as that wherewith you feed rumor. Madames, you are mute, vpon this new *metamorphosis*! but here stands shee, that has vindicated your fames. Take heed of such *infecta* hereafter. And let it not trouble you that you haue discouer'd any mysteries to this yong gentleman. He is (a'most) of yeeres, & will make a good visitant within this twelue-month. In the meanetime, wee'll all vndertake for his secrecie, that can speake so well of his silence.   Spectators, if you like this *comœdie*, rise cheerefully, and now Morose is gone in, clap your hands. It may be, that noyse will cure him, at least please him.
>
> THE END.

FIGURE 5.1 *Truewit's final speech.* Ben Jonson, Epicoene, *in* The Workes of Benjamin Jonson *(London: Will Stansby, 1616), sig. Ddd3r. The John Work Garrett Library, Sheridan Libraries, Johns Hopkins University.*

Jonson highlights the problems and the possibilities of MTF crossdressing. Through exploiting the connection between the gender of the boy actor and the gender of the character, Jonson has duped not only audiences but critics in misaligning the presentation of identity in the final moment. He demonstrates through his rupture the complicated interrelationship between conventions, and as Dutton explains, he 'keep[s] the audience', and I would add critics, 'questioning what is real and what is illusory, what is truth and what merely a convenient fiction'.[72] Therefore, the rupture interrupts our consideration of the plot and makes us question the foundation of theatrical artifice itself. As Richard Dutton again puts it, Jonson 'overturn[s] the whole convention of suspended disbelief and throw[s] the audience back on the first principles of literary judgment, the ability to discriminate truth from fiction'.[73] In this way, Jonson's prologue has prepared us; it was his reminder that the whole of the play will feed us for days. As stated earlier, the opening night's performance was potentially met with silence, a silence that Epicene too experiences, but its own meaning is just as complicated. Did the audience experience 'annoyance or bewilderment',[74] or did it lack the sense of control to speak up like Epicene? Perhaps, the silence was none of those more negative connotations, but rather was a silence of contemplation, one that indicated a fulfilment of Jonson's own desire for us to continue eating on what we had just witnessed. Even further, the silence might even be taken as a 'traditional sign of approval'.[75] Even if the silence argues against Truewit's desire for clapping and noise, it surely befits, in more ways than one, a play called 'The Silent Woman'.

To return briefly to this moment as a macrointerruption, it bears consideration of the continuation, which despite such a significant rupture is one that realigns with the premise. Jonson's *coup* did not disrupt theatre and introduce women onto the early modern stage, which Rackin's assertion that the ending 'rigidly enforced' sex roles would almost suggest. Rather, the continued vibrancy of the early modern theatre, though maybe not of the children's companies, attests to the reaffirmation of the convention that boys would play women on the early modern stage. Therefore, if we remove the rupture, the move from premise to continuation is direct, which once more illustrates Jonson's approach to interruptions. Jonson's rupture reveals the nature of the theatrical artifice, but does not overturn or destroy that artifice. Rather, in highlighting the conventions that allow for theatrical representation, Jonson supports their continuation.

Alinda/Archas

Shakespeare and Jonson used MTF cross-dressing sparingly, but Fletcher used this convention more than any other early modern playwright (see Table 5.1). With seven distinct usages, his plays show a sustained interest in this theatrical form.[76] While many of these moments use the disguise only briefly for comedy, two plays focus on the significance of the cross-dressing itself: *Love's Cure* (1615) and *The Loyal Subject* (1618). The earlier play, co-written with Massinger,[77] has a double cross-dressing scheme and provides, as Simone Chess explains, 'a fitting capstone that is also just another example of the pervasiveness and residual impact of MTF crossdressing, and of our persistent critical oversight when it comes to this type of queer gender presentation'.[78] While this play proves productive for Chess and for other scholars as well,[79] it highlights the cross-dressing at the beginning and works to consider the after-effects of such a gender swap. It presents what happens after *Epicene* or *The Shrew* is over, exploring how these boys break out of their acculturated gender roles. In this manner, Fletcher and Massinger present the convention and questions its outcomes, which challenges our expectations, but does not really rupture them.

In *The Loyal Subject*, however, Fletcher returns to this convention in a way that builds upon the legacy of Jonson while further interrupting his audience's expectations. *The Loyal Subject* presents the story of Archas, a general who retains his loyalty to the young Duke of Moscow despite a series of dishonourable accusations and almost fatal complications. The subplot follows the Duke's sister Olimpia and her relationship to a new gentlewoman at court named Alinda. The attraction between the two women is almost palpable and leads to a destructive moment of jealousy. At the end of the play, after the Duke has realized how wrong he has been, Olimpia discovers that Alinda is really Archas's son Young Archas in disguise. Olimpia marries Young Archas, the Duke marries one of Archas's daughters, and everything is healed in typical tragicomic reconciliation. The surprise of Alinda's gender and identity is a surprise almost as concealed as Epicene's, better in some ways and yet more obvious in others, but has garnered little critical attention. Philip Finkelpearl dismisses the play as 'one of Fletcher's weaker efforts',[80] and Nicholas Radel sees it as less complicated and therefore less worthwhile in comparison to

Shakespeare's cross-dressing plots.[81] So too, Daryl Palmer notes the 'opportunity for individuation' in Fletcher's subject matter, but then finds the conclusion 'royal and conservative'.[82] However, the artfulness of Fletcher's complicated interruption of the MTF cross-dressing demonstrates the need for careful re-evaluation. Through this play, Fletcher engages what Shakespeare only toyed with and what Jonson seriously developed. Fletcher theatrically complicates the problems at hand through a layering of character development. Importantly, unlike both previous plays, Fletcher not only gives the character two separate identities, both of which are specifically revealed with names, but also permits audiences to see both sides of the disguised gendered character. Fletcher takes the cross-dressing convention and ruptures it by opening it up to consider the playfulness and the paradox at the centre of the theatrical construction of character and gender. This play's macrointerruption of the MTF cross-dressing convention, therefore, exemplifies Fletcher's 'simultaneity of antitheses', a critical paradox found in his plays.[83]

The Loyal Subject begins by setting up the MTF cross-dressing scenario, but does so innocuously. Two men enter at the top of the play and have a brief exchange:

> THEODOR: Captaine, your friend's prefer'd, the Princesse has her,
> Who, I assure my selfe, will use her nobly;
> A prettie sweet one 'tis indeed.
> PUTSKIE: Well bred Sir,
> I doe deliver that upon my credit,
> And of an honest stock.
> THEODOR: It seemes so Captaine,
> And no doubt will doe well.
> PUTSKIE: Thanks to your care sir;[84]

The importance of this brief passage is its relative unimportance. The short exposition gives the audience a piece of needed information but then quickly moves on without further comment. This exchange significantly supports seeing Alinda as only Alinda: namely that she is 'prettie' and 'sweet', 'well bred' and 'of an honest stock'. All of these present a positive and feminine image of Alinda before she has been introduced. As with Bartholomew, the audience gets a preview and is prepared for her eventual entrance. Fletcher provides the seed of a premise, but gives no hint towards the eventual rupture that he pursues.

The second scene immediately complicates this opening description when Olimpia discusses Alinda's arrival with a group of waiting women. Unlike the men's assessment, the women hold a more complex examination, hinting at Alinda's disguise. Olimpia enters and comments upon Alinda's appearance, 'Is't not a handsome wench?' (1.2.1), which leads into a dissection of Alinda's attributes from her complexion to her gait. In this examination, the ultimate determination of her beauty as well as her grace is debatable as Petesca and the Second Woman tend to be harsher on Alinda than Olimpia is. Sandra Clark reads these assessments as clear indications of Alinda's gender identity,[85] but the dialogue is not so clear as it creates an unbalanced image. Alinda is 'a pretty Gentle-woman' but with 'a black eye', she has a 'good hand' that could 'strangle the neck of a Lute', and 'her strange pace' is because of her 'breeding' (1.2.3, 5, 9, 10, 13). The women cannot agree on how to assess her. Eventually, Olimpia falls in love with Alinda, and Petesca's jealousy drives her to get Alinda removed from court. These dynamics, therefore, are clearly at play in the opening exchange and complicate Clark's assumptions. Fletcher plays with his audience, suggesting the denouement's rupture in which the she is a he, but at the same time, the counter-assessment leads the audience to question such a deterministic conclusion. Our perception of her leaves us questioning what to expect upon her entrance. The exchange between the women culminates with a specific revelation:

> PETESCA: And what a manly body? me thinks she looks
>   As though she would pitche the Barre, or goe to Buffets.
> 2 WOMAN: Yet her behaviour's utterly against it,
>   For me thinks she is too bashfull.
>   (1.2.14-17)

Petesca reveals the surprise, and a perceptive audience member might remember this moment, predicting Fletcher's plot. However, Fletcher does not make this revelation overly obvious, nor does he make it clear within the construction of the scene. By placing it after the descriptions of Alinda as 'handsome' and 'pretty' with 'a good hand' and after the first descriptions that also emphasize her physical attractiveness by Theodor (her/his brother no less), the audience cannot read this statement as one of fact. Petesca further undermines herself by delivering a speech about how women are always cruel to other women who rival them in beauty and position (1.2.23-38). The harsh judgement then is unclear as to whether it actually characterizes Alinda or Petesca. So too, Alinda's demeanour supports her femininity as the Second Woman offers. The addition of the bashful observation renders the truth of the situation: that a man has taken on the actions/demeanours of a woman in order to pass as one. Alinda has been outed by Petesca and the Second Woman; however, like Bartholomew and Epicene before him, Alinda's cover only highlights the truth of the stage at the historical moment. In fact, Petesca, Olimpia, and the Second Woman all have 'manly bodies' hidden underneath a feminine demeanour. In this theatrical moment, Fletcher both highlights the artifice of theatre and reveals character information.

In many ways, this back and forth adds too much information to our pre-assessment of Alinda, and, in doing so, it clears the way for a fresh assessment of her once she enters. Even with the repeated negative assessments, Fletcher frames Alinda's entrance by emphasizing her beauty. After Petesca's speech about women's jealousies for each other, Olimpia responds:

> Thou art deceiv'd foole; now let your own eyes mock ye.
>   *Enter* GENTLEWOMAN *and* ALINDA.
> Come hither girle: Hang me and she be not a handsom one

(1.2.39-41)

Olimpia's response to Petesca's disparaging remarks is to show Petesca's lack of critical acumen through a demonstration of Alinda's beauty. Olimpia emphasizes that seeing Alinda will clearly disprove Petesca's remarks of jealousy as Petesca will see how beautiful Alinda is. Olimpia bolsters her assurances after the audience gets to see Alinda by offering once more her assessment of Alinda's beauty. These moments of prefiguration for Alinda, from the beginning of the play to her entrance, engender an image of a beautiful young woman. The disparaging remarks, even if they reveal the 'truth' of her disguise, become complicated through Petesca's intentions and thereby become dismissible as we engage in the tension over Olimpia's affections for one waiting woman or another. Petesca cryptically responds to Olimpia with 'I feare it will prove indeed so' (1.2.42). The unclear antecedent of 'it' means that Petesca might be hinting towards a tragic ending for Olimpia in which her love for Alinda does indeed get her 'hanged', or it might generally refer to Alinda's handsomeness, meaning that her attractiveness will eventually be proved through Olimpia's preference for Alinda over Petesca. Whether the line is a foreboding hint or a jealous quip, it registers the tonal inconsistency that Alinda's appearance has garnered from the first line of the play.

The characters surrounding Alinda colour and recolour the audience's reception of her, which means that when the audience sees her, they do so with several opinions already expressed.[86] Radel sees these moments as Fletcher playing a 'theatrical guessing game',[87] but then he dismisses such playfulness because of the ending in which the discourse becomes clearly heteroerotic. He explains that 'her transgressions are finally authorized in the voice of a man', which means that 'the text suppresses the subversion it invents as a titillating possibility'.[88] Sandra Clark too reads the whole play in light of knowing Alinda's gender identity, ultimately stating that the play argues that 'sex difference is natural, and that those qualities which define it, such as courage for men and timidity for women, can never be totally suppressed'.[89] While I agree that Fletcher is being playful in these moments, I disagree that the text suppresses its subversion or reifies gender determinations in light of the ending. Of course, having the transgressive couple be nothing more than a heterosexual one at the end reasserts a patriarchal heterosexuality (the same can be said of Shakespeare's great cross-dressing lovers in *Twelfth Night* and *As You Like It*), but to read the entire play in light of the ending discounts the productive *frisson* that Fletcher displays in the middle of the text. Fletcher, like Shakespeare and Jonson, lived in a world much different from ours, and to produce a completely homosexual couple on stage would have been too risky. However, Fletcher here does so in part, even having a character hint towards a tragic-lover ending in Petesca's warning. Playfully intense love-turned-tragedy was quotidian fodder for the early modern stage, but offering that plot for two young women is more subversive than critics have given Fletcher credit for. We might view Fletcher's work as Gordon McMullan does:

Fletcher repeatedly examines versions of utopia, brief alternative realms that cannot exist in the face of imperatives of practical living. Whether through the picaresque gentleman ... or through, for example, assertive and dominant women, he offers glimpses of possible new worlds which are much more appealing than the pragmatics that indicate how impossible they are.[90]

We might add to his list of examples: homosexual relationships. This interaction as Alinda takes the stage and all of the Alinda/Olimpia moments throughout offer the audience a glimpse at something just out of reach. While the ending may make the play not too subversive, Fletcher still displays the subversion. Furthermore, the presentation of Alinda complicates the understanding of gender. Alinda is both 'pretty' and 'handsome', 'sweet' and 'bashful'; she attracts both Olimpia and the Duke. Through this complicated presentation of a singular character, Fletcher clearly takes the idea of the *Epicene* surprise and retools it by considering its implications throughout a drama. This play does not want to be reassessed only in memory, in later feedings as Jonson's prologue puts it, but forces us to reconceptualize these problems in the moment by complicating our notions of character presentation and gender stability.

Fletcher's use of the Duke's love for Alinda as a complication for the relationship between Alinda and Olimpia reveals the depths of the relationship between the women. In these scenes especially, Fletcher drops most of the 'theatrical guessing game' over Alinda's identity and instead allows her to be read as an object of desire from both the Duke and Olimpia. In this construction, both Daniel McKeithan and Peter Berek argue that the play is a reconception of Shakespeare's cross-dressed love triangle in *Twelfth Night*.[91] Even though the set-up can be considered through that lens, the critical danger is in privileging the Shakespearean antecedent over the 'derivative' Fletcher play, which Berek does as he argues that Fletcher 'rewrites *Twelfth Night* to affirm subjects' obedience to sovereigns and women's subordination to men'.[92] In rehashing Coleridgean assumptions about the royalism of Beaumont and Fletcher plays with a gendered addition,[93] Berek dismisses the play without recognizing the playful valances of Fletcher's work. He furthermore ignores the work of Finkelpearl and McMullan in highlighting how Fletcher is a more complicated writer than such a reductive statement indicates. Given those complications, the comparison to *Twelfth Night* actually demonstrates more of Fletcher's theatrical macrointerruptive strategy as he reframes such a narrative by removing the layer of dramatic irony. Without us knowing for sure that Alinda is disguised, we cannot have the same reaction to the incorrect pairing of the Duke and Alinda as we might have in watching Viola/Cesario and Olivia. Shakespeare's usual ploy, as with Bartholomew, is to let the audience know explicitly what is going on and to allow the characters to be duped. However, Fletcher places us in the present, living the experience of the characters without an expectation of the events. We do not watch a boy cross-dressed as a girl being wooed by a lusty tyrant. Rather, we experience a young woman being the subject of predatory sexual behaviour, a scene played out once more when the Duke tries to seduce Alinda's sisters Honora and Viola (not to be confused with Shakespeare's heroine, but a name which bolsters McKeithan's conclusions). Fletcher forces us to evaluate the Duke's character in the repeated instances of sexual aggression and helps us to champion the love between Olimpia and Alinda.

One scene that demonstrates Fletcher's crafting of the women's relationship over that of the Duke is the scene where they exchange rings. While McKeithan argues that the ring is another *Twelfth Night* connection,[94] he overlooks how Fletcher uses multiple rings. After a Malvolio-like servant brings Alinda a ring that she does not want, Olimpia becomes jealous:

> OLIMPIA: But he that sent it, makes the vertue greater.
> ALINDA: I and the vice too Madam: goodnes blesse me:
>   How fit 'tis for my finger.
> 2 WOMAN: No doubt you'l find too
>   A finger fit for you.
> ALINDA: Sirrah, *Petesca*,
>   What wilt thou give me for the good that followes this?
>   But thou hast Rings enough, thou art provided:
>   Heigh ho, what must I doe now?
> PETESCA: You'l be taught that,
>   The easiest part that e're you learn't, I warrant you.
> ALINDA: Ay me, ay me.
> PETESCA: You will divide too, shortly,
>   Your voice comes finely forward.
> OLIMPIA: Come hither wanton,

>   Thou art not surely as thou saist.
> ALINDA   I would not:
>   But sure there is a witchcraft in this Ring, Lady,
>   Lord how my heart leaps.
>   PETESCA: 'Twill goe pit a pat shortly.
>   ALINDA: And now methinks a thousand of the Dukes shapes—
>   2 WOMAN: Will no lesse serve ye?
>   ALINDA: In ten thousand smiles—
>   OLIMPIA: Heaven blesse the wench.
>   (2.2.35-50)

This passage demonstrates the way in which Fletcher builds up the reaction of the four characters within this scene. Alinda receives the ring and puts it on her finger, immediately causing a physical response. She then tries to give it away quickly. The physical action of placing the ring on the finger seals her connection to the Duke, which goes against her burgeoning affection for Olimpia. In the realization of such betrayal, she tries to give it to a woman who would accept such attentions from the lusty Duke: Petesca. Petesca though has too many rings already. In the aforementioned passage, I have removed the editorial asides, because they are unnecessary. If the interruptive commentary from Petesca and the Second Woman is aloud, then their debauchery heightens Alinda's reaction and emphasizes the sexual actions that the ring portends. So too, it furthers the antagonism, and perhaps explains Alinda's own slight at Petesca, noting that she has too many rings already. Like Jonson's microinterruptions in the final scene of *Epicene*, Fletcher adds dialogic microinterruptions to build towards the significant and interruptive exchange that is about to occur between Alinda and Olimpia. Alinda's description of the Duke all around is sarcastically interrupted by the Second Woman, who reads the image as one of extensive lust; however, Alinda continues the description insinuating her horror, which provokes Olimpia's interruption asking for heavenly intervention. Alinda becomes overwhelmed at the thought of the Duke's sexual predation, and Olimpia interrupts the image, positioning herself as the object of desire. Olimpia's interruption wrests power not only from Alinda's imagination but also from her brother's pervasive sexuality.

This crescendo leads into a moment of heightened intimacy for Alinda and Olimpia as the women exchange rings, mimicking a wedding. This ritualized exchange has the impression of, but not the force of, marriage:

> ALINDA: With eyes that will not be denide to enter;
> And such soft sweet embraces; take it from me,
> I am undone else Madam: I'm lost else.
> OLIMPIA: What ailes the girle?
> ALINDA: How suddenly I'm alter'd?
> And growne my selfe againe? doe not you feele it?
> OLIMPIA: Weare that, and I'le weare this: I'le try the strength on't.
> ALINDA: How cold my bloud growes now? Here's sacred vertue:
> When I leave to honour this,
> Every houre to pay a kisse,
> When each morning I arise,
> Or I forget a sacrifice:
> When this figure in my faith,
> And the purenes that it hath,
> I pursue not with my will,
> Nearer to arrive at still:
> When I lose, or change this Jewell,
> Flie me faith, and heaven be cruell.
> OLIMPIA: You have halfe confirm'd me, keep but that way sure,
> And what this charme can doe, let me endure.
> (2.2.51-69)

Alinda insists upon ridding herself of the ring to rid herself of the image of the Duke and his pervasive gaze. She realizes that his token and her acceptance will make her identity crumble under the weight of his sexuality, which would destroy both her disguise and her love for Olimpia. After Olimpia takes the ring, Alinda asserts that its removal means she has 'growne [her] selfe againe', and then asks whether or not Olimpia can 'feele it'. The text focuses on her identity as character and its alterations under the Duke's sexual predation and then emphasizes the material reality of her body as Olimpia touches it. The text here requires the characters to touch. The physical encounter between the women leads Olimpia to offer her ring, which itself leads Alinda to deliver a set of more or less wedding vows. Her shift into a headless iambic tetrameter in rhyming couplets indicates the heightened moment in which Alinda promises herself fully to Olimpia. We might dismiss this charged moment if we read the play solely through the ending; however, if we consider that Fletcher presents a mock wedding of two women on stage in 1618, we can see the complicated subversion at work in Fletcher's drama, one that ruptures expectations. Fletcher presents us with situations that challenge our notion of accepted conventions and then recolours them. We see a step further than Shakespeare ever takes with Viola or Rosalind, as those cases contain subversion because of audience's knowledge. Even Fletcher's most cautious audience member could not guarantee that Alinda is in fact male.[95]

A later scene between the Duke and Alinda while Olimpia watches unobserved further heightens the gender dynamics of the play and develops Fletcher's build towards the rupture of the final moment. In this scene, Alinda has denied all of the Duke's advances, including another ring, but her seeming acceptance of payment leads Olimpia to misconstrue her words. In response to his blunt proposal to 'lye' with her, she responds:

> ALINDA: Nay, if we doe, sure wee'll doe for good fellowship,
>   For pure love, or nothing: thus you shall be sure sir
>   You shall not pay too deare for't.
> DUKE: Sure I cannot.
> ALINDA: By'r Lady but yee may: when ye have found me able,
>   To doe your work well, ye may pay my wages.
> PETESCA: Why does your Grace start back?
> OLIMPIA: I ha' seen that shakes me:
>   Chills all my bloud: O where is faith or goodness?
>   *Alinda* thou art false, false, false thou fair one,
>   Wickedly false; and (woe is me) I see it.
>   For ever false.
> PETESCA: [*aside*]   I am glad 't has taken thus right.
>   *Exeunt* [OLIMPIA, PETESCA].
>
> (3.3.93-102)

At the moment, when Alinda must confront the advances of the Duke, she playfully banters him away, seeming to accept his desire, while admitting that she will be unable to fulfil it. However playful, her language through the invocation of exchanging money reduces her to a courtesan or prostitute. For a moment, an audience too might be taken in, as is Olimpia, to think that the 'faire' Alinda is now 'false, false, false . . . Wickedly false', depending on how she delivers her previous two lines. However, the audience witnesses the final exchange between the Duke and Alinda:

> ALINDA: Ile goe aske my Lady, sir.
> DUKE: What?
> ALINDA: Whether I
> Shall lye with ye, or no; If I find her willing—
> For look ye sir, I have sworn, while I am in her service—
> ('Twas a rash oath I must confesse.)
> DUKE: Thou mockst me.
> ALINDA: Why, would yee lye with me, if I were willing?
> Would you abuse my weaknesse?
> DUKE: I would peece it,
> And make it stronger.
> ALINDA: I humbly thank your highnesse,
> When you piece me, you must piece me to my Coffin:
> When you have got my Maiden-head, I take it,
> 'Tis not an inch of an Apes taile will restore it;
> I love ye, and I honour yee, but this way
> Ile neither love nor serve yee: heaven change your minde sir.
> *Exit.*
> DUKE: And thine too: for it must be chang'd, it shall be.
> *Exit.*
> (3.3.103-15)

The tone wavers back and forth in a tragicomic register as Alinda playfully yet also seriously toys with the Duke. Firstly, she offers to get Olimpia's permission to sleep with him, but then highlights his desire to take her without her consent, and even invokes the possibility of death were she to lose her virginity to him. Her response to the Duke's disbelief over her assertion to ask Olimpia is a moment of self-interruption that crafts her character's interiority both comically and emotionally. Alinda is confronted with a dire situation that she makes a joke out of in reversing the expectations. The self-interruptions give us a brief glimpse into her love and desire for Olimpia. This tension in the usage of the double self-interruption demonstrates Fletcher's own tonal ambiguity, offering both a scene of high comedy and a scene of sexual aggression. In meshing together these alternatives, he does not make light of such situations; Fletcher highlights the complex negotiations we make within such situations and in rendering them on the stage. Alinda leaves the scene hoping that the Duke can change; the Duke leaves the scene demanding that Alinda be changed. Fletcher leads us to these transformations: one, into that which he always was, though in a different gender, and the other, into a completely new character. Importantly, the Duke is not changed here, only Olimpia is (in thinking that she has been betrayed). The threat of the heterosexual assignation overcomes the homosocial/sexual bond that the two women established in the previous scene.

In the subsequent break-up scene, Fletcher stages a fully homoerotic moment. When Olimpia confronts Alinda about her assignation with the Duke, she does not know that Alinda has rebuked him. Olimpia's language is suffused with epizeuxis, which Fletcher uses to indicate distress, but he further complicates the scenario in Olimpia's final dismissal:

> look on me,
> I love those eyes yet dearely; I have kiss'd thee,
> And now Ile doe't againe: farewell *Alinda*,
> I am too full to speak more, and too wretched.
>
> (4.1.53-56)

Not only do the two women kiss here on stage, but Olimpia's line asserts that they have kissed before, meaning that earlier moments, such as their mock wedding, could also have been a site of the two women kissing intimately. Notably, John Masefield's edition of the play provides a stage direction here that reads, '*Kisses him*'.[96] Masefield helps readers know that a kiss occurs, but subsumes the subversion within a heterosexual encounter. Clarifying Alinda's gender removes the almost-shocking nature of the moment as well as the complexity within which Fletcher crafts it. Even if an audience member knows that Alinda is Young Archas (through clues, a previous performance, or an over-obvious Dramatis Personae), the action they watch is two women kissing. On the early modern stage too, this image is always a homoerotic one as both characters would be played by boys. This statement might seem to render something obvious as all kisses on the early modern stage are such; however,

Fletcher's usage here is charged with a moment of uncertainty that is only rectified in the ending.

Fletcher leads us towards the truth while further moving us away when he has Alinda come back to court, but this time dressed as a man. While critics read this moment as confirmation of the identity beneath,[97] neither the first printing nor the first performance would have offered such a confirmation. The play states his entrance only as '*Ent. Alinda*' squeezed into the right-hand margin.[98] This scene, like Alinda's first, overworks the commentary on his/her appearance, though, instead of focusing on beauty, the conversation focuses on the young man's similarity to Alinda. A reader or an audience member would realize the convention of disguise immediately—but which disguise? Again, if we read the moment through the ending, then this scene only demonstrates what we are about to learn, that Alinda is really Young Archas; however, in the printed text and in the performed text, *Alinda* shows up in disguise as a young man. Fletcher then reuses the heroine-as-page disguise that he and Beaumont used in *Philaster* and *The Maid's Tragedy*, and which he saw in Shakespeare's *Twelfth Night* and *As You Like It*. Thinking of this moment as Alinda in disguise, and *not* as a revelation of Young Archas's 'true' gendered identity, illustrates the lengths to which Fletcher was willing to play around with the construction of genders and the use of MTF cross-dressing. He subsumes the MTF cross-dressing within the potentiality of FTM cross-dressing. Reading this scene as such renders the exchanges between Olimpia and Alinda-as-gentleman as transgressive as any in Shakespeare, if not more so for the seeming 'reality' of the female character within the man's attire that is sportively and not demurely attracting the attention of the other female character. Again, critics remove Fletcher's playful point of view when they reduce these moments to a reading that uses the ending as indicative of the whole. While the ending colours consideration, these moments allow for play itself to surface.

Fletcher eventually ruptures the convention by revealing the disguise in the final moments of the play. In order to get Archas to not kill his son Theodor, Archas's brother enters and reveals the disguise that he has put on Young Archas and threatens to kill her/him as well:

> *Enter* PUTSKIE (*alias* BRISKIE) *and* ALINDA (*alias* ARCHAS).
> PUTSKIE: Thou hast no child left *Archas*, none to inherit thee
> If thou strikst that stroke now: behold young *Archas*;

> Behold thy brother here, thou bloudy brother,
> As bloudy to this sacrifice as thou art:
> Heave up thy sword, and mine's heav'd up: strike *Archas*,
> And I'le strike too, as suddenly, as deadly:
> Have mercy, and I'le have mercy:
>
> (5.6.56-63)

The reveal is all. Unlike Jonson's build-up and focused removal, Putskie enters with Alinda ready to kill her/him. Fletcher reveals his rupture of the convention within a moment in which the audience does not have time to digest the new information. Whereas Jonson's surprise is the point of the final scene, Fletcher only wants it to be a part of the whole. In this way, we should not read the entirety of the preceding action as rewritten by this piece of information; it only adds more to the already-overflowing presence of information that Fletcher produces. Consider, for instance, the final stage direction that reveals the identity. The use of 'alias', according to Alan Dessen and Leslie Thomsen, means 'now known as', and they give several examples, a few even from other Fletcher plays.[99] However, several of their examples do not point to a disguise but rather indicate that the second name is another way to identify this character. For example, in Thomas Heywood's *If You Know Not Me, You Know Nobody Part Two*, a stage direction reads '*Enter Rowland alias Tawnicoate*', but neither Tawnicoate nor Rowland ever wore disguises.[100] Rather, Rowland is the name of the character now that he has become respectable and is no longer the down-on-his-luck Tawnicoate. The stage direction then is not reductive. It does not reveal disguise but offers another facet of identity, or another way to understand him. Fletcher gives us both Alinda and Young Archas in this final exchange; the character, as has been true throughout, is both male and female. If Fletcher rewrites *Twelfth Night*, he does so with a mind to coalescing Cesario/Viola/Sebastian into a single character.

The plotline of Alinda's disguise concludes when Putskie reveals why he used such a disguise. The Duke asks, 'Why was this boy concealed thus?' (5.6.69), and Putskie responds:

> Fearing the vow you made against my brother
> And that your anger would not only light
> On him, but find out all his familie,

This young boy, to preserve from after danger,
Like a young wench, hether I brought

(5.6.71-75)

Unlike either the Lord in *The Shrew* or Dauphine in *Epicene*, Putskie has Young Archas don this gendered disguise out of concern for the boy's own safety and not for his own advancement. Even if Young Archas does not have the agency in choosing this disguise initially, he takes it on because an adult wants to protect him. In this way, we might consider that the end of the play affirms Alinda/Young Archas's gender-bending role as a safe and protective place, one that allows openness in gender expression that is free from political harm. Even if it draws the eye of a sexual predator like the Duke, Alinda also possesses the power to draw the affection and love of a character like Olimpia.[101] So too, Fletcher uses the disguise not as the ends of a homosexual joke, like *The Shrew* and *Epicene*. Here the disguise is protection in a politically dangerous world, and the danger only surfaces in the revelation of identity in the end. The reveal is a moment of almost tragedy and not one of uproarious comedy. Through disrupting a correlation between biological gender and gender identity, Alinda is kept safe. Thus, we too might find security in the power of a playful theatricality.

While Shakespeare gives us Bartholomew's name but shows us the Lady and Jonson names Epicene and only briefly shows us the character underneath, Fletcher provides names—specific subjective identities—to both aspects of the character and presents scenes in which the audience meets both of them interacting with the other characters. Fletcher ruptures the reveal of the MTF cross-dressing by opening up our reception of what the relationship between Olimpia and Alinda/Young Archas is. Fletcher's continuation highlights how this convention is endlessly exploitable on the early modern stage. The audience can never assume the gendered identity of a character, because it might be a disguise. Yet this is true for all theatres, as all roles are disguises and all characters are represented. When interrupting conventions, the artificial nature of the theatrical endeavour is ultimately at stake. This goal is what Fletcher's play and the character of Alinda/Archas reveals to audiences and readers alike: that theatricality is pervasive, flexible, and playful. *The Loyal Subject* foregrounds the problems of embodiment and character within the theatre, and Fletcher once more demonstrates his extensive theatricality that invests in the playfulness of performance. The assumed stability of a character and their gender identity can never be fixed into a certainty. Audiences must accept the fictions that the actors present, and gender, like all other theatrical fictions, is one of the myriad fictions that we interpret.

These three plays and their varying usages of MTF cross-dressing all demonstrate the playwrights interrupting conventions of their theatre. They take the received versions of such conventions, engender expectations around them, and then rupture those expectations, potentially changing audience's ideas about the conventions itself, sometimes creating new conventions in such a continuation. In this way, we can see the development from Shakespeare to Jonson to Fletcher: from Shakespeare's Bartholomew, who is anticipated but never revealed, to Jonson's Epicene, who is not anticipated but ruptures the entire play, to Fletcher's Alinda, who is regularly shifting our expectations and ultimately disrupts our notions of static gender identity in the theatre. Ultimately though, conventional macrointerruptions possess an indeterminate continuation as that part of the form resides solely within the audiences' developed expectations for the next play that they encounter.

Continuation

In light of the form as I have offered it, I end this book not with a conclusion—because this work is not over—but with a continuation. The preceding work opens up dramatic and theatrical texts to further explorations by offering insight into one particular form: the interruption. This study excavates the important information, both dramatic and theatrical, that derives from considering interruptions as a specific form within these texts. While I have focused on early modern English drama, this type of work is not limited historically. Later dramatists and theatre makers have used it in many other ways that have enlivened and complicated their texts, and all I can say is that more work needs to be done. What constitutes a Suzan-Lori Parks interruption or a Harold Pinter one? Their work provides fertile raw material.

Furthermore, early modern drama scholars might object to my dramatis personae of Shakespeare, Jonson, and Fletcher, noting that Marlowe's rupturing of theatrical style in *Tamburlaine* or Middleton's use of the surprise ending in *The Widow* or Beaumont's macrointerruptive masterpiece *The Knight of the Burning Pestle* merited consideration. I accede these points with the same gesture I just made towards modern writers: more work needs to be done. In limiting my discussion to Shakespeare, Jonson, and Fletcher, I hope to have explored their particular art in crafting interruptions, especially in comparison to each other. Doing so allows the study of interruptions to be not only about noticing such moments within a play but also about considering how a creative mind deploys such moments: How does that mind alter power in rupturing certain premises? What characters are privileged? How much is the audience trusted or knowledgeable? These questions are important as we continue to reassess our canonical writers. Past praise does not equal continued pride of place: remember Fletcher's fall from grace.

In that vein, I freely admit that I intend this study to provoke conversations about Fletcher and his plays. To do this, I have used his solo-authored plays and plays that are generally not well known. Their unfamiliarity for contemporary audiences provides space to consider the work these plays do in a way that can no longer happen with Shakespeare's plays. Fletcher's plays possess ideas and themes that Shakespeare's do not, ones that often speak to a contemporary sensibility. As Celia Caputi has lamented: 'Why read Shakespeare's *The Taming of the Shrew* and not John Fletcher's *The Tamer Tamed, or the Woman's Prize?*'.[1] One answer to this question is because Fletcher's texts need to be performed. While this aspect of Shakespeare's plays has become a truism, Fletcher's delightful theatricality is pervasive, making his texts for a reader seemingly less 'poetic' than his predecessor. Studying them in the confines of a literature classroom renders them somewhat vague. However, his methodologies for construction, especially through interruptions, provide a way in. Interruptions are a form through which Fletcher's text can be read, as I have done, with an eye towards the theatre.

Anecdotally, I offer two elaborations to my aforementioned conclusions. Recently, I taught Fletcher's *The Island Princess* in an Introduction to Shakespeare course. We read it at the end of the term after studying three plays by Shakespeare. I included the play so the students might understand what Shakespeare is not. Not only did my students love the play, several insisted that they would like to read more Fletcher, and even suggested beginning the term with the play. Therefore, Fletcher might do well in a literature class alongside his sometimes collaborator. Second, as an independent research project, I edited Fletcher's play *The Mad Lover* with two undergraduate students. In doing so, we discovered that while Fletcher's syntax and images roll into the mind quite facilely, indicating a directness and ease that feels uncomplicated, his language is actually highly complicated and knotty when trying to determine the best recourse to modern punctuation. His syntactic construction elides subjects and verbs, quickly alters tenses, and, like his interruptions, abruptly changes. The beauty of his poetry is the way in which a reader's mind quickly understands the ideas within the lines but that when parsed out specifically they become over complicated. This almost paradoxical construction reminds me of Stephen Booth's reading of *Twelfth Night*. Instead of 'nonsense that we read as sense',[2] Fletcher gives us complicated language that we read as simplicity itself. Perhaps this is another way in which we can see Fletcher's antitheses as McMullan puts it, or the strange and familiar as Waith does. Such density, which has bolstered Shakespeare and other writers for years, seems to be overlooked and undervalued when approaching Fletcher.

But this is not a study of Fletcher; it is a study of a form and of three writers who use that form significantly, importantly, and unexpectedly. As any reader would note, Jonson proves himself with significant examples to be an important writer of interruptions. With this in mind, I give the last word to him through one more reading of one more scene in one more play.

Jonson's second comical satire after *Every Man Out* was the more linear, though perhaps more otiose, endeavour known fully as *The Fountain of Self-Love or Cynthia's Revels* (1600). While the play tells the story of allegorical figures who drink from the titular fountain and whose follies are mostly exposed before a final masque for Cynthia the queen, it opens with another one of Jonson's complicated framing devices. The Praeludium begins, like the Induction to *Every Man Out*, at the second sounding, but instead of a continual Grex, we instead encounter three boy actors each vying to deliver the play's Prologue. This structure mimics Marston's *Antonio and Mellida*,[3] but it transforms it in Jonsonian fashion. Like Marston's iteration, Jonson presents actor as character, but instead of focusing on this aspect as Marston does (whose boy actors lament the roles they are to play), Jonson's induction leads to a discussion of dramaturgy. The Third Child, out of dissatisfaction, becomes determined to ruin the play by revealing the argument:

> THIRD CHILD: Stay, Jack. 'Slid, I'll do somewhat now afore I go in, though it be nothing but to revenge myself of the author, since I speak not his prologue. I'll go tell all the argument of his play aforehand, and so stale his invention to the auditory before it come forth.
> FIRST CHILD: Oh, do not so.
> SECOND CHILD: By no means.[4]

Before looking at the speech itself and its interruptive 'breaches' as Jonson terms them,[5] we should note the Third Child's purpose. He claims that revealing the 'argument' of the play will 'stale [the author's] invention', thereby exacting some revenge for not getting to deliver the prologue. The Third Child claims that if he tells the whole story, then the audience will not experience any interruptions in the plot because they will already expect them; he believes that removing the potentiality for rupture and establishing a solid premise make the theatrical endeavour less satisfying. Of course, what Jonson and presumably his audience realized, though the character does not, is that this cannot be the case. As we will see, the boy does deliver the 'argument', and if that did thoroughly 'stale' the play, then Jonson's work would fold in on itself, which is surely not Jonson's purpose in writing the Praeludium. Many critics read this induction sequence as a way of illustrating the play's desire to place 'Words above action, matter above words'.[6] Anne Barton argues that the play has 'no discernable plot line', John Sweeney iterates that it 'has no plot to reveal, at least in the conventional sense of the term', and Richard Dutton says the child 'outlines such plot as there is . . . effectively removing the what-comes-next element that we normally think crucial in a dramatic performance'.[7] However, they miss the complicated interrelation between the dramaturgy at stake and the dialogue/action of the moment, which the interruptions reveal.

Notably, the boy calls what he says to the audience not a plot or story but an 'argument'. Arguments were usually found in classical texts or closet dramas, though some printed versions of works from the public stage also had them.[8] Jonson used arguments, significantly adding one to the published text of *The New Inn*, which reveals the surprise identities in the final act. In *Cynthia's Revels*, however, the text is not printed but spoken by the boy for the audience. While not in the same detail, Shakespeare used a similar device at the beginning of *Romeo and Juliet*. This is not to say that Shakespeare does not toy with suspense (he left several details out of his argument) or that Jonson is not trying to dissipate expectation (he clearly is); rather, Jonson's usage of this verbal argument as a rare theatrical moment merits further consideration than most scholars have allowed. Tiffany Stern explains that textual arguments were meant to help the audience follow the story of a complicated performance and make, as Jonson himself put it, 'spectators understanders'.[9] While she overlooks this moment in *Cynthia's Revels*, it presents several complicated issues surrounding Jonson's own need for and use of arguments, all of which is further enmeshed within his deployment of interruptions in this scene.

The scene's interruptive quality is underscored in the printed text through the wording of the stage direction, which indicates the interpretation of the dashes. Jonson's stage direction before the speech in the Folio reads, 'At the breaches in this speech following, the other two interrupt him, still.'[10] The direction offers two significant aspects. Firstly, all the breaches or dashes in the following section of text are to be read as interruptions or more specifically as ruptures in which the other two boys must try and stop the third boy from continuing. The subsequent eleven dashes of the text, therefore, are staged moments in which the boys must actively try to stop the third child. Secondly, the Folio stage direction adds an additional note that brings the number of interruptions up to twelve. The final adjective of 'still' implies that the two previous lines by the First and Second Child are themselves ruptures of the Third Child beginning to speak. The Quarto leaves this small addendum out and, thereby, loses a bit of clarification on Jonson's part. The breaches are interruptive, but that form precedes this speech. The 'still' then illustrates the pervasive sense of interruption to the Praeludium.

The eleven breach-marked interruptions in the following speeches exhibit three differing types of interruptive moments. Two are speeches by the Second and First Child, which are dialogic microinterruptions.[11] Four provoke specified responses by the Third Child, which resemble both action and self-interruptions.[12] The other five are only breaches, which in their openness are completely theatrical spaces.[13] Here, Jonson presents the reader with the loss of a theatrical moment that a reader must create. He insinuates that action takes place here with the stage direction, but he does not imply what these actions must be. They obviously become aggressive or perhaps sexual as the Third Child exclaims, 'What, will you ravish me?', but even that is an open-ended suggestion whose seriousness can only be decided in performance.[14] Despite the boisterous or rude attempts to interrupt the Third Child, he tells the whole story from the entrances of Mercury and Cupid to the final masque with Cynthia. Therefore, despite the eleven, or twelve, ruptures, the Third Child successfully continues his premise, leaving the other two children with, shall we say, impotent ruptures. This scene centrally illustrates Jonson's approach to interruptions because, as with Celia and Volturcius, if we remove the ruptures, the premise survives; therefore, what becomes important is not a perceived destruction of the premise but the addition of the ruptures and the regular continuations in spite of those ruptures. Jonson may be using an argument here to clarify a complicated story, but he does so in a form that makes it hard to follow as the audience most likely watches the competition between the boys. If this is a moment to tell us the story, as a typical argument would, it loses its ability to do so, which seems to be Jonson's point. As he suffuses the scene with all types of interruptions (playing with Inductions, characters, dialogue, monologue, actions, and dramaturgy), he insists that interruptions and the competitive nature of the power underneath them are the basis for drama and theatre and story. The tension between two speakers makes drama happen and leads to the action of the theatre. With this scene, we arrive back at Derrida, at the basis of interruption as the basis for communication, at the relation of interruption.

This study begins an investigation into a form that is central to dramatic representation and theatrical action. Through studying an important era of dramatic output and its central figures, I illustrate how such a focus can reinvigorate our understanding of these texts. This work provides the basis for further work both in dramatic literature beyond this period and in theatrical performance and practice because it asks questions of the dynamics not only among characters but also between a text and a performance, a performer and an audience. So too, it offers several questions about the relationships of text that should influence editors and book historians, especially in regards to typography of specific moments and choice of copy text. I have also offered specific readings of the works of Shakespeare, Jonson, and Fletcher, noting their radical differences when using a similar form. Even though each playwright approaches interruptions differently, they all three share an interest that speaks of the connection and influence among them, and———

NOTES

Introduction

1 Oliver Morgan comes close in his book *Turn-Taking in Shakespeare*, but, even as he outlines how dialogue functions via 'turns', he relies heavily on interruptions for examples but never clearly defines interruptions specifically (6–10). Oliver Morgan, *Turn-Taking in Shakespeare* (Oxford: Oxford University Press, 2019). For interruptions in general, see David Hillman and Adam Phillips, eds. *The Book of Interruptions* (New York: Peter Lang, 2007), and Kate McLoughlin, 'Interruption Overload: Telephones in Ford Madox Ford's "4692 Padd", *A Call* and *A Man Could Stand Up*—', *Journal of Modern Literature* 36, no. 3 (2013): 50–68. For interruptions in early modern literature, see Joe Moshenka, 'Sir Kenelm Digby's Interruptions: Piracy and Lived Romance in the 1620s', *Studies in Philology* 113, no. 2 (2016): 424–83 and Gavin Alexander, 'Sidney's Interruptions', *Studies in Philology* 98, no. 2 (2001): 184–204.

2 Friedrich Nietzsche, *The Birth of Tragedy and the Case of Wagner*, trans. Walter Kaufmann (New York: Vintage Books, 1967), 66 and *passim*. Grazielle Vinh mentions that tragedy should be seen as 'a succession of choral songs interrupted by spoken interludes and not the other way around', 'Athens in Euripides' *Suppliants*: Ritual, Politics, and Theatre', in *Why Athens?: A Reappraisal of Tragic Politics*, ed. D. M. Carther (Oxford: Oxford University Press, 2011), 326. See also Marjorie Garber, 'Third Person Interruption', in *The Book of Interruptions*, ed. David Hillman and Adam Phillips (New York: Peter Lang, 2007), 24.

3 Frederic V. Bogel, *New Formalist Criticism: Theory and Practice* (New York: Palgrave, 2013), 7.

4 Caroline Levine, *Forms: Whole, Rhythm, Hierarchy, Network* (Princeton: Princeton University Press, 2017), 3.

5 Bogel, *New Formalist Criticism*, 7.

6 Garber, 'Third Person Interruption', 17. For more on New Formalism, see Verena Theile and Linda Tredennick, eds., *New Formalisms and Literary Theory* (New York: Palgrave Macmillan, 2013), and Bogel, *New Formalist Criticism*. Additionally, Caroline Levine's *Forms*, which aims to 'produce a new formalist method' (3), was featured in the 'Theories and Methodologies' section of *PMLA* (Oct 2017).

7 Levine, *Forms*, 6–7. A pertinent observation: Levine uses a self-interruption to uncover something and/or clarify her point. She turns the reader away from the main thought to a secondary thought that ruptures the premise, but then offers a continuation that returns with new information. In this she exemplifies the form of an interruption as I will lay out here.

8 André Jolles, *Simple Forms*, trans. Peter J. Schwartz (New York: Verso, 2017), 18.

9 This bifurcation relies upon Schechner's delineations. Richard Schechner, 'Drama, Script, Theatre and Performance', *The Drama Review: TDR* 17, no. 3 (1973): 5–36. For a further consideration of the tension between theatre and drama as it relates to interruption, see Michael M. Wagoner, 'Ofelia's Interruption of Ophelia in *Hamlet*', *Critical Survey* 31, no. 1/2 (2019): 43–57.

10 For a powerful reading of the importance of this interruption, see H.R. Woudhuysen, '"Dead, for My Life": Stopping, Starting and Interrupting in *Love's Labour's Lost*,' *Actes des congrès de la Société française Shakespeare* 32 (2015): para. 1–37.

11 Such as when someone is talking and you say, 'Yes,' to agree with them but do not intend to take over the conversation or add more than that single word. Jack Bilmes notes that such moments are not interruptions in a sociological perspective, but from a dramatic one, they almost always are. Jack Bilmes, 'Being Interrupted,' *Language in Society* 26, no. 4 (1997): 508. Bilmes's sociological work, through his argument that interruptions are not an analyst's but a participant's phenomenon, demonstrates that despite the linguistic work that has been done on this form, the literary deployment of it is different from its everyday usage.

12 'interrupt, v.,' *OED Online*, Oxford University Press, January 2018.

13 Aristotle, *Aristotle's* Poetics, trans. George Whalley, ed. John Baxter and Patrick Atherton (Montreal: McGill-Queen's University Press, 1997), 81, 80.

14 Ibid., 87.

15 Puttenham terms aposiopesis as the 'the figure of interruption' and categorizes it as a 'figure of defect.' Elsewhere, he praises forms as

'most excellent' that exist 'without any . . . interruption.' George Puttenham, *The Arte of English Poesie* (London: Richard Field, 1589), sig. T4v, sig. N3r. Sidney relies on Aristotle to aver, 'the stage should always represent but one place, and the uttermost time presupposed in it should be, both by Aristotle's precepts and common reason, but one day.' Philip Sidney, 'A defence of poetry (1595),' in *English Renaissance Literary Criticism*, ed. Brian Vickers (Oxford: Oxford University Press, 1999), 381.

16 Shakespeare of course left no treatise on drama, but his plays regularly change locations (*Henry V*), have subplots (*Cymbeline*), and cover large swaths of time (*The Winter's Tale*). John Fletcher's plays like Shakespeare's also do not adhere to the unity of time, place, and action. Furthermore, his definition of tragicomedy indicates his desire to break unities. He says tragicomedy 'is not so called in respect of mirth and killing, but in respect it wants deaths . . . yet brings some neere it . . . which must be a representation of familiar people . . . so that a God is as lawful in this as in a tragedie, and mean people as in a comedie.' His negative constructions and the playful usage of proximity, of almost-ness, demonstrates Fletcher's interest in disrupting expectations for his audience, his readers, and his critics. John Fletcher, *The Faithful Shepherdess by John Fletcher: A Critical Edition*, ed. Florence Ada Kirk (New York: Garland Publishing, 1980), 15.

17 Such as Coleridge's Person from Porlock. Hugh Haughton, 'Xanadu and Porlock: Thoughts on Composition and Interruption,' in *The Book of Interruptions*, ed. David Hillman and Adam Phillips (New York: Peter Lang, 2007), 27–43.

18 See Richard Dutton, *Licensing, Censorship, and Authorship in Early Modern England* (New York: Palgrave, 2000), and Annabel Patterson, *Censorship and Interpretation: The Conditions of Writing and Reading in Early Modern England* (Madison: The University of Wisconsin Press, 1984).

19 The *Cambridge Edition of the Works of Ben Jonson* (*CWBJ*) contains all four endings. Randall Martin uses the 1599 'original' theatrical ending as printed in the quarto, having it immediately follow the end of the final scene. Ben Jonson, *Every Man Out of His Humour*, ed. Randall Martin, in *The Cambridge Edition of the Works of Ben Jonson*, ed. David Bevington, Martin Butler, and Ian Donaldson, vol. 1 (Cambridge: Cambridge University Press, 2012), 417–18.

20 In this way, we may analogously consider the texts as representing the problems of theatre and print. In the critical truisms of their

studies, one provides absence, the other presence. One is lacking of completion, haunted by loss and absences (theatre), and the other provides multiple considerations that can all be contained at the same time (print).

21 Gary Taylor, ed., *The History of Cardenio adapted as 'Double Falsehood'* by John Fletcher and William Shakespeare, in *The New Oxford Shakespeare: Modern Critical Edition*, ed. Gary Taylor, et al. (Oxford: Oxford University Press, 2016), 3136.
22 Ibid., 3136.
23 Ibid., 1.1.5–15.
24 Any audience interaction that the author or producer necessitates would not be an external interruption but would rather be internal.
25 *Gesta Grayorum: Or, the History of the High and Mighty Prince Henry* (London: W. Canning, 1688), sig. D3v.
26 Sarah Neville, ed., *The Comedy of Errors*, in *The New Oxford Shakespeare: Modern Critical Edition*, ed. Gary Taylor, et al. (Oxford: Oxford University Press, 2016), 726.
27 See also, Margaret Knapp and Michal Kobialka, 'Shakespeare and the Prince of Purpoole: The 1594 Production of The Comedy of Errors at Gray's Inn Hall,' in *The Comedy of Errors: Critical Essays*, ed. Robert S. Miola (New York: Garland Publishing, 1997), 431–45. A more contemporary example of external interruption would be the opening night of Alfred Jarry's *Ubu Roi*. Stephen Tifft, 'Catharsis Interrupta,' in *The Book of Interruptions*, ed. David Hillman and Adam Phillips (New York: Peter Lang, 2007), 107.
28 For more on audience responses, see Richard Preiss, *Clowning and Authorship in Early Modern Theatre* (Cambridge: Cambridge University Press, 2014), 27–47.
29 Preiss, *Clowning and Authorship*, 30.
30 See *Hamlet* Q2 3.2.37–44. For more on clowning practice in the period, see Preiss, *Clowning and Authorship*, and Robert Hornback, '"But I Do It More Naturally.": Falstaff's "Original Clowning Practice" vs. Theatrical Naturalism,' *The Hare* 2, no. 1 (2014).
31 The American Shakespeare Center in Staunton, Virginia, provides a site for such research as the company has encouraged their audiences to engage the actors when prompted or even when not prompted. For example, I attended a performance of *Othello* in Fall 2010 in which one emboldened audience member started enthusiastically yelling 'Devil!' at the actor playing Iago when he was alone on stage. Fortunately, the actor Benjamin Curns handled it as if she were a

scene partner, adjusting his delivery of lines to acknowledge the interruption. Such dexterity is required of an actor when an audience can employ external interruptions at will. Curns's ability made the external, internal to the performance, demonstrating the way in which a performance can be a text, which complicates the notion of external versus internal interruptions in a performance.

32 See, Katherine Acheson, 'Introduction: Marginalia, Reading, and Writing,' in *Early Modern English Marginalia* (London: Routledge, 2019), 1–12.

33 Arlynda Boyer, 'Actors Annotations and Paradoxical Editions of Shakespeare's Texts,' *Actes des congrès de la Société française Shakespeare* 39 (2021): para. 15–16.

34 Nicholas Rowe in his 1709 edition first supplied this dash. For more on early modern print punctuation, see John Jowett, 'Full Pricks and Great p's: Spelling, Punctuation, Accidentals,' in *Shakespeare and Textual Studies*, ed. Margaret Jane Kidnie and Sonia Massai (Cambridge: Cambridge University Press, 2015), 317–31.

35 Bilmes, 'Being Interrupted,' 508–9 and *passim*, and Maggie Koerth, 'How Many Times Did Trump Interrupt Clinton in the First Debate? Depends on How You Count,' *FiveThirtyEight: Politics*, 9 October 2016, FiveThirtyEight.

36 Jacques Derrida and Pierre-Jean Labarrière, *Altérités: Jacques Derrida et Pierre-Jean Labarrière, avec des études de Francis Guibal et Stanislas Breton* (Paris: Osiris, 1986), 82. Translation mine: 'Pour entrer en rapport avec l'autre, il faut que l'interruption soit possible; il faut que le rapport soit un rapport d'interruption.'

37 For an overview of punctuation in the period, see M. B. Parkes, *Pause and Effect: An Introduction to the History of Punctuation in the West* (Berkeley: University of California Press, 1993); however, he does not much discuss the dash. Claire M. L. Bourne fully explores the development of the theatrical dash in her book, *Typographies of Performance in Early Modern England* (Oxford: Oxford University Press, 2020). Importantly, Ben Jonson and John Fletcher have two unique relationships to the dash. Jonson, as the editors of the *CWBJ* note, was an early user and adopter of the punctuation mark, which means that their placement in his texts, especially ones which he oversaw publication of, indicates his authorial choice. David Bevington, Martin Butler, and Ian Donaldson, General Introduction to *The Cambridge Edition of the Works of Ben Jonson*, vol. 1 (Cambridge: Cambridge University Press, 2012), lxxxi. Fletcher's play texts contain enough interruptive moments that the various printers

of the Beaumont and Fletcher Folio of 1647 used more dashes in his solo plays than in the other plays contained in the volume (see Chapter 1).

38 Puttenham, *The Arte of English Poesie*, sig. T4v.

39 For example, Derrida's description of Levinas, as discussed in Garber, 'Third Person Interruption,' 17. So too, the feigned stuttering in Fletcher and Massinger's *Beggars' Bush*, which prompts one character to respond, 'I understand no word he says.' John Fletcher and Philip Massinger, *Beggars' Bush*, ed. Fredson Bowers, in *The Dramatic Works in the Beaumont and Fletcher Canon*, ed. Fredson Bowers, vol. III (Cambridge: Cambridge University Press, 1976), 2.1.199.

40 See Mariko Ichikawa, *Shakespearean Entrances* (London: Palgrave Macmillan, 2002), 21–32, and Steven Urkowitz, 'Interrupted Exits in *King Lear*,' *Educational Theatre Journal* 30 (1978): 203–10.

41 My examination of the manuscripts associated with the Fletcher canon indicates that dashes were more often used in manuscript to point towards a stage direction. This usage suggests the interruptive nature of all entrances and exits within written scripts; they are a place where action interrupts language/speech. This habit is sometimes, though not always, retained within the printed text. For a consistent example of a manuscript with stage direction dashes, see *Honest Man's Fortune* (Dyce MS 9); for a play text with stage direction dashes, see *The Tragedy of Valentinian* in the Beaumont and Fletcher 1647 Folio.

42 Every performance is itself an adaptation. So too, the understanding of source, of even what constitutes a source, may be invigorated through the form of the interruption.

43 A production of *Hamlet* in 2011 at the Blackfriars Playhouse eliminated the 'To be or not to be' soliloquy after the famous first line, which elicited audible reactions from the audience. This external interruption on the part of the director—he claimed that he could not hurt *Hamlet*, so why not try the excision—created a macrointerruption and a microinterruption that enlivened a text that most people in the audience had seen countless times before. Similarly, he removed all language of Claudius confessing to the murder of Old Hamlet and removed the bulk of Claudius' prayer monologue. This intervention—while not provoking the audience in the same manner—had a macrointerruptive effect by significantly altering that audience's comprehension and understanding of Claudius. Per the text of that performance, Claudius was potentially innocent, which changed the characterization of Hamlet

as he enacts a revenge not clearly justified. Zach Brown, dir. *Hamlet* by William Shakespeare, Blackfriars Playhouse, Staunton, VA, October 2011.

44 Fletcher, *The Faithful Shepherdess*, 15.

45 Jeremy Lopez, 'Hard Pastoral,' *The Hare* 4, no. 1 (2018).

46 Karen Britland, 'Queen Henrietta Maria's Theatrical Patronage,' in *Henrietta Maria: Piety, Politics and Patronage*, ed. Erin Griffey (Aldershot: Ashgate, 2008), 64–6.

47 Lopez, 'Hard Pastoral.'

48 Hirschfeld's overview of the scholarship is incredibly thorough, and her stance at the end invoking an understanding that does not dismiss the individual author but also does not overlook collaboration is well balanced. Heather Hirschfeld, 'Early Modern Collaboration and Theories of Authorship,' *PMLA* 116, no. 3 (2001): 618–19.

49 Michel Foucault, 'What is an Author?,' in *Textual Strategies: Perspectives in Post-Structuralist Criticism*, ed. Josuè V. Harari (Ithaca: Cornell University Press, 1979), 148. See also Jeffrey Masten, *Textual Intercourse: Collaboration, Authorship, and Sexualities in Renaissance Drama* (Cambridge: Cambridge University Press, 1997), 14–15 and *passim* and Gary Taylor, 'Artiginality: Authorship after Postmodernism,' in *The New Oxford Shakespeare: Authorship Companion*, ed. Gary Taylor and Gabriel Egan (Oxford: Oxford University Press), 3–26.

50 Kathleen McLuskie, *Renaissance Dramatists: Feminist Readings* (New York: Harvester Wheatsheaf, 1989), 222–3. Gordon McMullan advocates for an 'attempt to locate a working distinctiveness for the orchestrator of voices, influences, sources, and contexts known to literary history as Fletcher.' Gordon McMullan, *The Politics of Unease in the Plays of John Fletcher* (Amherst: The University of Massachusetts Press, 1994), 155.

51 McMullan, *The Politics of Unease*, 155.

52 Hoy's study appeared in seven parts from 1956 to 1962. Each section examines Fletcher's work in connection to another playwright and groups the plays accordingly. Cyrus Hoy, 'The Shares of Fletcher and His Collaborators in the Beaumont and Fletcher Canon (I-VII),' *Studies in Bibliography*, 8–15 (1956–1962).

53 Martin Wiggins, with Catherine Richardson, *British Drama 1533–1642: A Catalogue*, vols. II–VII (Oxford: Oxford University Press, 2012–2016).

54 Ian Donaldson writes, 'For throughout the seventeenth and much of the eighteenth century Shakespeare was frequently seen not as a solitary genius but as one of a group, or, more pointedly, on of a *pair* of celebrated English writers. . . . The writer with whom Shakespeare was regularly compared was Ben Jonson.' Ian Donaldson, *Jonson's Magic Houses: Essays in Interpretation* (Oxford: Oxford University Press, 1997), 7.

55 I begin at 1580 to include the burgeoning commercial theatre, leading into Shakespeare, and I stop at 1647 because of the publication of the Beaumont and Fletcher First Folio. These tallies are based upon searches within *Early English Books Online*.

56 Arthur Colby Sprague, *Beaumont and Fletcher on the Restoration Stage* (Cambridge, MA: Harvard University Press, 1926), 24–5. Sprague counts the number of performances and also quotes Dryden (1668): '[Beaumont and Fletcher's] plays are now the most . . . frequent entertainment of the stage; two of theirs being acted through the year for one of Shakespeare's or Jonson's.'

57 Randall Martin, introduction, *Every Man Out of His Humour* by Ben Jonson, in *The Cambridge Edition of the Works of Ben Jonson*, ed. David Bevington, Martin Butler, and Ian Donaldson, vol. 1 (Cambridge: Cambridge University Press, 2012), 235.

58 Garber, 'Third Person Interruption,' 24.

Chapter 1

1 M. B. Parkes, *Pause and Effect: An Introduction to the History of Punctuation in the West* (Berkeley: University of California Press, 1993), 1.

2 Jennifer DeVere Brody, *Punctuation: Art, Politics, and Play* (Durham, NC: Duke University Press, 2008), 4.

3 H. R. Woudhuysen, 'The Foundations of Shakespeare's Text', *Proceedings of the British Academy: 2003 Lectures*, vol. 125 (Oxford: Oxford University Press, 2004), 90.

4 Claire Bourne's work on the action implied by the dash fills in much of this missing history. Claire M. L. Bourne, *Typographies of Performance in Early Modern England* (Oxford: Oxford University Press, 2020), 82.

5 Ibid., 90.

6 Jeff Schieble, *Digital Shift: The Cultural Logic of Punctuation* (Minneapolis: University of Minnesota Press, 2015), 22.

7 Ibid., 22.

8 For more work on punctuation, see Geoffrey Nunberg, *The Linguistics of Punctuation* (Stanford, CA: Center for the Study of Language and Information, 1990), and Marjorie Garber, *Quotation Marks* (London: Routledge, 2003).

9 One of the least interruptive usages of a dash in modern texts for drama is as a change of addressee. While one might argue that this is an interruption, and sometimes it is, it is not always so. Often, the change of addressee is a logical extension of a thought following the completed previous thought. Therefore, in counting interruptions, especially when using modernized texts, I have only counted those that were interruptive of the speaker's premise.

10 Burrows argues for the potentiality of commas as interruptive punctuation. I. R. Burrows, '"The Peryod of My Blisse": Commas, Ends and Utterances in *Soliman and Perseda*', *Textual Cultures* 8, no. 2 (2013): 105–10. Bourne also discusses the development of dashes as verbally interruptive punctuation. Bourne, *Typographies of Performance*, 108 and *passim*.

11 A. Lynne Magnusson, 'Interruption in "The Tempest"', *Shakespeare Quarterly* 37, no. 1 (1986): 52–65. Brian Gibbons, '*The Tempest* and Interruptions', *Cahiers Elisabéthains* 45 (1994): 47–58.

12 David Bevington, Martin Butler, and Ian Donaldson, general introduction to *The Cambridge Edition of the Works of Ben Jonson*, vol. 1 (Cambridge: Cambridge University Press, 2012), lxxxi.

13 See also Bourne, *Typographies of Performance*, 77–136.

14 Gibbons, '*The Tempest* and Interruptions', 48.

15 Louis Althusser, *Positions (1964–1975)* (Paris: Editions Sociales, 1976), 115–16, 113.

16 While most readers will be familiar with the plots of *Volpone* and *The Tempest*, *The Humorous Lieutenant* is not a widely read text. Therefore, for those not familiar with Fletcher's play, here is a brief plot summary: King Antigonus sends his son Demetrius to war, and while his son is gone, the King discovers that Demetrius has been courting Celia. The King has his bawd Leucippe convince Celia to come to court and attempts to corrupt her. After she refuses his advances, he has a potion made to make her fall in love with him, which is accidentally consumed by the eponymous Lieutenant (who in the meantime has been fighting in the wars with Demetrius and the General Leontius). The Lieutenant makes a fool of himself in proclaiming his love for the King. Demetrius accuses Celia of infidelity, so she rebukes him. The King is transformed by Celia's

goodness, Celia forgives Demetrius, the Lieutenant recovers from the potion, and Celia turns out to be a neighbouring princess. For a fuller synopsis, see Wiggins and Richardson #1898 (Vol VII, 173–4).

17 Both the first Quarto and second Quarto texts of *Hamlet* only use full stops in this exchange. However, Ann Thompson and Neil Taylor add the dash to the end of Hamlet's line about Roscius in their Arden editions of those texts. Notably, neither the first nor the second Quarto contain any dashes in their printed texts.

18 John Jowett uses this dash in his *New Oxford* edition based on the Q2 text.

19 William Shakespeare, *Hamlet*, ed. John Jowett, in *The New Oxford Shakespeare*, ed. Gary Taylor et al. (Oxford: Oxford University Press, 2016), 7.303–310.

20 Some contemporary playwrights such as Caryl Churchill and Paula Vogel opt for the solidus or slash '/' to indicate interruption while allowing overlapping dialogue in an effort to effect layering of speech.

21 Gibbons, '*The Tempest* and Interruptions', 47.

22 John Dryden, 'An Essay on Dramatic Poesy', in *John Dryden: The Major Works*, ed. Keith Walker (Oxford: Oxford University Press, 2003), 111.

23 Richard Dutton, '*Volpone*: Textual Essay', in *The Cambridge Edition of the Works of Ben Jonson Online* (Cambridge: Cambridge University Press), 4.

24 Ibid., 5.

25 For the Quarto, I examined the Scolar Press facsimile (1968). Ben Jonson, *Volpone 1607* (Menston, England: The Scolar Press Limited, 1968). For the Folio, I examined David Gants's personal copy, which is in state 1 as indicated by the dashes in the conversation between Mosca and Volpone in 1.1 (see Dutton's textual notes in the *CWBJ*). As for other Jonson plays, *The Alchemist* is closest in its usage of dashes, with 141 in the Folio text. As a comparison, the Folio play with the fewest microinterruptive dashes is *Catiline His Conspiracy* with only forty-one. Jonson's quartos usually use even fewer as demonstrated by *Every Man in His Humour*, which only has fifteen microinterruptive dashes.

26 I use the scene breaks in the Folio, which Dutton uses in the *CWBJ*. Jonson, unlike most English dramatists of the period, used the French or neoclassical scene which has a new scene anytime a character enters. As it currently is printed, the play has thirty-nine scenes. If one were to reorganize *Volpone* into English scenes (governed by a cleared stage), then the play would have an average of twenty-one

interruptions per scene and only twelve scenes. For more on Jonson's scenes, see Chapter 3.

27 *Act Three*, scene six with only four lines and zero interruptions is an anomaly.

28 That solitary dash occurs on sig. A1v (TLN 44) within the Boatswain's line. It reads, '*Botes*. Downe with the Top-Mast: Yare, Lower, Lower,/Bring Her to Try with Maine-Course. A Plague—/A Cry Within. Enter Sebastian, Anthonio & Gonzalo' (TLN 43–5). What is significant is that the Boatswain's sentence is 'A plague upon this howling', which the printed text interrupts with the sound of the howling itself. Through this usage, the text simultaneously represents the sound alongside the line. Furthermore, this text is most likely a Ralph Crane transcript, and he is not known to use dashes outside of those he connected to stage directions. Margaret McLaren Cook and F. P. Wilson, eds., *Demetrius and Enanthe*, ed. John Fletcher (Oxford: Malone Society, 1951), ix. As this dash connects the stage direction to the text, it aligns with Crane's habits. T. H. Howard-Hill, *Ralph Crane and Some Shakespeare First Folio Comedies* (Charlottesville: University Press of Virginia, 1972), 16–68. Also see Chapter 3 for more on dashes connecting to off-stage sounds.

29 The two modern editions are Cyrus Hoy's in *The Dramatic Works in the Beaumont and Fletcher Canon* (1982) and Philip Oxley's *A Critical Edition of John Fletcher's The Humorous Lieutenant* (1987). Both editors use B&F F1 as copy text but add in missing text from MS; Hoy, however, prefers variants from the MS, while Oxley sticks to B&F F1.

30 Ben Jonson, *Volpone, or The Fox*, ed. Richard Dutton, in *Cambridge Edition of the Works of Ben Jonson*, ed. David Bevington, Martin Butler, and Ian Donaldson, vol. 3 (Cambridge: Cambridge University Press, 2012).

31 Dutton notes that exclamation marks, like dashes, have a questionable authority because of their grouping. Dutton, '*Volpone*: Textual Essay', 4. However, the fact that this piece of pointing remains stable between texts gives it a better claim to authority.

32 Martin Butler, 'Introduction: from *Workes* to Texts', in *Re-Presenting Ben Jonson: Text, History, Performance*, ed. Martin Butler (New York: St. Martin's Press, 1999), 4.

33 Robert Watson, 'The Fox and his Pause: Punctuating Consciousness in Jonson's *Volpone*', in *Shakespeare Up Close: Reading Early Modern Texts*, ed. Russ McDonald, Nicholas D. Nace, and Travis D. Williams (London: Arden Shakespeare, 2012), 206.

34 Magnusson, 'Interruption in "The Tempest"', 54.
35 He gives a dash, clearly indicating microinterruption, only at lines 13, 15, 20, 23, 31, 34, 36, and 53. Rory Loughnane, ed., *The Tempest* by William Shakespeare, in *The New Oxford Shakespeare: Modern Critical Edition*, ed. Gary Taylor, et al. (Oxford: Oxford University Press, 2016).
36 William Shakespeare, *The Tempest*, in *The Norton Facsimile: The First Folio of Shakespeare*, prep. Charlton Hinman, 2nd ed. (New York: W.W. Norton & Co., 1996), TLN 701–716.
37 All three lines without final punctuation end with the word 'yet', which may have indicated to a compositor that a sentence was not complete, in a way that 'Though this island seem to be desert' does not. The only other line in the text of the play that has no terminal punctuation is in 1.1 when Antonio says, 'Let's All Sinke with' King' (TLN 74). Sebastian's rejoinder of 'Let's take leave of him' (TLN 75) could easily be an interruption of Antonio's noble purpose, though it does not have to be.
38 If this part of the scene contains twenty-one microinterruptions, then the rate for that section of lines per interruption becomes 5, which makes it similar to the scenes in both *Volpone* and *The Humourous Lieutenant*.
39 All modern editions generate consensus around the interruptive nature of the first seven microinterruptions within the scene, which is also where the Folio gives its moments of no punctuation.
40 Quoted in Magnusson, 'Interruption in *The Tempest*', 54.
41 David Bevington, ed., *The Tempest* by William Shakespeare, in *Shakespeare's Romances and Poems* (New York: Pearson, 2007), 2.1.17.
42 Loughnane, ed., *The Tempest*, 2.1.14.
43 Loughnane, ed., *The Tempest*, 2.1.14.
44 For more on editors and stage directions, see Chapter 3.
45 T. W. Craik, '"Tell" in *The Tempest*, II.i.15: Speech or Stage Direction?', *Notes and Queries* 44 (1997): 514. I must thank Tiffany Stern to alerting me to this this possibility.
46 For more on that unique moment, see the Continuation.
47 Loughnane adds stage directions in this sequence indicating who the addressee is for each speech; however, that does not remove the interruptive nature of the passage. Neither the Vaughns nor Bevington nor Sherman in the Norton third edition add the stage directions '*to* [character]" in this sequence.

48 For example, scenes 2.2, 3.5, and 4.2 have moments where characters convince the Lieutenant to act in opposition to his own will. The entire character seems constructed upon the idea of removal of subjectivity and personal identity: case in point, he is never given a proper name. For more on the Lieutenant's subjected position, see Vimala C. Pasupathi, 'The King's Privates: Sex and the Soldier's Place in *The Humorous Lieutenant* (ca. 1618)', *Research Opportunities in Medieval and Renaissance Drama* 47 (2008): 25–50.

49 I disagree with Hoy's use of the MS in assigning 'when I consider' to the Lieutenant. While this creates another interruption, the awkward self-interruption that would be required of the Lieutenant seems unnecessary. John Fletcher, *The Humorous Lieutenant*, ed. Cyrus Hoy, in *The Dramatic Works in the Beaumont and Fletcher Canon*, ed. Fredson Bowers, vol. V (Cambridge: Cambridge University Press, 1982), 4.6.8–9. All citations come from this edition and will be cited parenthetically.

50 Leontius enters with the Lieutenant asking, 'Hast thou cleane forgot the wars?' to which the Lieutenant responds, 'Prethee Hold Thy Peace' (4.6.1–2).

51 The cutting off of the love protestations results in a playfully Fletcherean construction, in that the openness and honesty of the Lieutenant's love for a man is demonstrated but also contained. It allows the potential of subversion but veers away from upsetting decorum for the period.

52 This creates a very distinct pattern among the first six interruptions of the scene, perhaps indicating that Leucippe's lines at either 23 or 25 could interrupt the Governess to complete the pattern for a third pass. This pattern is not necessary or indicated through grammar or punctuation; however, it follows a specific rhythm. Unless Fletcher intended to interrupt a rhythm after establishing it.

53 Eugene Waith, *The Pattern of Tragicomedy in Beaumont and Fletcher* (New Haven: Yale University Press, 1952), 36.

Chapter 2

1 While a dialogic microinterruption surely possesses a thought that drives the second character's rupture (meaning their interrupting voice), the external movement away from the premise elides that thought. Actors and directors may query that thought process in a

way that readers and audience members do not. However, the self-interruption becomes the signifier of a character's thought processes that actors, directors, readers, and audience members alike notice and consider.

2 Katharine Eisaman Maus, *Inwardness and Theater in the English Renaissance* (Chicago: University of Chicago Press, 1995), 32.
3 Ibid., 31.
4 Wolfgang Iser, 'Interaction between Text and Reader', in *The Reader in the Text: Essays on Audience and Interpretation*, ed. Susan Rubin Suleiman and Inge Crosman (Princeton: Princeton University Press, 1980), 113, 112. See also, Laurie Maguire, *The Rhetoric of the Book* (Oxford: Oxford University Press, 2020), who adopts the term 'blanks' to explore 'the positive, creative potential of the blank in printed texts' (5).
5 Maguire, *The Rhetoric of the Book*, 7. Maguire completes this line with 'we supply the continuation' (7), which, while using the same terminology as I do, differs in that I see the self-interruptions in particular as signalling rupture not continuation.
6 Gary Taylor, *Moment by Moment by Shakespeare* (London: Macmillan, 1985), 73. Taylor notes this only about Shakespeare, but as my analysis indicates, self-interruptions render this true of at least all three playwrights of this study, if not others as well.
7 Iser, 'Interaction', 119.
8 While neither the Q2 text nor the F text provide a dash here (Q2 has no punctuation and F has a period), beginning with Rowe, and in most modern editions, this self-interruption is marked with a dash, indicating a consensus about its status.
9 George Puttenham, *The Arte of English Poesie* (London: Richard Field, 1589), sig. T4v.
10 Ibid., sig. T4v.
11 The Folio uses a comma here, which is consistent with its relative dearth of dashes. Alexander Pope was the first to add the dash here, which modern editors retain.
12 Ben Jonson, *The Workes of Beniamin Jonson* (London: Will Stansby, 1616), sig. Rrr4r.
13 The Quarto text (1611) has the dashes but not the stage direction, but Bevington argues that the marginalia such as this line should be seen as authorial. David Bevington, '*Catiline*: Textual Essay', in *The Cambridge Edition of the Works of Ben Jonson Online* (Cambridge: Cambridge University Press), 5.

14 Again, the breaches in the 1616 Folio give a sense of a substantial pause or break to indicate Volturcius's fear. But that is only hypothesized from their length, which has no clear semantic meaning.

15 Karen Pirnie, 'In Changèd Shapes: The Two Jonsons' Volpones and Textual Editing', *Comitatus* 27, no. 1 (1996): 43, 54. Richard Dutton, '*Volpone*: Textual Essay', 4.

16 Dutton, '*Volpone:* Textual Essay', 4. The Quarto text contains a total of 186 dashes, and even though the Folio eliminates them from this speech, overall it has 189. The compositors of both texts set a lot of dashes as they composed the play. For more on dashes and this play, see Chapter 1.

17 Bevington, '*Catiline*: Textual Essay', 1–2.

18 Ibid., 3.

19 David Gants, 'The 1616 Folio (F1): Textual Essay', in *The Cambridge Edition of the Works of Ben Jonson Online* (Cambridge: Cambridge University Press), 8.

20 Ibid., 6.

21 The final phrase too might be discounted because it is not a self-interruption as Volpone speaks next. As a dialogic microinterruption, its shortness is less part of her speech and more part of the dialogue's construction as Volpone wrests back power from his victim. The shortest segment, therefore, in the second half of the speech is the doubly interruptive moment within the parentheses that comes in at seven words.

22 In this manner, it functions like Volturcius's speech, which, like the Folio rendering of Celia's speech, demonstrates a clear logical set of images and ideas.

23 Jeremy Lopez, 'Fletcher's *Mad Lover* and Late Shakespeare', in *Shakespeare Up Close: Reading Early Modern Texts*, ed. Russ McDonald, Nicholas D. Nace, and Travis D. Williams (London: Arden Shakespeare, 2012), 184–5.

24 For those not familiar with the plot of *The Mad Lover*, here is a brief synopsis: Memnon returns from war and, upon seeing the Princess Calis, falls madly in love with her, offering her his heart. She playfully accepts, but he takes her literally and seeks out someone to cut his heart out. His brother Polydore agrees to help by taking a fake heart to Calis and berating her for her treatment of his brother, which makes her fall in love with Polydore. Memnon's soldiers use a masque and a dressed-up whore to try to heal the general's wits, which eventually works. Polydore is being

pressed to love Calis and falls ill. Calis appeals to Venus, who tells her that she will have a dead lover. Polydore's funeral arrives at the temple, bearing directions for Calis to marry Memnon, but his brother's death drives Memnon crazy again. So, Polydore leaps up, agrees to wed Calis, Memnon gives up his claim to her and agrees to go back to war. For the full synopsis with the subplot about Syphax and Chloe, see Wiggins and Richardson, *British Drama*, vol. VI, #1809 (545).

25 John Fletcher, *The Mad Lover*, ed. Robert Kean Turner, in *The Dramatic Works in the Beaumont and Fletcher Canon*, ed. Fredson Bowers, vol. V (Cambridge: Cambridge University Press, 1982), 2.1.1–24. All subsequent citations will be parenthetical.

26 Pirnie, 'In Changèd Shapes', 43.

27 The Second Folio of 1679 gives two: one in line 23 after 'Regiments' and one at the end of the speech when Chilax enters. While interruptive, one is an action microinterruption, and the other is only one of many options. The original spelling edition in the Cambridge *Dramatic Works* only retains the final dash for Chilax's interruptive entrance. R. Warwick Bond's *Variorum* from 1908 (the only modern spelling edition) adds five but only in the final seven lines: two around 'staie there', one after 'Dead once', one after 'know there?', and one after 'there it goes'. R. Warwick Bond, ed., *The Mad Lover* by John Fletcher, in *The Works of Francis Beaumont & John Fletcher: Variorum Edition*, ed. A. H. Bullen, vol. III (London: George Bell and Sons, 1908), 2.1.1–24.

28 Like Celia's, the final interruption is not self-imposed but results from the interference of another character. However, in *Volpone*, the interference is a direct interjection and stopping of the speech by Volpone, while in *The Mad Lover*, the interference is inadvertent, as Chilax finds Memnon after searching for him.

29 Lopez, 'Fletcher's *Mad Lover*', 184–5.

30 Even the first quarto version, 'Ay, there's the point', asserts a clear acceptance and understanding of his subject.

31 Lopez, 'Fletcher's *Mad Lover*', 183.

32 Constantin Stanislavski, *Building a Character*, trans. Elizabeth Reynolds Hapgood (New York: Theatre Arts Books/Routledge, 1989), 113 and *passim*.

33 Gary Taylor, 'A History of *The History of Cardenio*', in *The Quest for Cardenio: Shakespeare, Fletcher, Cervantes, and the Lost Play*, ed. David Carnegie and Gary Taylor (Oxford: Oxford University Press, 2012), 19. Terri Bourus, 'Poner en escena *The History of Cardenio*',

in *The Creation and Re-Creation of Cardenio*, ed. Terri Bourus and Gary Taylor (London: Palgrave Macmillan, 2013), 215.

34 The end is potentially self-interruptive as he stops himself with 'Soft you now'. However, he does so at the end of a logical conclusion to his postulations:

> Thus conscience does make cowards of us all
> And thus the native hue of resolution
> Is sicklied o'er with the pale cast of thought,
> And enterprises of great pitch and moment
> With this regard their currents turn away
> And lose the name of action.
> (Q2 3.1.83–88)

35 Edward Pechter, '"Iago's Theory of Mind": A Response to Paul Cefalu', *Shakespeare Quarterly* 64, no. 3 (2013): 298.

36 William Hazlitt (1815), S. T. Coleridge (1819), and Stephen Orgel (2003). All three are quoted in the introductory bricolage to *Othello, or The Moor of Venice*, ed. Gary Taylor, in *The New Oxford Shakespeare: Modern Critical Edition*, ed. Gary Taylor et al. (Oxford: Oxford University Press, 2016), 2111–14.

37 Paul Cefalu, 'The Burdens of Mind Reading in Shakespeare's *Othello*: A Cognitive and Psychoanalytic Approach to Iago's Theory of Mind', *Shakespeare Quarterly* 64, no. 3 (2013): 265–94. While the use of Theory of Mind brings out one possibility, Cefalu never gets beyond the complicated notions of character, especially within drama and its theatrical potential. Therefore, he overlooks how language constructs this Theory of Mind as much as he uses the language to craft it.

38 The Folio text of *Othello* has only five dashes, two of which are in this scene.

39 Graham Bradshaw notes the usage of triple hyphens in the Quarto and their reduction in the Folio, arguing that they connect to verse line shifts. While he reads several of these moments, and notes that the Folio uses only two em rules, he does not consider this moment as one where the Folio uses a dash not found in the Quarto. Graham Bradshaw, *Misrepresentations: Shakespeare and the Materialists* (Ithaca: Cornell University Press, 1993), 259–60 and *passim*.

40 Madeline Doran, *Shakespeare's Dramatic Language* (Madison: The University of Wisconsin Press, 1976), 63. Her analysis of Iago is related to mine, but she focuses on the disruptive power of conditional syntax found throughout and how that relates to the overall structure.

41 Cefalu, 'The Burdens of Mind Reading', 290.
42 The Folio text reads 'dilations', meaning amplification, which Honigmann changes to 'delations', meaning accusations. I revert to the Folio wording as it best approaches the oxymoronic moment of an opening out of a secret thought, which is a way to consider a self-interruption. For a thorough explication of this particular crux, see Patricia Parker, 'Shakespeare and Rhetoric: "dilation" and "delation" in *Othello*', in *Shakespeare and the Question of Theory*, ed. Patricia Parker and Geoffrey Hartman (London: Metheun, 1985), 55–74.
43 Cefalu, 'The Burdens of Mind Reading', 290.
44 John Calderwood, *The Properties of Othello* (Amherst, MA: University of Massachusetts Press, 1989), 113.
45 The Folio actually places the phrase in parentheses.
46 Arden 3 uses several moments of ellipses as another form of interruptive pointing, related to but different from a dash. Here is a key example. The Folio text uses a full stop.
47 Laura Salisbury, 'Beside Oneself: Beckett, Comic Tremor and Solicitude', *parallax* 11, no. 4 (2005): 83–4.
48 Ibid., 85.
49 As with most of my examples, they are not limited to early modern drama. In fact, early cinema and screwball comedies such as *Bringing Up Baby* (1938) provide several great examples.
50 That speech in particular has several dashes included in the Folio text itself.

Chapter 3

1 Tiffany Stern has argued that using 'stage direction' to describe all paratext that is not the dialogue lacks a historical basis and obfuscates the differing pieces of texts. Tiffany Stern, 'Inventing Stage Directions; Demoting Dumb Shows', in *Stage Directions and Shakespearean Theatre*, ed. Sarah Dustagheer and Gillian Woods (London: Bloomsbury, 2018), 40–1. Pascale Aebischer and other writers have used the term *didascalia*, which comes from the Greek, as a term to identify all text that is not the speeches themselves in a play. Pascale Aebischer, 'Didascalia and Speech in the Dramatic Text', *Journal of Dramatic Theory and Criticism* 17, no. 2 (2003): 28; Ronald W. Vince, 'Didascalia', *The Oxford Encyclopedia of*

Theatre and Performance (Oxford: Oxford University Press, 2005), *Oxford Reference*, Accessed 5 February 2019. *Didascalia* helps us to think historically, as Aebischer encourages, and it highlights the entire text's participation in a consideration of stage business. Aebischer, 'Didascalia', 33, 38; Anthony Hammond, 'Encounters of the Third-Kind in Stage-Directions in Elizabethan and Jacobean Drama', *Studies in Philology* 89, no. 1 (1992): 73. While all stage directions are *didascalia*, not all *didascalia* are stage directions; some are speech prefixes or scene breaks or other paratextual pieces of information.

2 Sarah Dustagheer and Gillian Woods, *Introduction: Stage Directions & Shakespearean Theatre* (London: Bloomsbury, 2018), 2.

3 For more on-stage directions in general, see Michael Issacharoff, *Discourse as Performance* (Stanford: Stanford University Press, 1989), 16–27, and Marvin Carlson, 'The Status of Stage Directions', *Studies in the Literary Imagination* 24, no. 2 (1991): 37–48. For an overview of early modern stage directions, see Linda McJannet, *The Voice of Elizabethan Stage Directions: The Evolution of a Theatrical Code* (Newark, DE: University of Delaware Press, 1999), and the essays in Dustagheer and Woods, eds., *Stage Directions & Shakespearean Theatre*.

4 Carlson, 'The Status', 46.

5 Entrances and exits are two of the most common actions that interrupt or are interrupted. See Mariko Ichikawa, *Shakespearean Entrances* (London: Palgrave Macmillan, 2002), 21–32, and Steven Urkowitz, 'Interrupted Exits in *King Lear*', *Educational Theatre Journal* 30 (1978): 203–10.

6 John Jowett has articulated that 'the challenge presented to editors lies in the identification and correction of error', indicating that the earliest texts are not themselves indisputably original. However, in what follows, my analysis aims to demonstrate that the considerations I offer are not 'errors' and that understanding them as interruptions help to 'release' them into their 'intended clarity'. John Jowett, 'Shakespeare and the Kingdom of Error,' in *The New Oxford Shakespeare: Critical Reference Edition*, ed. Gary Taylor, John Jowett, Terri Bourus, and Gabriel Egan, vol. 1 (Oxford: Oxford University Press, 2017), lviii, lxii.

7 Leah Marcus, *Unediting the Renaissance: Shakespeare, Marlowe, Milton* (London: Routledge, 1996), 16–17.

8 For more on entrances and exits, see Ichikawa, *Shakespearean Entrances*. Importantly, she notes that 'There is much evidence that

Elizabethans did not use either "*enter*" or "*exit/exeunt*" in the same way that we normally understand these terms' (3). While she uses this to explain the latitude of some marked entrances and exits, it does not change the phenomenological quality of an entrance into or exit from the dramaturgical space of the play.

9 The idea of a cleared stage governs the definition of 'scene' in the *OED*, see *The Oxford English Dictionary Online* (2016), 'scene'. Claire M.L. Bourne questions whether such a strict logic would occur to an early modern audience. She argues that the print history of such demarcations shows that scene is an unstable form that cannot be succinctly defined. Claire M. L. Bourne, *Typographies of Performance in Early Modern England* (Oxford: Oxford University Press, 2020), 139–40, 184, and *passim*.

10 Bruce R. Smith, 'Scene', in *Early Modern Theatricality*, ed. Henry S. Turner (Oxford: Oxford University Press, 2013), 110.

11 Bourne, *Typographies*, 138, 150–1. The two dramas of the period that most regularly use French scenes are academic and closet dramas, both deriving this structure from classical precedent. For more on closet drama and space, see Michelle Dowd, 'Dramaturgy and the Politics of Space in *The Tragedy of Mariam*', *Renaissance Drama* 44, no. 1 (2016).

12 Richard Cave, 'Script and Performance', in *Ben Jonson and Theatre: Performance, Practice, and Theory*, ed. Richard Cave, Elizabeth Schafer, and Brian Woolland (London: Routledge, 1999), 25. Cave's essay provides an excellent reading of the theatrical nature of the mise-en-page for Jonson's Folio and especially *The Alchemist*. While he tries to recover the theatrical text, he misses Jonson's more overall idiosyncrasy, see 25–7, 29.

13 For an analysis of the tension between dramatic presentation and textual presentation in Jonson, see Helen Ostovich, '"To Behold the Scene Full": Seeing and Judging in *Every Man Out*', in *Re-Presenting Ben Jonson: Text, History, Performance*, ed. Martin Butler, 76–92 (Houndmills: Macmillan Press Ltd, 1999). While Ostovich champions the 'long full scenes' of *Every Man Out* in the Quarto, as opposed to the Folio's 'choppy "single scenes"' (90), what she underserves is Jonson's choice in effecting this particular movement and effect. Her own analogy of the dance, rather than support the Quarto 'scene', emphasizes Jonson's choice of movements by showing the groupings that occur within the whole. She seems to acknowledge this in part, praising Jonson's 'multiple complex tensions' (90); however, her phrasing again, especially the repetitive 'chop', emphasizes her approval of one and denigration of the other.

14 I use the term 'dramaturgical space' to mean 'the nexus that exists among the plot-structure, the written part, the physical theatre, and the actor's body', Michael M. Wagoner, 'The Dramaturgical Space of Solo Scenes, or a Study of the Jailer's Daughter', *Shakespeare Bulletin* 35, no. 1 (2017): 97. This combination among the theatrical and the written animates this exploration between the theatrical and the written in Jonson.

15 The Quarto versions of the *Every Man* plays both contain unclear usage of French scenic structure: *Every Man In* has twenty-one possible French scenes and *Every Man Out* has twenty. These early printed texts though, while moving towards his scenic structure, do not reflect the divisions that he would later embrace.

16 The only other Jonson play to do so is *The Devil is an Ass*.

17 Peter Holland and William Sherman, Introduction, *The Alchemist* by Ben Jonson, in *The Cambridge Edition of the Works of Ben Jonson*, ed. David Bevington, Martin Butler, and Ian Donaldson, vol. 3 (Cambridge: Cambridge University Press, 2012), 553.

18 *The Alchemist* only specifically notes seven entrances and two exits.

19 William Sherman, 'The Alchemist: Textual Essay', *The Cambridge Edition of the Works of Ben Jonson Online* (Cambridge: Cambridge University Press), 4.

20 Ben Jonson, *The Alchemist*, ed. Peter Holland and William Sherman, in *The Cambridge Edition of the Works of Ben Jonson*, ed. David Bevington, Martin Butler, and Ian Donaldson, vol. 3 (Cambridge: Cambridge University Press, 2012).

21 Nine of the forty-five marginal directions are for knocking, meaning that twenty per cent of all the given stage directions are for a character to knock or for the sound of knocking to occur. Notably, no stage direction appears for the ring noise.

22 Ben Jonson, *The Alchemist*, ed. F. H. Mares, *The Revels Plays* (London: Metheun & Co., 1967), I.ii.0sd. This usage accords with several other Jonson texts that use the phrase 'to them' to indicate who joins the grouping of the French scene. See, for example, the Folio text of *Every Man Out* 3.4, 3.5, and 3.6.

23 Ben Jonson, *The Alchemist*, ed. W. Gifford, in *The Works of Ben Jonson*, vol. IV (London: G. and W. Nicol, et al., 1816), 25.

24 This differs from Francis Beaumont's text of *The Knight of the Burning Pestle*, which concludes every Act with a 'Finis', thereby closing it off and neatly containing the onstage action as separate from the interlude commentary of the Citizen and Wife. Francis

Beaumont, *The Knight of the Burning Pestle*, ed. Michael Hattaway (London: Methuen Drama, 2002).

25 So too, this analysis may further indicate a control over form that the playwright loses in the live performance of the text. Something that Jonson seems often to have wanted to recover.

26 It has six, as does 5.5. Only 4.5 has more with seven.

27 Ben Jonson, *The Works of Beniamin Jonson* (London: Will Stansby, 1616), sig. 3G2r-3G2v.

28 Mares even notes that this break is so clear and clean that it is the most likely place for an overall interval break, arguing that the other act breaks elide over with continuous action and recognition, Jonson, *The Alchemist*, ed. Mares, xlv–xlvi. While I agree about *Act Three/Act Four*, as I will discuss, his sense of the necessity of the break for time to pass seems overly determined.

29 Gary Taylor, 'The Structure of Performance: Act Intervals in the London Theatres, 1576–1642', in *Shakespeare Reshaped, 1606–1623*, ed. Gary Taylor and John Jowett (Oxford: Clarendon Press, 1993), 4, 36. See also, Lucy Munro '*The Alchemist*: Stage History', *The Cambridge Edition of the Works of Ben Jonson Online*, 1–3, and Elizabeth Schafer and Emma Cox, '*The Alchemist* on the Stage: Performance, Collaboration and Deviation,' in *The Alchemist: A Critical Reader*, ed. Erin Julian and Helen Ostovich (London: Bloomsbury, 2013), 45–6.

30 Mark Hutchings, 'The Interval and Indoor Playmaking', *Studies in Theatre and Performance* 33, no. 3 (2013): 266, 269, 270. Hutchings specifically refers to Fitzdotterl's line in *The Devil is an Ass*, as well as passages in Jonson's notes to the reader for *The New Inn* and *The Magnetic Lady*. All these plays postdate *The Alchemist* and so may express later disappointment after problems with even such a popular play as *The Alchemist*. In fact, in both *The Staple of News* and *The Magnetic Lady*, Jonson crafts 'intermeans' as dramatized pieces to cover the interval. For more on these 'intermeans', see Hutchings, 'The Interval', 270–2.

31 Bourne, *Typographies*, 138.

32 The only other example in Jonsonian dramaturgy is the break between *Act 1* and *Act 2* in *The Devil is an Ass*, which M.J. Kidnie in her edition notes as being 'unusual' as 'the action is continuous'. Ben Jonson, *The Devil is an Ass*, in *The Devil is an Ass and Other Plays*, ed. Margaret Jane Kidnie (Oxford: Oxford University Press, 2000), 1.7.29-30n. She is of course correct, but as with this moment in *The Alchemist*, it is not beyond Jonson to craft such

oddities, providing alternative experiences for performance and readerly text.

33 One might even hypothesize that if the candles were getting low or burning unevenly by the end, it could add a mood to enhance the feeling of devastation post-explosion. And with the arrival of the master and the movement outdoors, the lights would be brightened once again.

34 Jonson, *The Alchemist*, ed. Mares, xlv.

35 Sherman, '*The Alchemist*: Textual Essay', 1.

36 Sarah Outterson-Murphy, '"Remember Me:" The Ghost and Its Spectators in *Hamlet*,' *Shakespeare Bulletin* 34, no. 2 (2016): 259.

37 Ibid., 253.

38 For more on Shakespeare's use of ghosts, generally see John Jump, 'Shakespeare's Ghosts', *Critical Quarterly* 12 (1970): 339–51, and F. W. Moorman, 'Shakespeare's Ghosts', *The Modern Language Review* 1, no. 3 (1906): 192–201. For a consideration of the ghosts in performance, see Stanley Wells, 'Staging Shakespeare's Ghosts', in *The Arts of Performance in Elizabethan and Early Stuart Drama: Essays for G.K. Hunter*, ed. Murray Biggs, Philip Edwards, Inga-Stina Ewbank, and Eugene M. Waith (Edinburgh: Edinburgh University Press, 1991), 50–69, and Outterson-Murphy, 'Remember Me'. Finally, Catherine Belsey has offered two important articles on the uniqueness of Shakespeare's ghosts and especially their connection to a tradition of fireside stories. Catherine Belsey, 'Beyond Reason: *Hamlet* and Early Modern Stage Ghosts', in *Gothic Renaissance: A Reassessment*, ed. Elizabeth Bronfen and Beate Neumeier (Manchester: Manchester University Press, 2014), 32–54, and 'Shakespeare's Sad Tale for Winter: *Hamlet* and the Tradition of Fireside Ghost Stories', *Shakespeare Quarterly* 61, no. 1 (2010): 1–27. The chronology of these plays is contested; *Hamlet* might be Shakespeare's earliest use of a stage ghost. See Terri Bourus, *Young Shakespeare's Young Hamlet: Print, Piracy, and Performance* (London: Palgrave Macmillan, 2014), and Gary Taylor 'Shakespeare's Early Gothic Hamlet', *Critical Survey* 31, no 1/2 (2019): 4–25.

39 Horatio possesses an alacrity in noticing ghostly entrances; in all but one of the ghost's appearances, Horatio speaks up first on noting the spirit's arrival.

40 The Arden Shakespeare editions (edited by Ann Thompson and Neil Taylor) of both Q2 and F *Hamlet* make the same choice that I will

be critiquing from older editors of *Macbeth*. Namely, they move the Ghost's entrance from where it appears in the text of both Q2 and F to after Hamlet's line, in order to occur just before the reaction of 'Save me'. While this makes Hamlet's reaction immediate, it downplays the build-up of dramatic irony and suspense (even briefly) that Shakespeare more fully explores later in *Macbeth*. Also, in the First Quarto (Q1) of *Hamlet* the Ghost is immediately addressed by Hamlet. That dramaturgy accords with all of Shakespeare's early ghosts. If Q1 represents Shakespeare's first version of the play from the late 1580s, as Terri Bourus has argued, then the revision of Hamlet as represented in Q2 and F introduced a bit of dramaturgy that he would develop in *Macbeth*, namely not acknowledging the ghost immediately upon its entrance. See Bourus, *Young Shakespeare's Young Hamlet*.

41 Simon Forman recounts in his diary seeing the play performed. He mentions that the Ghost appeared when Macbeth specifically mentioned the missing Banquo, which has led some editors to move the stage direction as close to that line as possible. While this placement may make the dramatic irony immediately apparent, it lessens the suspense that Shakespeare builds into the dramatic irony. For Forman's diary entry, see Robert Miola, ed., *Macbeth* by William Shakespeare (New York: W.W. Norton & Co., 2014), 225–7.

42 William Shakespeare, *The Norton Facsimile: The First Folio of Shakespeare*, prepared by Charlton Hinman, 2nd ed., New York: W.W. Norton & Co., 1996.

43 The Ghost is completely Shakespeare's invention as several commentators note. In this move, he goes back to his invention of ghosts in *Richard III* and *Hamlet*, differing from his use of Plutarch in *Julius Caesar*. For more on Shakespeare's ghosts and sources, see Wells, 'Staging Shakespeare's Ghosts', 53; Taylor, 'Shakespeare's Early Gothic *Hamlet*', 5–7; and Belsey, 'Beyond Reason', 35, 49.

44 I borrow the term 'jump scare' from film because moving the ghost's entrance closer to Macbeth's reaction allows the on-stage audience to better mimic what the offstage audience might feel if the ghost's entrance is particularly alarming or spectacular.

45 For more on editors and error, see Jowett 'Shakespeare and the Kingdom of Error'.

46 Nick de Somogyi, ed., *Macbeth* by William Shakespeare (London: Nick Hern Books, 2003), 177.

47 George Steevens, ed., *The Plays of William Shakespeare. In fifteen volumes* (London: T. Longman, et al., 1793) *Eighteenth Century*

Collections Online, vol. I, 446. This anecdote occurs in the fourth edition of the works as an explanation of his attempt to explore all extant copies of the First Folio.

48 The other moment Steevens alludes to is the Ghost's invasion of Gertrude's closet in *Hamlet*. As discussed earlier, this is the only other ghost in Shakespeare that is not immediately acknowledged. What Steevens picks up on is Shakespeare's development of his later ghostly dramaturgy, ignoring the immediate ghosts and commenting upon the ones that engender greater suspense.

49 They slightly emended the wording—substituting the more descriptive 'rises' for 'Enter'—but they retained the placement.

50 The one outlier is Thomas Johnson's pirated edition, printed in the Hague but sent over to London. He moved the entrance down eight lines to after Macbeth's line, 'Who may I rather challenge for Unkindness,/Than pity for Mischance', bringing the entrance of the Ghost closer to the sighting of the Ghost. William Shakespeare, *The Tragedy of Macbeth* (London [the Hague], [T. Johnson], 1711), 44/sig. C6v. While this might clear up some confusion, uniting the action of the stage direction with the immediate response, it lessens suspense. Johnson's edition had no effect on subsequent editions, as it is not until Capell fifty years later that another edition moves the entrance. For more on Thomas Johnson, see Andrew Murphy, *Shakespeare in Print: A History and Chronology of Shakespeare Publishing* (Cambridge: Cambridge University Press, 2003), 103–5; Judith Milhous and Robert D. Hume, *The Publication of Plays in London 1660–1800: Playwrights, Publishers, and the Market* (London: The British Library, 2015), 245–8; and, B. J. McMullin, 'T. Johnson, Bookseller in the Hague,' in *An Index of Civilisation: Studies of Printing and Publishing History in Honour of Keith Maslen*, ed. R. Harvey, W. Kirsop and B. J. McMullin (Clayton, Victoria: Centre for Bibliographical and Textual Studies, Monash University, 1993), 99–112.

51 Murphy, *Shakespeare in Print*, 86.

52 Alan Galey and Rebecca Niles, 'Moving Parts: Digital Modeling and the Infrastructures of Shakespearean Editing', *Shakespeare Quarterly* 68, no. 1 (2017): 45.

53 For an examination of another peculiar aspect of Capell's edition that defied the editorial tradition but also did not necessarily follow the earliest texts, see Paul Menzer, 'Dislocating Shakespeare: Scene Locators and the Place of the Page', *Shakespeare Bulletin* 24, no. 2 (2006): 1–19.

54 William Shakespeare, *Mr. William Shakespeare, His Comedies, Histories, and Tragedies*, ed. Edward Capell (London: J. and R. Tonson, 1768), vol. IV, 44.

55 Murphy, *Shakespeare in Print*, 85.

56 This is not to say that Capell's emendation does not work in performance, nor that Capell was not thinking about performance when he emended the text. What the move effects is a more streamlined presentation of the scene that would help readers in a way that audiences do not need. When the audience sees the Ghost, they begin to realize the impending problems and would not be confused about what was happening. The physical presence of the actor as ghost would give a spectator a point of reference from which they could understand the irony of the scene. With only the one stage direction, readers must keep the silent ghost in mind while reading dialogue not about the Ghost.

57 William Shakespeare, *The Plays and Poems of William Shakespere*, ed. Edmund Malone, vol. III (London: J. Rivington and Sons, et al., 1790), 57. Presumably this is because the move seemed self-evident. Alternatively, it might have reflected Shakespearean practice elsewhere, such as in the theatre. Edmund Kean's 1853 promptbook follows the Capell/Malone placement. Charles Kean, *Shakespeare's Tragedy of Macbeth* (London: John K. Chapman & Co., 1853): 55.

58 William Shakespeare, *Macbeth*, in *The Plays of William Shakespeare*, ed. Thomas Keightley, vol. 6 (London: Bell and Daldy, 1864), 41.

59 In departing from the more immediately interruptive ghosts, Banquo's early entrance accords with Shakespeare's overall investment in dramatic irony within interruptive forms. Again, it might also express a developing interest in changing spectral dramaturgy.

60 Kenneth Muir, ed. *Macbeth* by William Shakespeare (London: Arden Shakespeare, 2nd Series, 1951), 91.

61 Miola, ed., *Macbeth*, 227.

62 Ibid., 225.

63 Because of its closer proximity to the reaction, the re-entrance has experienced much less editorial fiddling than the first.

64 Muir, ed., *Macbeth*, 91.

65 Middleton's aesthetic is of course the most important one to consider in this text, and the Folio stage direction could have been placed by him. However, his use of ghosts in *The Changeling* (4.1, 5.1) align with the paradigm of immediate recognition of the ghostly visitor. Thomas Middleton and William Rowley, *The Changeling*, ed. Douglas

Bruster, in *Thomas Middleton: The Collected Works*, ed. Gary Taylor and John Lavignino (Oxford: Oxford University Press, 2007), 4.1.0, 5.1.58.

66 Catherine Henze's dissertation and subsequent article both establish the importance of music in Fletcher's plays. Catherine Henze, '"With the Power of my Enchanting Song": Functions of Music in the Drama of Beaumont and Fletcher' (PhD dissertation, University of Chicago, 1995), 112; and 'Unraveling Beaumont from Fletcher with Music, Misogyny, and Masque'. *SEL: Studies in English Literature 1500–1900* 44, no. 2 (2004): 383. However, Henze's goal is to use music to consider attribution, often deriding Fletcher for amplifying the misogyny of the text within his songs. She sums up Fletcher's use of songs in her dissertation as such: 'Fletcher—by associating music with fantastical effects—intensifies scenes, adds important nuances, and causes the audience and characters to believe things it ordinarily would not, such as that a courtesan is a desirable marriage partner, or that suitors can come running out of the woods by wishing—and singing—their desire into being. Not unlike alcohol, and sometimes in conjunction with it, music enchants the consciousness of both character and audience, allowing the plot to move forward along its already determined path.' Henze, 'With the Power', 113. This assessment begins to consider what Fletcher does theatrically with music; however, she eliminates this paragraph from the published article, intensifying the case for Beaumont as the more interesting and unique user of music. Furthermore, while she notes some examples from *Valentinian* and *The Faithful Shepherdess* in her analysis, she does not explicate why she only looks at those two plays, as they are not inherently unique as far as the music is concerned, and she leaves out two songs in *Faithful Shepherdess*. These omissions weaken her argument. As I hope to show, Fletcher's music and usage of it more often asserts power for his female characters rather than amplifying misogynistic tendencies.

67 Gary Taylor uses this staging, along with other evidence, to argue that the offstage song in *Double Falsehood* 4.2 represents a Fletcherean moment. Gary Taylor, 'A History of *The History of Cardenio*', in *The Quest for Cardenio: Shakespeare, Fletcher, Cervantes, and the Lost Play*, ed. David Carnegie and Gary Taylor (Oxford: Oxford University Press, 2012), 45. He specifically likens it to the moment in *The Chances*, but the similarly constructed moments in *The Woman's Prize* and *Women Pleas'd* further strengthen his observation. For an analysis of how powerful such staging can be, see Terri Bourus, 'Poner en escena *The History of Cardenio*', in *The Creation and Re-Creation of Cardenio*, ed. Terri

Bourus and Gary Taylor (London: Palgrave Macmillan, 2013), 212–13.

68 John Fletcher, *Women Pleas'd*, ed. Hans Walter Gabler, in *The Dramatic Works in the Beaumont and Fletcher Canon*, ed. Fredson Bowers, vol. V (Cambridge: Cambridge University Press, 1982), 4.2.6–16.

69 John Fletcher, *The Chances*, ed. George Walton Williams, in *The Dramatic Works in the Beaumont and Fletcher Canon*, ed. Fredson Bowers, vol. IV (Cambridge: Cambridge University Press, 1979), 2.2.13–47 and 4.3.7–71.

70 The plot of the play follows Shakespeare's play by having a newly widowed Petruccio marry a new woman, Maria. While he assumes she will be easier than his first wife, she sets out to tame him, which she accomplishes through a series of tricks beginning with a sex strike. The offstage song occurs as the men of play, included Petruccio come to the house where the women have ensconced themselves.

71 Stern, 'Inventing Stage Directions', 38.

72 For more about songs and their placements/usages in early modern drama, see Tiffany Stern, *Documents of Performance in Early Modern England* (Cambridge: Cambridge University Press), 120–73.

73 For more about dashes and pointing, see Chapter 1.

74 See David Bevington, Martin Butler, and Ian Donaldson, general introduction to *The Cambridge Edition of the Works of Ben Jonson*, vol. 1 (Cambridge: Cambridge University Press, 2012), lxxxi; and Bourne, *Typographies of Performance*, 77–136.

75 Laurie Maguire, 'The Boundaries of Stage Directions', in *Stage Directions and Shakespearean Theatre*, ed. Sarah Dustagheer and Gillian Woods (London: Bloomsbury, 2018), 45–67.

76 Stern notes that the MS seems to have the remnants of a wax seal and fibres near the direction 'Song', which perhaps indicates that the lyrics were at one time appended to that text but were subsequently removed. Stern, *Documents*, 159. If so, we might imagine an overlapping and interruptive text where the lyrics lived alongside the dialogue, akin to the moment of overlapping dialogue in *The Alchemist* 4.5.

77 Gary Taylor, '*The Tamer Tamed*: Dating Fletcher's Interactions with Shakespeare', *Memoria di Shakespeare* no. 5 (2018): 144–8.

78 Celia Caputi, 'A Tale of Two Tamings: Reading the Early Modern Shrew Debate from a Feminist Transnationalist Perspective', in

Shakespeare, Italy, and Transnational Exchange: Early Modern to Present, ed. Chris Stamatakis and Enza De Francisci (London: Routledge, 2017), 42–3.

79 While he is usually the one given credit, Lupić and Greatley-Hirsch show that his involvement is still unclear as there may have been others to contribute to the notes of this edition. Ivan Lupić and Brett Greatley-Hirsch, '"What Stuff is Here?" Edmond Malone and the 1778 Edition of Beaumont and Fletcher', *Papers of the Bibliographical Society of America* 111, no. 3 (2017): 294–5.

80 Arnold Glover, ed. *The Works of Francis Beaumont and John Fletcher: Cambridge English Classics*, vol. I (Cambridge: Cambridge University Press, 1905), v-vi.

81 Ferguson, ed. *John Fletcher The Woman's Prize*, 211.

82 Hammond, 'Encounters of the Third-Kind', 72. Hammond brings up Bowers' defense of stage direction placement to argue that the logic sometimes creates 'unactable' texts that ignore 'theatrical necessity'. Oddly enough, the placement of the song in *The Woman's Prize* is a moment where Bowers does the opposite: in that he ignores the early texts, which have a theatrical necessity, and instead follows an editorial logic.

83 Fredson Bowers, ed. *The Woman's Prize, or the Tamer Tamed*, in *The Dramatic Works in the Beaumont and Fletcher Canon*, vol. IV (Cambridge: Cambridge University Press), 2.6.44–57n.

84 Celia R. Daileader and Gary Taylor also use the MS for the basis of their edition, but they give no indication of the MS's placement of the song. Celia R. Daileader and Gary Taylor, eds., *The Tamer Tamed, or, The Woman's Prize* by John Fletcher (Manchester: Manchester University Press, 2006), 2.5.40–57.

85 Lucy Munro, ed., *The Tamer Tamed* by John Fletcher (London: Methuen Drama, 2010), 2.5.43. The other twenty-first-century edition is by Barry Gaines and Margaret Maurer, who place the text of the song after 'Pray, silence', and give the following note: 'Although both F1 and MS have stage directions calling for a song, they do not include it. The text of the song is taken from F2'. Barry Gaines and Margaret Maurer, eds., *Three Shrew Plays* (Indianapolis: Hackett Publishing Company Inc., 2010), 178. Despite using the folio text and 'incorporat[ing] some manuscript readings' (xxii), Gaines and Maurer give no textual note about the song otherwise or provide clear reasoning for their choices in relation to the song.

86 Munro, ed., *The Tamer Tamed*, 2.5.43n.

87 Ibid., 2.5.43n.
88 Ibid., 2.5.1.
89 Daileader and Taylor, eds., *The Tamer Tamed*, 5.4.97.

Chapter 4

1 José A. Pérez Díez, 'The Wide Gap of Sixteen Years: The Performance of Time in The Winter's Tale in Britain, 2001–2017', *Shakesepare Bulletin* 36, no. 2 (2018): 299.
2 For more on 'spoilers', see Anne-Charlotte Mecklenburg, 'The Sensational Temporality of Spoilers in *The Woman in White* and *Avengers: Endgame*', *Nineteenth-Century Contexts* 43, no. 1 (2021): 57–9, and Sarah Beck, 'Let There Be No More Woe for Jon Snow: The Dramaturgy of Spoilers', in *Vying for the Iron Throne: Essays on Power, Gender, Death, and Performance in HBO's Game of Thrones*, ed. Lindsay Mantoan and Sara Brady (Jefferson, NC: McFarland & Co., 2018), 184–5.
3 Jan Kott, *Shakespeare Our Contemporary*, trans. Boleslaw Taborski (New York: W.W. Norton, 1974), xii and *passim*. The phrase 'Shakespeare, our contemporary' is the title to Jan Kott's book that demonstrates the modern-ness of Shakespeare's plays. I offer the title ironically as I use it to emphasize our overfamiliarity, but Kott intended the title to show how Shakespeare can be saved from overfamiliarity and made pertinent again.
4 Randall Martin, introduction, *Every Man Out of His Humour* by Ben Jonson, in *The Cambridge Edition of the Works of Ben Jonson*, ed. David Bevington, Martin Butler, and Ian Donaldson, vol. 1 (Cambridge: Cambridge University Press, 2012), 235.
5 Anne Barton, *Ben Jonson, Dramatist* (Cambridge: Cambridge University Press, 1984), 65.
6 Martin, introduction, 235. Bill Angus, *Metadrama and the Informer in Shakespeare and Jonson* (Edinburg: Edinburgh University Press, 2016), 74.
7 Helen Ostovich, introduction, *Every Man Out of His Humour* by Ben Jonson (Manchester: Manchester University Press, 2001), 40.
8 F. P. Wilson, introduction, *Every Man Out of His Humour, 1600*, by Ben Jonson (London: Malone Society Reprints, 1920), v.
9 Martin, introduction, 235.

10 Randall Martin, '*Every Man Out of His Humour*: Stage History', *The Cambridge Edition of the Works of Ben Jonson Online* (Cambridge: Cambridge University Press), 1. Ostovich, introduction, 40.

11 Ibid., 1.

12 Jonson reuses this framing structure in two later plays, *The Staple of News* (1626) and *The Magnetic Lady* (1632).

13 Both are found, for instance, in *The Taming of the Shrew* and *The Taming of a Shrew*, as I discuss in Chapter 5.

14 Much of the criticism on the play focuses on the play's engagement with satire. For more on the satiric angle, see Robert N. Watson, *Ben Jonson's Parodic Strategy: Literary Imperialism in the Comedies* (Cambridge, MA: Harvard University Press, 1987), 53–7.

15 Ben Jonson, *Every Man Out of His Humour*, ed. Randall Martin, in *The Cambridge Edition of the Works of Ben Jonson*, ed. David Bevington, Martin Butler, and Ian Donaldson, vol. 1 (Cambridge: Cambridge University Press, 2012), ind.0SD. All citations come from the *CWBJ*, unless otherwise noted, and will be provided parenthetically. This edition is based on the 1600 Quarto, though it notes readings in the Folio that differ. I have consulted David Gant's personal copy of the 1616 Folio to check for variances where they are important and will cite or indicate Folio readings with an F and citation of a signature. Here, the Folio reads, 'After the second Sounding', sig. G5r.

16 Richard Hosley, 'Was There a "Dramatic Epilogue" to *The Taming of the Shrew*?', *Studies in English Literature, 1500–1900* 1, no. 2 (1961): 22.

17 Andrew Gurr states, 'If we can credit the Swan drawing, alongside the hut was a small platform level with the gallery roof, from which a trumpeter announced the imminent start of a performance, to hurry any latecomers', Andrew Gurr, *The Shakespearean Stage 1574–1642*, 4th ed. (Cambridge: Cambridge University Press, 2013), 151. Tiffany Stern clarifies Gurr's work laying out the evidence supporting the sounding of the trumpet and asks, 'Is the trumpet the last sound heard before the play starts, or is it actually the play's start?', Tiffany Stern, 'Before the Beginning; After the End: When Did Plays Start and Stop?', in *Shakespeare and Textual Studies*, ed. Margaret Jane Kidnie and Sonia Massai (Cambridge: Cambridge University Press, 2015), 367.

18 Hosley, 'Was There a "Dramatic Epilogue"', 32–3.

19 Heywood, Thomas, *The Four Prentices of London*, ed. William N. West. *The Routledge Anthology of Early Modern Drama*, ed. Jeremy Lopez (London: Routledge, 2020), Prol.1–3.

20 John Marston, *The History of Antonio and Mellida, the First Part* (London: Matthew Lownes and Thomas Fisher, 1602), sigs. A3r, B1v, B2r.

21 Alan C. Dessen and Leslie Thomsen, *A Dictionary of Stage Directions in English Drama 1580–1642* (Cambridge: Cambridge University Press, 1999), 209. The only other plays from the period to seemingly use the entrance at the second sounding are two works in manuscript by William Percy: *The Cuck-Queanes and Cuckolds Errant, or the Bearing Down the Inne* (1601) and *The Aphrodysiall or Sea-Feast* (1602). Both post-date *EMO* and therefore might be influenced by it. These manuscript plays are difficult to find. *The Cuck-Queanes* has a transcription of its published edition from the nineteenth century included in *Literature Online: English Drama*, but *The Aphrodysiall* only recently received an edition in an unpublished PhD Dissertation by Caroline Carpenter.

22 While the two other comical satires, *Cynthia's Revels* and *Poetaster*, both have inductions followed by prologues, neither play's quarto texts indicate any information about the sounding of the trumpets. However, the Folio texts of both plays indicate that the inductions begin, as in *EMO*, at the second sounding.

23 The breaking down of the actor/character barrier is the most important development of the Marstonian Inductions, which attempt to stage the players themselves getting ready for the play. Marston, *Antonio and Mellida*, sig. A3r-B1r. John Webster's added induction to Marston's *The Malcontent* mimics this same issue. John Webster, *The Induction to the Malcontent*, in *The Malcontent* by John Marston (London: William Aspley, 1604), sig. A3r–A4v.

24 Neither the 1600 quarto nor the 1616 Folio use dashes, though Randall Martin does, but the incompletion indicates clear interruption.

25 William Blisset, 'The Oddness of *Every Man out of his Humour*', in *The Elizabethan Theatre XII*, ed. A. L. Magnusson and C. E. McGee (Toronto: PD Meany, 1993), 166.

26 Blissett, 'The Oddness', 167.

27 Russ McDonald, *Shakespeare & Jonson/Jonson & Shakespeare* (Lincoln, NE: University of Nebraska Press, 1988), 58.

28 Ibid., 58.

29 Heywood, *Four Prentices*, Prologue.37–41.

30 Jonson preferred to have his plays printed in French scenes, meaning a new scene begins when a new character enters, to mimic classical precedents; however, most drama of the period used the cleared stage as the demarcation for a new scene (see Chapter 3). Importantly in performance, this play highlights its English not French scenes because of the commentary from the Grex. Their longer sections of dialogue take place during cleared stages, while they usually only exchange a line or two if other characters are on stage. Therefore, the structure is different depending on who experiences the play, audience or reader. Furthermore, one of the cleared stages that the Grex does not speak during is not treated as a scene break in the Folio version of the play (between 4.1/4.2 in *CWBJ*); therefore, there is even a difference in how the readers would experience the Grex and the scene breaks. For another aspect of the difference of scene breaks and their importance to *Every Man Out* in print, see Helen Ostovich, '"To Behold the Scene Full": Seeing and Judging in *Every Man Out*', in *Re-Presenting Ben Jonson: Text, History, Performance*, ed. Martin Butler (New York: St. Martin's Press, 1999), 76–7, 90.

31 The only two cleared stages without Grex commentary are between 4.1/4.2 and 5.5/5.6. The former is not treated as a scene break in the Folio and gives the implication that the stage is not really cleared as Delirio and Macilente enter in the same space as the preceding scene and speak a short three-line exchange before exiting. The second break changes locations and characters and so should have Grex commentary, but neither Cordatus nor Mitis speak until after the first line of the scene. The delayed nature of this Grex commentary plays with our expectations.

32 This contrasts Beaumont's *Knight of the Burning Pestle* (1607). The Wife and the Citizen there are more regularly and incessantly interruptive in their engagement with the theatrical material. Their over-involvement actually reduces their interruptive qualities as they become clearly part of the play itself. Consider for example, a production of *Every Man Out* without the Grex; it is a play that could stand on its own without much alteration. However, *The Knight of the Burning Pestle* is a play that cannot exist without the Wife and the Citizen. As much as Beaumont's play is about audience interruption, it ultimately becomes indistinguishable from the play because of its thorough integration.

33 The variety of people attendant in a public playhouse like The Globe would mean that fewer people would have had the education to easily follow the Latin delivered; hence the usual delivery of a brief

translation. Macilente's first line as well is a Latin phrase without translation.

34 As theatrical footnotes, the Grex are always interruptive. However, unlike a footnote that can be ignored, the Grex would have to be acknowledged in either reading or performance.

35 Barton says that the Cordatus/Mitis exchange 'serves to trivialize and undercut a repentance that already seems oddly stilted and artificial'. Barton, *Ben Jonson*, 67. Watson notes that the scene 'has been condemned as an unrealistic piece of dramatic convenience' and uses Mitis's line to support such a reading. Watson, *Ben Jonson's Parodic Strategy*, 60. What both critics miss is how Jonson plays a theatrical game of interruption that has to do with audience expectation, which questions all theatrical moments and their artificial natures.

36 Fletcher's letter to the reader of his tragicomedy *The Faithful Shepherdess* famously defined the genre as 'not so called in respect of mirth and killing, but in respect it wants deaths . . . yet brings some neere it'. John Fletcher, *The Faithful Shepherdess by John Fletcher: A Critical Edition*, ed. Florence Ada Kirk (New York: Garland Publishing, 1980), 15.

37 For more on this prologue, see Chapter 5.

38 Watson, *Ben Jonson's Parodic Strategy*, 47.

39 John Gordon Sweeney, *Jonson and the Psychology of Public Theater: To Coin the Spirit, Spend the Soul* (Princeton: Princeton University Press, 1985), 25.

40 Robert Kean Turner and Virginia Westling Haas, ed. *A New Variorum Edition of Shakespeare's The Winter's Tale* (New York: The Modern Language Association of America, 2005), 745.

41 Alison Findlay, 'Ceremonies and Time in Shakespeare', *Shakespeare* 15, no. 3 (2019): 230.

42 Wiggins and Richardson date *The Woman Hater*, *Cupid's Revenge*, and *The Faithfull Shepherdess* to 1607–8 and place *Philaster* and *The Coxcomb* in 1609, which is the year that *The New Oxford Shakespeare* argues for the best guess to dating *The Winter's Tale*. Both *The Woman Hater* and *Cupid's Revenge* are collaborative plays written with Beaumont. Wiggins and Richardson place *The Winter's Tale* in 1611, which would premiere after *Philaster* and *The Coxcomb*, as well as after *The Woman's Prize* and *The Scornful Lady*, and in the same year as *A King and No King* and *The Maid's Tragedy*. The Wiggins and Richardson date then further emphasizes the idea that Beaumont and Fletcher influenced Shakespeare.

43 Lee Bliss, 'Tragicomic Romance for the King's Men, 1609–1611: Shakespeare, Beaumont, and Fletcher', in *Comedy from Shakespeare to Sheridan: Change and Continuity in the English and European Dramatic Tradition, Essays in Honor of Eugene M. Waith*, ed. A. R. Braunmuller and J. C. Bulman (Newark, DE: University of Delaware Press, 1986), 148–9.

44 Geoffrey Bullough, *Narrative and Dramatic Sources of Shakespeare*, vol. 8 (New York: Columbia University Press, 1975), 118. Terri Bourus, ed. *The Winter's Tale* by William Shakespeare, in *The New Oxford Shakespeare: Critical Reference Edition*, ed. Gary Taylor et al., vol. 2 (Oxford: Oxford University Press, 2017), 2217.

45 For more on surprise endings, see Chapter 5.

46 Yayoi Miyashita lays out the significant critical voices concerning both the beginning and Leontes's jealousy. Yayoi Miyashita, 'Authorial Design in *The Winter's Tale*: Evaluation of the Statue Scene from a Narrative Point of View', *The Annual Report on Cultural Studies: Hokkaido University* 122 (2007): 64 and *passim*.

47 Turner and Haas, ed. *A New Variorum Edition*, 620.

48 Inga-Stina Ewbank, 'From Narrative to Dramatic Language: *The Winter's Tale* and Its Source', in *Shakespeare and the Sense of Performance: Essays in the Tradition of Performance Criticism in Honor of Bernard Beckerman*, ed. Marvin and Ruth Thompson (Newark, DE: University of Delaware Press, 1989), 32.

49 Turner and Haas, ed. *A New Variorum Edition*, 620–1.

50 The printed version of *Every Man Out* included a series of 'Characters' that describe the qualities and attributes for each character within the play.

51 Turner and Haas, ed. *A New Variorum Edition*, 621.

52 This paragraph is separated from the main body of text by a white space. No other such separations occur until the text of the oracle is completely offset several pages later.

53 Such an opening closely resembles Beaumont and Fletcher's *Philaster*, *A King and No King*, and *The Maid's Tragedy* as well as Shakespeare's *Cymbeline*. This type of exposition is prefigured in *King Lear* with Gloucester and Kent, but even they are not quite the same as they are less functionary and more integral to both plot and subplot that are begun in their exchange.

54 Charles Frey, 'Tragic Structure in *The Winter's Tale*: The Affective Dimension', in *Shakespeare's Romances Reconsidered*, ed. Carol McGinnis Kay and Henry E. Jacobs (Lincoln, NE: University of Nebraska Press, 1978), 120.

55 Fitzroy Pyle, *The Winter's Tale: A Commentary on the Structure* (London: Routledge & Kegan Paul, 1969), 10.
56 Turner and Haas, ed. *A New Variorum Edition*, 15.
57 While the Folio and the Arden 3 place a full stop here, Terri Bourus in the *New Oxford* uses a dash, beginning the interruptive quality of the exchange even earlier.
58 The Arden 3 text eliminates this dash, which is one of the few clearly interruptive dashes found in the 1623 Folio.
59 Steven R. Mentz, 'Wearing Greene: Autolycus, Robert Greene, and the Structure of Romance in *The Winter's Tale*', *Renaissance Drama* 30 (1999–2000): 73.
60 M. M. Mahood, *Bit Parts in Shakespeare Plays* (Cambridge: Cambridge University Press, 1992), 35.
61 Miyashita, 'Authorial Design', 62.
62 C. B. Hardman, 'Theory, Form, and Meaning in Shakespeare's *The Winter's Tale*', *The Review of English Studies* 36, no. 142 (1985): 229.
63 The bear in particular provides further consideration of rupture as it has no antecedent in *Pandosto* or any other source material other than bears generally in the culture at the time. William Blissett offers that a recent bear fighting event might have precipitated the inclusion. William Blisset, 'This Wide Gap of Time: *The Winter's Tale*', *English Literary Renaissance* 1, no. 1 (1971): 57.
64 Bertrand Evans, *Shakespeare's Comedies* (Oxford: Oxford University Press, 1960), 310.
65 Ibid., 296. Evans's beautifully narrative consideration of the play and this rupture often returns to his assertion that Shakespeare lied to the audience about Hermione's death. His reiteration of this lie seems as if Evans takes it personally that Shakespeare chose not to avoid such a dilemma. In fact, he spends most of his time on the play comfortably, and seemingly more happily, discussing *Act Four* when Perdita's true identity is known only to the audience, thereby creating dramatic irony (298–309).
66 Charles W. Hieatt, 'The Function of Structure in *The Winter's Tale*', *The Yearbook of English Studies* 8 (1978): 17.
67 While the oracle alerts us to the reunion of the end of the play, specifically addressing Perdita, it does not address Hermione. As Mamillius remains dead and as Greene did not revive Hermione, we have no reason to assume that the resolution includes the reunion of Hermione with husband and daughter.

68 Pyle presents another reading in which he sees all of the structure as not only intentional but rather fully mystical in crafting a 'delusion' for the audience so that we might get a 'sense of the miracle'. Pyle, *The Winter's Tale*, 136.

69 Evans, *Shakespeare's Comedies*, 314. Even before the scene with the statue, Paulina clearly hints at Hermione's survival through her insistence that Leontes not remarry without her express permission (see 5.1.69–84).

70 For an insightful reading of this play in performance at the Blackfriars, see Farah Karim-Cooper, 'To Glisten in a Playhouse: Cosmetic Beauty Indoors', in *Moving Shakespeare Indoors: Performance and Repertoire in the Jacobean Playhouse*, ed. Andrew Gurr and Farah Karim-Cooper (Cambridge: Cambridge University Press, 2014), 197–200.

71 The Arden 3 edition by John Pitcher places the descent after line 103, and *The New Oxford Shakespeare* places it at line 99. The Folio gives no stage direction and Paulina's entire speech gives various options for Hermione's movement and descent.

72 Helena Faucit, Lady Martin, *On Some of Shakespeare's Female Characters*, 7th ed. (Edinburgh: Blackwood and Sons, 1904), 386.

73 Evans, *Shakespeare's Comedies*, 312.

74 Jess Hamlet provides an insightful reading of this final scene but argues that Perdita loses power in Hermione's restoration. Jess Hamlet, '"Born in a Tempest When My Mother Died": Shakespeare's Motherless Daughters', in *The Absent Mother in the Cultural Imagination: Missing, Presumed Dead*, ed. Berit Åström (London: Palgrave Macmillan, 2017), 121. While Perdita does not have any speeches once her mother revives, the interaction between the two would be theatrically powerful as a moment of reunion.

75 Shakespeare's interruptions in dramaturgy are perhaps harder than most all other playwrights to perceive because they have been excavated from so many angles and their dramaturgies iterated and reiterated through reading, teaching, and performance. I have attempted here to examine his perhaps most significant contribution to the dramaturgical interruption by focusing on *The Winter's Tale*. One other place where he explores this complication is *Love's Labours Lost*. For a reading of this work's usage of interruption, see H. R. Woudhuysen '"Dead, for My Life": Stopping, Starting and Interrupting in *Love's Labour's Lost*'. *Actes des congrès de la Société française Shakespeare* 32 (2015): para. 1–37, DOI: 10.4000/shakespeare.2892.

76 Cyrus Hoy, 'Fletcherean Romantic Comedy', *Research Opportunities in Renaissance Drama* 27 (1984): 11. Hoy also thought the play was Fletcher's final one, but recent dating places it in 1617, just after *The Mad Lover* (1616), and before *The Loyal Subject* (1618) and *The Humorous Lieutenant* (1619).

77 Charles L. Squier, *John Fletcher* (Boston: Twayne Publishers, 1986), 131.

78 Joyce Boro and Diana de Armas Wilson denigrate Fletcher's handling of the maternal images found in Cervantes, while Mary Bjork and Celia Caputi have explored Fletcher's complicated presentation of characters. Bjork notes that Fletcher was 'an iconoclast committed to tearing down myths about honor' (41), and Caputi avers that the play is 'more subversive' upon further inspection and argues that a 'more sexualized, earthy Madonna . . . means a less dichotomized view of womankind' ('A Whore' 7, 5). Joyce Boro, 'Blessed with a Baby or "Bum-Fidled with a Bastard"? Maternity in Fletcher's *The Chances* and Cervantes' *Novela de la señora Cornelia*', in *The Creation and Re-Creation of* Cardenio: *Performing Shakespeare, Transforming Cervantes*, ed. Terri Bourus and Gary Taylor (London: Palgrave Macmillan, 2013), 61–72. Diana de Armas Wilson, 'Of Piracy and Plackets: Cervantes' *La señora Cornelia* and Fletcher's *The Chances*', in *Cervantes for the 21st Century/Cervantes para el siglo XXI: Studies in Honor of Edward Dudley*, ed. Francisco La Rubia Prado (Newark, DE: Juan de la Cuesta Hispanic Monographs, 2000), 49–60. Mary Lucille Dudy Bjork, 'Golden Age Spanish Prose and Jacobean Drama' (PhD diss., University of California, Santa Barbara, 2005). Celia Caputi, '"A Whore You Are, Madam", or the Binary that Wasn't: Female Dyads and Doubling in John Fletcher's *The Chances* and *Women Pleased*', *Early Modern Literary Studies* 27 (2017): 1–15.

79 John Jones and John Macklin, ed. *Exemplary Novels IV: Lady Cornelia, The Deceitful Marriage, The Dialogue of the Dogs*, by Miguel de Cervantes Saavedra (Warminster: Aris & Phillips Ltd, 1992), 2.

80 Bjork, 'Golden Age Spanish Prose', 57.

81 For a fuller account of the plot, see Martin Wiggins with Catherine Richardson, *British Drama 1533–1642: A Catalogue*, vol. VII (Oxford: Oxford University Press), #1819, 12–13.

82 Bjork, 'Golden Age Spanish Prose', 38.

83 Jones and Macklin, ed. *Exemplary Novels IV*, 15.

84 The closest other play out of all the plays with even a bit of Fletcher's hand is *The Night Walker* with eight scenes in its first act. George Walton Williams's edition of *The Chances* erases the numbers of scenes within the first act by grouping the Folio's scene 4 with the preceding scene 3. He does so without brackets, presenting the stage direction for what should be scene 5 as '[I.]iv', which indicates his editorial inclusion of the act but his following of the Folio with the scene, which is inaccurate. In the introduction, he explains that the dialogue gives no indication of a location shift and though earlier editors use the Folio's scene break with the stage direction 'Another street', he finds that unnecessary. John Fletcher, *The Chances*, ed. George Walton Williams, in *The Dramatic Works in the Beaumont and Fletcher Canon*, ed. Fredson Bowers, vol. IV (Cambridge: Cambridge University Press, 1979), 547. Williams furthermore notes that the scene break also breaks up a line of verse. However, John's line before the exit, 'If it hit right, Ile blesse this night', gives a compacted exit couplet that would seem to close out the scene. This simply means that Frederick begins the scene with a short line ''Tis strange'. Furthermore, the short scene that he wants to fold into scene 3 is a solo scene, which is a unique Fletcherean dramaturgy and here occurs twice in the act, further displaying the odd structures at play. See Michael M. Wagoner 'The Dramaturgical Space of Solo Scenes, or a Study of the Jailer's Daughter', *Shakespeare Bulletin* 35, no. 1 (2017): 97–118. While I will quote from Williams's edition, I place his scene numbers in brackets after the Folio's, which hold more authority in designating the dramaturgy of the act.

85 While Jonson's use of French scenes drives up the number of scenes in some later plays like *The Magnetic Lady* (with eight), as they have few cleared stages, they possess significantly fewer English scenes. Also, Shakespeare did not use act breaks with his plays until the move to Blackfriars and all such designations are generally editorial. Even with such divisions, his later plays like *Cymbeline* (with six) and *Macbeth* (with seven) come closest. *Coriolanus* has the most with eleven as it features several alarums in the first act that add to the many scene breaks; this most closely resembles the second highest in the Shakespeare canon *1 Henry VI* with eight, but that play's entire first act was written by Thomas Nashe. However, Claire Bourne's work argues against seeing the alarums as creating scene breaks, which would reduce the number in both plays. Claire M. L. Bourne, *Typographies of Performance in Early Modern England* (Oxford: Oxford University Press, 2020), 149. Therefore, *The Chances* presents an anomaly in its first act dramaturgy by including a barrage of scenes with cleared stages and no alarums.

86 The play is Fletcher's shortest trailing *The Mad Lover* by about 170 lines. The first act has 479 lines, *Act Two* has 399 lines, *Act Three* has 422, *Act Four* has 246, and *Act Five* has 281.

87 For the complete opposite effect in exposition, consider Shakespeare's *The Tempest*, which stalls out in the second scene of *Act One* and its 500 lines of narrative exposition. Even amid Prospero's self-interruptions in his story to Miranda, the tale tumbles forward and is succeeded by a pageant of important characters as we meet first Ariel, then Caliban, and then Ferdinand.

88 *The Oxford English Dictionary Online* (2018), 'chance'.

89 *Twelfth Night* also does not help the audience orient itself unless it alludes to the festival nature of Christmas and Epiphany, towards which the subtitle *What You Will* might lead an audience. Shakespeare's title then points towards genre, in a way that *The Chances* does not. Chance can be good or bad. Furthermore, *Twelfth Night* also gives a sense of ordered structure: *Twelfth Night* indicates a regular, repeated sequence. *The Chances* emphasizes unpredictability.

90 In the twentieth century, Samuel Beckett will do this.

91 All citations are from John Fletcher, *The Chances*, ed. George Walton Williams, in *The Dramatic Works in the Beaumont and Fletcher Canon*, ed. Fredson Bowers, vol. IV (Cambridge: Cambridge University Press, 1979) and will be parenthetically cited. However, the scene numbers follow the Folio with Williams's numbers in brackets afterward; see note 84.

92 As the issue of an audience's knowledge of names is important to my ensuing analysis, I here put names that an audience member does not know in square brackets to call attention to that ambiguity.

93 Consider *The Winter's Tale*, which clearly articulates the position of the masters as part of their names, Camillo's name, and Mamillius's name. We do not learn Archidamus's name, but he does not appear again. Also, consider *Cymbeline*. It begins with two unnamed lords who deliver a heavy dose of narrative exposition full of names and rank identifiers for the audience to follow. My emphasis on names here comes from Fletcher's overemphasis on an unimportant name. Admittedly, in performance other signifiers, especially non-linguistic ones, would aid in identification of character; however, that does not help when trying to identify characters who are not on stage and whom we need to know.

94 Bjork, 'Golden Age Spanish Prose', 38.

95 Ibid., 54.

96 Fletcher returns to the uncertainty and doubling of naming later in the play when the whore who is mistaken for Constantia has the exact same name. Caputi, 'A Whore', 7–8. Additionally, Fletcher did not seem overly invested in printing his plays during his lifetime. Only nine plays that he worked on were printed before his death in 1625, and the only solo play of his to receive publication was *The Faithful Shepherdess*, printed in 1610. Meaning that he might not have thought about how the plays work as reading texts, while he surely was considering how they worked as theatrical ones.

97 Megan Snell in her reading of this scene points out the baby's connection to objects and things, connecting this moment to Middleton's use of a baby in *A Chaste Maid in Cheapside*. Megan Snell, 'Shakespeare's Babies: "Things to Come at Large"', in *Shakespeare's Things: Shakespearean Theatre and the Non-Human World in History, Theory, and Performance*, ed. Brett Gamboa and Lawrence Switzky (New York: Routledge, 2019), 81–3.

98 Boro, 'Blessed with a Baby', 68.

99 Wagoner, 'The Dramaturgical Space', 108.

100 That speech is the Duke's in scene 10[9].13–30. Note: Williams' line numbering in this scene is wrong: he skips line 11.

101 The closest corollary is the Jailer's Daughter in 2.6, with thirty-nine lines.

102 James Hirsch, *The Structure of Shakespearean Scenes* (New Haven: Yale University Pres, 1981), 51.

103 Why four of the six plays with on stage infants are collaborative is unclear. Shakespeare wrote the infant scenes in *Titus Andronicus*, *3 Henry VI*, and *Pericles*, but Fletcher wrote the one for *All is True*. Both *Four Plays in One* and *The Knight of Malta* have infants on stage, but both appear in sections written by Nathan Field and not Fletcher.

104 Snell, 'Shakespeare's Babies', 79–80.

105 Andrew Sofer, '"Take up the Bodies": Shakespeare's Body Parts, Babies, and Corpses', *Theatre Symposium* 18 (2010): 138–9.

106 Ibid., 138.

107 Randall Martin, 'Stepping into Risky Business: Jonson's Canine Ventures in *Every Man Out of His Humour*', *The Ben Jonson Journal* 12 (2005): 1–2 and *passim*.

108 The availability of such a proposed prop is uncertain and merits further examination. The only cry from a Shakespearean infant is of Aaron's son offstage in *Titus Andronicus*, but that is merely reported not heard.

109 Jennifer Higginbotham, *The Girlhood of Shakespeare's Sisters: Gender, Transgression, Adolescence* (Edinburgh: Edinburgh University Press, 2013), 104.

110 Anne Varty discusses the perils of using a live baby, noting a performance when Ellen Terry was interrupted in a climatic moment by a live infant crying. Anne Varty, 'The Rise and Fall of the Victorian Stage Baby', *New Theatre Quarterly* 21, no. 3 (2005): 218–19 and *passim*. Notably, the interruption caused laughter from the audience; therefore, using a baby in a comedy as in *The Chances* would yield the proper affective response, like Crab in *TGV*. See also Andrew Sofer, *The Stage Life of Props* (Ann Arbor: University of Michigan Press, 2003), 51–7.

111 Once more I must disagree with Williams's edition, which adds asides to both Frederick's line before this one and to the first half of this line and places a dash in between 'perish'd' and 'Sir'. The aside here would undo the scene as, especially in the dark, Constantia's hearing Frederick's voice should be part of the cue that this is the wrong man. Also, there is no reason why Frederick cannot hear her brief lament. Her inability to conceal such thoughts would bolster the expediency of the moment.

112 Caputi, 'A Whore', 4 and *passim*. Her readings of this play and *Women Pleas'd*, as well as her work on *The Tamer Tamed* in 'A Tale of Two Tamings', argue that Fletcher's treatment of women, while not making him anachronistically a feminist, suggests that he had some feminist ideas, so she offers the term 'proto-feminist.' This assessment is one that I repeatedly come back to in reading his plays, especially in comparison to Shakespeare and Jonson.

113 Frederick is finally identified by John in the scene before as he talks to the landlady about the baby. Constantia is not identified as Constantia until the end of *Act Two*.

Chapter 5

1 See Chapter 4.
2 Bert O. States, *Great Reckonings in Little Rooms: On the Phenomenology of Theater* (Berkeley: University of California Press, 1985), 12.

3 Jeremy Lopez, *Theatrical Convention and Audience Response in Early Modern Drama* (Cambridge: Cambridge University Press, 2003), 98–9.

4 Pamela Allen Brown, 'Why Did the English Stage Take Boys for Actresses?' *Shakespeare Survey*, vol. 70 (Cambridge: Cambridge University Press, 2017), 186–7. Stephen Orgel, *Impersonations: The Performance of Gender in Shakespeare's England* (Cambridge: Cambridge University Press, 1996). Michael Shapiro, *Gender in Play on the Shakespearean Stage: Boy Heroines and Female Pages* (Ann Arbor: University of Michigan Press, 1994). Juliet Dusinberre, *Shakespeare and the Nature of Women* (New York: Barnes and Noble Books, 1975), 231–71. For cross-dressing issues more generally, see Marjorie Garber, *Vested Interests: Cross-dressing & Cultural Anxiety* (New York: Routledge, 1992), and Laurence Senelick, *The Changing Room: Sex, Drag, and Theatre* (New York: Routledge, 2000). Simone Chess provides a useful bibliography of this scholarship: Simone Chess, *Male to Female Cross-Dressing in Early Modern English Literature: Gender, Performance, and Queer Relations* (New York: Routledge, 2016), 26 n12.

5 David Kathman, 'How Old were Shakespeare's Boy Actors?' *Shakespeare Survey* 58 (Cambridge: Cambridge University Press, 2005), 220–1.

6 Orgel, *Impersonations*, 53.

7 Simone Chess's work, which I will discuss later, highlights the potential queered gendered identities that this type of performance produces regardless of the actor's own identification. The negotiation between audience and actor in the mode of character becomes an area of gendered assumption that only adds to the overall matrix of character that itself is communally crafted. See Michael M. Wagoner, 'Imaginative Bodies and Bodies Imagined: Extreme Casting in Shakespeare's *The Tempest* and Fletcher and Massinger's *The Sea Voyage*', in *The Bear Stage: Shaping Shakespeare for Performance*, ed. Sid Ray and Catherine Loomis (Madison: Farleigh Dickinson University Press, 2016), 111.

8 Chess, *Male to Female Cross-Dressing*, 2.

9 Shapiro, *Gender in Play*, 34. Victor Oscar Freeburg, *Disguise Plots in Elizabethan Drama: A Study in Stage Tradition* (New York: Columbia University Press, 1915), 101. Linda Woodbridge argues that the difference was because it was 'less attractive than female transvestism' and further connects this to the idea that 'Men had a greater horror of effeminacy than women of mannishness'. Linda

Woodbridge, *Women and the English Renaissance: Literature and the Nature of Womankind, 1540–1620* (Urbana-Chicago: University of Illinois Press, 1984), 157.

10 Shapiro, *Gender in Play*, 37.
11 Chess, *Male to Female Cross-Dressing*, 3.
12 Ibid., 1. Garber, *Vested Interests*, 125. Shapiro, *Gender in Play*, 34. Chess particularly notes the violence and danger of Falstaff's choice to cross-dress, as well as the misogynistic discourse that ensues.
13 Wiggins and Richardson date *The Shrew* to 1592, but the *New Oxford* offers 1591. If *The Shrew* is from 1591, then the final two plays are contemporaneous with it. Gary Taylor and Rory Loughnane, 'The Canon and Chronology of Shakespeare's Works', in *The New Oxford Shakespeare: Authorship Companion*, ed. Gary Taylor and Gabriel Egan (Oxford: Oxford University Press, 2017), 499.
14 This reflects Middleton's usage in *A Mad World, My Masters*, which Chess analyses alongside *Epicene*. Chess, *Male to Female Cross-Dressing*, 74–85.
15 Anonymous, *The Wars of Cyrus King of Persia, against Antiochus King of Assyria, with the Tragicall ende of Panthea* (London: Edward Allde for William Blackwal, 1594), sig. C3v.
16 Instead of being discovered, Libanio kills his would-be seducer Dinon, displaying a moment of agency in protecting herself. The stage direction reads 'She kills him', which, like Shakespeare's speech prefixes discussed later, participates in the theatrical layering of the gendered page. Anonymous, *The Wars of Cyrus*, sig. D4v.
17 Robert Greene, *The Historie of Orlando Furioso: One of the Twelve Pieres of France* (London: John Danter for Cuthbert Burby, 1594), sig. F1v–F2r.
18 Anonymous, *A Pleasant Conceyted Comedie of George a Greene, the Pinner of VVakefield* (London: Simon Stafford for Cuthburt Burby, 1599), sig. D1v.
19 Michael Shapiro, 'Framing the Taming: Metatheatrical Awareness of Female Impersonation in "The Taming of the Shrew"', *The Yearbook of English Studies* 23 (1993): 151.
20 The Arden 3 text supplies an exit for the Hostess before Sly's line, which eliminates this moment, but the Folio gives no such exit.
21 Lopez, *Theatrical Convention*, 81, 94.
22 Ibid., 95.

23 These transformative lines also reflect the transformation of Vincentio into the 'young budding virgin' by first Petruccio and then Katherine (4.5.29–42). There, however, the language is only imaginatively powerful as it does not effect the change that the Lord's language does over Bartholomew's identity.
24 The *New Oxford* retains the Folio speech prefixes both for Sly as 'Beggar' and for Bartholomew as 'Lady'. The Arden 3 edition changes the speech prefixes to Sly and Bartholomew.
25 Ind.1.4; Ind.2.17–19.
26 Peter Stallybrass argues that costumes in the theatre function as a type of naming. Peter Stallybrass, 'Naming, Renaming and Unnaming in the Shakespearean Quartos and Folios', in *The Renaissance Text: Theory, Editing, Textuality*, ed. Andrew Murphy (Manchester: Manchester University Press, 2000), 110.
27 See the discussion of exposition and Fletcher's *The Chances* in Chapter 4.
28 Graham Holderness and Bryan Loughery, ed. *A Pleasant Conceited Historie, Called The Taming of a Shrew* (New York: Harvester Wheatsheaf, 1992), 45.
29 Keri Elam, '"Wanton Pictures": The Baffling of Christopher Sly and the Visual-Verbal Intercourse of Early Modern Erotic Arts', in *Shakespeare and the Italian Renaissance: Appropriation, Transformation, Opposition*, ed. Michele Marrapodi (Burlington, VT: Ashgate, 2014), 123, 126–34.
30 This is not true in *A Shrew*, where the audience is introduced to the Boy as Boy before he enters as Lady.
31 Because of the thoroughness of the central MTF cross-dressing characters in this chapter, I use gendered pronouns appropriate to their gender in the moment that I am discussing.
32 Both *The Wars of Cyrus* and *George a Greene* use speech prefixes that align with the character beneath the disguise.
33 Stallybrass, 'Naming, Renaming and Unnaming', 111.
34 As this line and the Lord's line of taking Sly to his bed might indicate, there could be a bed on the stage. I have found no performative precedent as to whether this was done in the period, especially in the 'aloft' area as the stage directions indicate. Celia Daileader explores the tension of the off-stage bedroom in the above space. Celia Daileader, *Eroticism on the Renaissance Stage: Transcendence, Desire, and the Limits of the Visible* (Cambridge: Cambridge University Press, 1998), 40 and *passim*.

35 While the Folio does not contain an exit for the Lord, as he is no longer necessary, most editors include an exit after Sly's command.
36 After a brief bawdy exchange in *A Shrew*, the Lord steps in to keep any further encounter from happening. The two conventions—disguise and MTF cross-dressing—achieve their joke and are no longer necessary. Furthermore, the Boy returns to the acting troupe to be part of the play-within-a-play, perhaps playing one of the several female characters, or, just as the fool Sanders plays Sanders during the play-within-the-play, the Boy might play the 'Boy'. If this is true, then the artificiality of the women characters in the play would never be specifically ruptured because we would never see them as otherwise. Furthermore, the Boy as Lady would only be seen in the one scene of the Induction, and in the rest of the play, he would remain the Boy. The text as is requires four boy actors because the final scene stages all three sisters with the Boy on stage at the same time. Therefore, while the Boy certainly could double as one of the three sisters, he does not have to, and the play almost wants to avoid that. Because of this structured use of the boy as Lady, *A Shrew* specifically makes the MTF cross-dressing a brief comedic bit that removes further complications.
37 Shapiro, *Gender in Play*, 136–7. Chess, *Male-to-Female Crossdressing*, 55–9. Freeburg, *Disguise Plots*, 87. Both Chapman and Jonson participated in a wave of plays employing MTF cross-dressing in light of the renewed children's companies between 1599 and 1610. Gurr, *The Shakespearean Stage*, 66–71. During that period, fifteen plays contained an instance of MTF cross-dressing, and of those plays, twelve were performed by children's companies. See Table 5.1.
38 Sean McEvoy, *Ben Jonson: Renaissance Dramatist* (Edinburgh: Edinburgh University Press, 2008), 85–91.
39 Jenny C. Mann, '"The 'Figure of Exchange"': Shakespeare's "Master Mistress," Jonson's *Epicene*, and the English Art of Rhetoric', *Renaissance Drama* 38 (2010): 185–6.
40 Sweeney, *Jonson and the Psychology of Public Theater*, 7.
41 Richard Dutton, *Ben Jonson: To the First Folio* (Cambridge: Cambridge University Press, 1983), 105.
42 Katharine Eisaman Maus, Introduction, *Epicene* by Ben Jonson, in *English Renaissance Drama: A Norton Anthology*, ed. David Bevington (New York: W.W. Norton & Co., 2002), 780.
43 William W. E. Slights, *Ben Jonson and the Art of Secrecy* (Toronto: University of Toronto Press, 1994), 81.

44 Lucy Munro, *Children of the Queen's Revels: A Jacobean Theatre Repertory* (Cambridge: Cambridge University Press, 2005), 51.

45 Tiffany Stern, *Documents of Performance in Early Modern England* (Cambridge: Cambridge University Press, 2009), 56.

46 Bevington, '*Epicene*: Textual Essay', in *The Cambridge Edition of the Works of Ben Jonson Online* (Cambridge: Cambridge University Press), 1.

47 William Drummond, 'Ben Jonson's Conversations with William Drummond of Hawthornden', in *Ben Jonson*, ed. C. H. Herford and Percy Simpson, vol. I (Oxford: Oxford University Press, 1925), 151.

48 A more complex example is Fletcher's *The Humorous Lieutenant*, which also has two completely different titles: *Demetrius and Enanthe* and *The Noble Enemy* or *Noble Enemies*.

49 Wiggins with Richardson, *British Drama*, vol. VI, 36.

50 A quick search on the *MLA International Bibliography* reveals that critical discourse over the play has preferred to use *Epicoene* rather than *Epicene*; however, the most recent editions of the play (Maus 2002, Dutton 2003, and Bevington 2012) all use the 'modernized' spelling of the title.

51 Wiggins with Richardson, *British Drama*, vol. VI, 36.

52 'epicene, adj. and n', *Oxford English Dictionary Online*, January 2018, www.oed.com/view/Entry/63248. Accessed 22 January 2018.

53 Jonson's other plays *Volpone, or The Fox* and *Poetaster, or The Arraignment* provide two analogues in title construction. Wiggins notes that *Poetaster* was a printed addition to the performance title of *The Arraignment*, which would accord with his reading of *Epicoene*. However, he does not offer the same for *Volpone*, which is the closer parallel as the first word is not a title but a specific character's name: a name, importantly, that indicates specific information about the character that is useful to an audience member. Again, the only source I can find for thinking that the performed play only had the title of *The Silent Woman* is Drummond's *Informations*, which to make his keen quip does not necessarily record the full title. The jest is lost or muddied with the addition of *Epicoene* into the joke.

54 'epicene, adj. and n', *Oxford English Dictionary Online*.

55 Slights, *Ben Jonson*, 99. Bevington, Introduction, *Epicene, or The Silent Woman* by Ben Jonson, in *The Cambridge Edition of the Works of Ben Jonson*, ed. David Bevington, Martin Butler, and Ian Donaldson, vol. 3 (Cambridge: Cambridge University Press, 2012), 383.

56 Reuben Sanchez, '"Things Like Truths, Well Feigned": Mimesis and Secrecy in Jonson's *Epicoene*', *Comparative Drama* 40, no. 3 (2006): 318.
57 Sanchez almost advocates that the play functions through dramatic irony, in which we clearly see Epicene's disguise. I do not completely agree because just knowing what epicene means does not mean that we can know what Jonson wants to do with gender ambiguity as I will demonstrate in reading the interruptions and constructions of the final scene.
58 One example of a truly surprise ending that has to do with gendered disguise is Beaumont and Fletcher's *Philaster*, which does not give any indication of Bellario's identity as a woman until she reveals it at the end. Jonson would later use this convention in *The New Inn*, which in performance disguises the true identity of Franck as the long-lost sister of Lady Frampul, making his/her marriage to Beaufort genuine. In the printed version, Jonson removes the surprise by adding an argument that specifically delineates the reveal. Jonson seems to then want his audiences to figure out what are seeming surprises in a way that Beaumont and Fletcher do not.
59 Ben Jonson, *Epicene, or The Silent Woman*, ed. David Bevington, in *The Cambridge Edition of the Works of Ben Jonson*, ed. David Bevington, Martin Butler, and Ian Donaldson, vol. 3 (Cambridge: Cambridge University Press, 2016), 1.2.24–26. All citations come from this edition and will be cited parenthetically.
60 Bevington, Introduction, 383.
61 Ben Jonson, *The Workes of Beniamin Jonson*. Will Stansby, 1616, sig. Xx6v.
62 Slights, *Ben Jonson*, 79.
63 Ibid., 79.
64 Shapiro, in his reading of the play, states, 'In the following pages, I describe the audience's attitudes and behaviour and examine the dramatists' efforts to prevent the audience from disrupting their plays. Whereas many playwrights addressed themselves extra-dramatically to this problem in prologues and inductions, others—Ben Jonson in *Epicoene*, most notably—tried to elicit sympathetic attentiveness by dramaturgical manipulation of the audience.' Michael Shapiro, 'Audience v. Dramatist in Jonson's *Epicoene* and Other Plays of the Children's Troupes', *English Literary Renaissance* 3 (1973): 401. I agree with this general assessment, though as I have just demonstrated, I think the Prologue here significantly participates in the game that Jonson sets out to play. Additionally,

Shapiro's article sounds like a reading of the structure of the drama and its method of affecting the audience, but it avoids a discussion of Mistress Epicene and instead focuses on the three wits and their connection to gentleman types in the audience.

65 Simon Palfrey and Tiffany Stern, *Shakespeare in Parts* (Oxford: Oxford University Press, 2007), 163 and *passim*.

66 This reflects the Mosca/Volpone relationship that I discuss in Chapter 1. Jonson wrote *Epicene* just after *Volpone*.

67 Phyllis Rackin, 'Androgyny, Mimesis, and the Marriage of the Boy Heroine on the English Renaissance Stage', *PMLA* 102, no. 1 (1987): 31.

68 Richmond Barbour, '"When I Acted Young Antinous": Boy Actors and the Erotics of Jonsonian Theater'. *PMLA* 110, no. 5 (1995): 1016.

69 Jean Howard, 'Crossdressing, The Theatre, and Gender Struggle in Early Modern England', *Shakespeare Quarterly* 39, no. 4 (1988): 430.

70 Chess, *Male-to-Female Crossdressing*, 85.

71 Ibid.

72 Dutton, *Ben Jonson*, 102.

73 Ibid., 105.

74 Maus, Introduction, 780.

75 Philip Mirabelli, 'Silence, Wit, and Wisdom in *The Silent Woman*', *Studies in English Literature* 29 (1989): 336.

76 José A. Pérez-Díez, introduction, *Love's Cure, or the Martial Maid* by John Fletcher and Philip Massinger (Manchester: Manchester University Press, 2021), 39.

77 Pérez-Díez, introduction, 14–19.

78 Chess, *Male-to-Female Crossdressing*, 169.

79 Ibid., 184 n.9.

80 Philip J. Finkelpearl, *Court and Country Politics in the Plays of Beaumont and Fletcher* (Princeton: Princeton University Press, 1990), 219.

81 Nicholas F. Radel, 'Fletcherian Tragicomedy, Cross-dressing, and the Construction of Homoerotic Desire in Early Modern England', *Renaissance Drama* 26 (1995): 76 and *passim*.

82 Daryl W. Palmer, *Writing Russia in the Age of Shakespeare* (Burlington, VT: Ashgate, 2004), 203, 232.

83 Gordon McMullan, *The Politics of Unease in the Plays of John Fletcher* (Amherst: The University of Massachusetts Press, 1994), 260.

84 John Fletcher, *The Loyal Subject*, ed. Fredson Bowers, in *The Dramatic Works in the Beaumont and Fletcher Canon*, ed. Fredson Bowers, vol. V (Cambridge: Cambridge University Press, 1982), 1.1.1–6. All citations to this play are from this edition and will be cited parenthetically.

85 Sandra Clark, *The Plays of Beaumont and Fletcher: Sexual Themes and Dramatic Representation* (1994; repr., London: Routledge, 2013), 66–7. Peter Hyland briefly examines the play, saying that Fletcher must have used this disguise for no reason other than novelty. Furthermore, he cannot decide if we are to know about the gendered identity or not and concludes, 'Of course, since no audience is uniform, it is possible that Fletcher expected both responses'. Peter Hyland, *Disguise on the Early Modern Stage* (Burlington, VT: Ashgate, 2011), 65–6. Despite his almost negative tone, I think that is precisely the point.

86 Potentially, a production could highlight her lack of beauty to make Olimpia's infatuation seem ridiculous or even emphasize her masculinity to make the disguise apparent; however, as I am arguing, both approaches seem counter to the subtle presentation that Fletcher creates in playing around with our expectations and perceptions of character.

87 Radel, 'Fletcherian Tragicomedy', 74.

88 Ibid., 73.

89 Clark, *The Plays of Beaumont and Fletcher*, 67.

90 McMullan, *The Politics of Unease*, 76.

91 Daniel Morley McKeithan, *The Debt to Shakespeare in the Beaumont and Fletcher Plays* (1938; repr. New York: AMS Press, 1970), 115–18. Peter Berek, 'Cross-Dressing, Gender, and Absolutism in the Beaumont and Fletcher Plays', *Studies in English Literature 1500–1900* 44, no. 2 (2004): 366–8.

92 Berek, 'Cross-Dressing, Gender, and Absolutism', 366.

93 In this assessment, Berek ignores the dual interview of the Duke with first Alinda and then with Honora and Viola. Notably, it is the second group, the female characters not the male, that effect the change in the Duke's behaviour. Alinda becomes submissive and unclear, while Honora corrects the Duke's behaviour.

94 McKeithan, *The Debt to Shakespeare*, 116.

95 This part of the plot is found in neither of the play's major sources. McKeithan, *The Debt to Shakespeare*, 115.
96 John Masefield, ed. *The Loyal Subject* by John Fletcher, in *The Works of Francis Beaumont & John Fletcher: Variorum Edition*, ed. A. H. Bullen, vol. III (London: George Bell and Sons, 1908), IV.i.55SD.
97 Clark even says his appearance reassures audiences of a happy outcome. Clark, *The Plays of Beaumont and Fletcher*, 68.
98 Francis Beaumont and John Fletcher, *Comedies and Tragedies* (London: Humphrey Robinson and Humphrey Moseley, 1647), sig. Fff3v. Bowers adds '*as a young gentleman*', which supports the text's portrayal of him as Alinda.
99 Dessen and Thomsen, *A Dictionary of Stage Directions*, 4.
100 Thomas Heywood, *The Second Part of If You Know Not Me, You Know Nobody* (London: Nathanial Butter, 1606), sig. H2v.
101 This makes this play fully align with Chess's goal of seeing the positive and productive space for MTF cross-dressers in the period's literature.

Continuation

1 Celia Caputi, 'A Tale of Two Tamings: Reading the Early Modern Shrew Debate from a Feminist Transnationalist Perspective', in *Shakespeare, Italy, and Transnational Exchange: Early Modern to Present*, ed. Chris Stamatakis and Enza De Francisci (London: Routledge, 2017), 40.
2 Stephen Booth, *Precious Nonsense: The Gettysburg Address, Ben Jonson's Epitaphs on His Children, and Twelfth Night* (Berkeley, CA: University of California Press, 1998), ix.
3 *Cynthia's Revels* is usually considered part of the so-called Poet's War, mostly between Jonson and Marston, which may explain his decision to mirror Marston's Induction in *Antonio and Mellida*. However, *Antonio* is usually seen as not participating in the attacks, and commentators about Jonson's attacks in this Induction do not focus on its structure. James P. Bednarz, *Shakespeare and the Poets' War* (New York: Columbia University Press, 2001), 9, 157–8. If Heywood's *Four Prentices* predates *Cynthia's Revels*, then it too offers a precedent for Jonson; however, Wiggins and Richardson argue persuasively for a 1602 date for *Four Prentices*, which would mean that Heywood's play responds to Jonson's. Martin Wiggins, with

Catherine Richardson, *British Drama 1533–1642: A Catalogue*, vol. IV (Oxford: Oxford University Press, 2012–16), #1351, 408.

4 Ben Jonson, *Cynthia's Revels: Quarto Version*, ed. Eric Rasmussen and Matthew Steggle, in *The Cambridge Edition of the Works of Ben Jonson*, ed. David Bevington, Martin Butler, and Ian Donaldson, vol. 1 (Cambridge: Cambridge University Press, 2012), Praeludium.27–32.

5 For a thorough investigation of Jonson's development of this unique typography, see Bourne, *Typographies of Performance*, 94–7. She provides a reading of this same moment, but while her argument is ultimately that the breaches provide Jonson a typographical way to render stage action in print, she also states that the breaches 'functioned as textual correlatives for interruptions of the body (or, in this case, bodies) interrupting speech that would have been otherwise clear and sound' (96). I disagree with the final suggestion about the speeches being 'clear and sound'. As my reading shows, the issue at stake here in the Praeludium is the clarity of the performance, which both is and is not there because of the interruptions.

6 Jonson, *Cynthia's Revels*, Prologue.20.

7 Anne Barton, *Ben Jonson, Dramatist* (Cambridge: Cambridge University Press, 1984), 74. John Gordon Sweeney, *Jonson and the Psychology of Public Theater: To Coin the Spirit, Spend the Soul* (Princeton: Princeton University Press, 1985), 31. Richard Dutton, *Ben Jonson: To the First Folio* (Cambridge: Cambridge University Press, 1983), 43.

8 Tiffany Stern, *Documents of Performance in Early Modern England* (Cambridge: Cambridge University Press), 63–5.

9 Ibid., 66.

10 Ben Jonson, *The Works of Beniamin Jonson* (London: Will Stansby, 1616), sig. Q1v.

11 Jonson, *Cynthia's Revels*, Praeludium.58, 66.

12 Ibid., Praeludium.39, 51, 76, 79.

13 Ibid., Praeludium.43, 47, 54, 63, 64.

14 Ibid., Praeludium.77. The typographical representation seems pertinent, and here Rasmussen and Steggle (or perhaps Bevington, Butler, and Donaldson) do a disservice to their readers. Both the Q and F provide thick long black lines that give weight and space to the interruptive actions; however, the *CWBJ* only uses the smallest of em dashes, making these breaches almost imperceptible, whereas they are unmistakable in the early texts.

BIBLIOGRAPHY

Aebischer, Pascale. 'Didascalia and Speech in the Dramatic Text'. *Journal of Dramatic Theory and Criticism* 17, no. 2 (2003): 25–44.
Acheson, Katherine. 'Introduction: Marginalia, Reading, and Writing'. In *Early Modern English Marginalia*, edited by Katherine Acheson, 1–12. London: Routledge, 2019.
Alexander, Gavin. 'Sidney's Interruptions'. *Studies in Philology* 98, no. 2 (2001): 184–204.
Althusser, Louis. *Positions (1964–1975)*. Paris: Editions Sociales, 1976.
Angus, Bill. *Metadrama and the Informer in Shakespeare and Jonson*. Edinburgh: Edinburgh University Press, 2016.
Anonymous. *A Pleasant Conceyted Comedie of George a Greene, the Pinner of VVakefield*. London: Simon Stafford for Cuthburt Burby, 1599.
Anonymous. *The Wars of Cyrus King of Persia, against Antiochus King of Assyria, with the Tragicall ende of Panthea*. London: Edward Allde for William Blackwal, 1594.
Aristotle. *Aristotle's Poetics*. Translated by George Whalley. Edited by John Baxter and Patrick Atherton. Montreal: McGill-Queen's University Press, 1997.
Barbour, Richmond. '"When I Acted Young Antinous": Boy Actors and the Erotics of Jonsonian Theatre'. *PMLA* 110, no. 5 (1995): 1006–22.
Barton, Anne. *Ben Jonson, Dramatist*. Cambridge: Cambridge University Press, 1984.
Beaumont, Francis. *The Knight of the Burning Pestle*. Edited by Michael Hattaway. London: Methuen Drama, 2002.
Beaumont, Francis and John Fletcher. *Comedies and Tragedies*. London: Humphrey Robinson and Humphrey Moseley, 1647.
Beck, Sarah. 'Let There Be No More Woe for Jon Snow: The Dramaturgy of Spoilers'. In *Vying for the Iron Throne: Essays on Power, Gender, Death, and Performance in HBO's Game of Thrones*, edited by Lindsay Mantoan and Sara Brady, 182–96. Jefferson, NC: McFarland & Co., 2018.
Bednarz, James P. *Shakespeare and the Poets' War*. New York: Columbia University Press, 2001.

Belsey, Catherine. 'Beyond Reason: *Hamlet* and Early Modern Stage Ghosts'. In *Gothic Renaissance: A Reassessment*, edited by Elizabeth Bronfen and Beate Neumeier, 32–54. Manchester: Manchester University Press, 2014.

Belsey, Catherine. 'Shakespeare's Sad Tale for Winter: *Hamlet* and the Tradition of Fireside Ghost Stories'. *Shakespeare Quarterly* 61, no. 1 (2010): 1–27.

Berek, Peter. 'Cross-Dressing, Gender, and Absolutism in the Beaumont and Fletcher Plays'. *Studies in English Literature 1500–1900* 44, no. 2 (2004): 359–77.

Bevington, David. '*Catiline*: Textual Essay'. In *The Cambridge Edition of the Works of Ben Jonson Online*, 1–11. Cambridge: Cambridge University Press. http://universitypublishingonline.org/cambridge/benjonson/k/essays/Catiline_textual_essay/1/.

Bevington, David. '*Epicene*: Stage History'. In *The Cambridge Edition of the Works of Ben Jonson Online*, 1–16. Cambridge: Cambridge University Press. http://universitypublishingonline.org/cambridge/benjonson/k/essays/stage_history_Epicine/1/.

Bevington, David. '*Epicene*: Textual Essay'. In *The Cambridge Edition of the Works of Ben Jonson Online*, 1–12. Cambridge: Cambridge University Press. https://universitypublishingonline.org/cambridge/benjonson/k/essays/Epicene_textual_essay/1/.

Bevington, David. 'Introduction. *Epicene, or The Silent Woman* by Ben Jonson'. In *The Cambridge Edition of the Works of Ben Jonson*, edited by David Bevington, Martin Butler, and Ian Donaldson, vol. 3, 375–83. Cambridge: Cambridge University Press, 2012.

Bevington, David, ed. '*The Tempest* by William Shakespeare'. In *Shakespeare's Romances and Poems, 1570–1603*, 1570–603. New York: Pearson, 2007.

Bevington, David, Martin Butler, and Ian Donaldson. *General Introduction to The Cambridge Edition of the Works of Ben Jonson*, vol. 1, lx–lxxxvi. Cambridge: Cambridge University Press, 2012.

Bilmes, Jack. 'Being Interrupted'. *Language in Society* 26, no. 4 (1997): 507–31.

Bjork, Mary Lucille Dudy. 'Golden Age Spanish Prose and Jacobean Drama'. PhD diss., University of California, Santa Barbara, 2005.

Bliss, Lee. 'Tragicomic Romance for the King's Men, 1609–1611: Shakespeare, Beaumont, and Fletcher'. In *Comedy from Shakespeare to Sheridan: Change and Continuity in the English and European Dramatic Tradition, Essays in Honor of Eugene M. Waith*, edited by A. R. Braunmuller and J. C. Bulman, 148–64. Newark, DE: University of Delaware Press, 1986.

Blissett, William. 'The Oddness of *Every Man out of his Humour*'. In *The Elizabethan Theatre XII*, edited by A. L. Magnusson and C. E. McGee, 157–79. Toronto: PD Meany, 1993.

Blissett, William. 'This Wide Gap of Time: *The Winter's Tale*'. *English Literary Renaissance* 1, no. 1 (1971): 52–70.
Bogel, Fredric V. *New Formalist Criticism: Theory and Practice*. New York: Palgrave, 2013.
Booth, Stephen. *Precious Nonsense: The Gettysburg Address, Ben Jonson's Epitaphs on His Children, and Twelfth Night*. Berkeley, CA: University of California Press, 1998.
Bond, R. Warwick, ed. '*The Mad Lover* by John Fletcher'. In *The Works of Francis Beaumont & John Fletcher: Variorum Edition*, edited by A. H. Bullen, vol. III, 111–219. London: George Bell and Sons, 1908.
Boro, Joyce. 'Blessed with a Baby or "Bum-Fidled with a Bastard"? Maternity in Fletcher's *The Chances* and Cervantes' *Novela de la señora Cornelia*'. In *The Creation and Re-Creation of Cardenio: Performing Shakespeare, Transforming Cervantes*, edited by Terri Bourus and Gary Taylor, 61–72. London: Palgrave Macmillan, 2013.
Bourne, Claire M. L. *Typographies of Performance in Early Modern England*. Oxford: Oxford University Press, 2020.
Bourus, Terri. 'Enter Shakespeare's Young Hamlet, 1589'. *Actes des congrès de la Société française Shakespeare* 34 (2016): paras 1–36, DOI : 10.4000/shakespeare.3736.
Bourus, Terri. 'Poner en escena *The History of Cardenio*'. In *The Creation and Re-Creation of Cardenio*, edited by Terri Bourus and Gary Taylor, 197–221. London: Palgrave Macmillan, 2013.
Bourus, Terri. *Young Shakespeare's Young Hamlet: Print, Piracy, and Performance*. London: Palgrave Macmillan, 2014.
Bourus, Terri, ed. '*The Winter's Tale* by William Shakespeare'. In *The New Oxford Shakespeare: Critical Reference Edition*, edited by Gary Taylor et al., vol. 2, 2217–99. Oxford: Oxford University Press, 2017.
Bowers, Fredson, ed. 'The Woman's Prize, or the Tamer Tamed'. In *The Dramatic Works in the Beaumont and Fletcher Canon*, edited by Fredson Bowers, vol. IV, 1–148. Cambridge: Cambridge University Press.
Boyer, Arlynda. 'Actors Annotations and Paradoxical Editions of Shakespeare's Texts'. *Actes des congrès de la Société française Shakespeare* 39 (2021): paras 1–32. DOI: 10.4000/shakespeare.5993.
Bradshaw, Graham. *Misrepresentations: Shakespeare and the Materialists*. Ithaca: Cornell University Press, 1993.
Britland, Karen. 'Queen Henrietta Maria's Theatrical Patronage'. In *Henrietta Maria: Piety, Politics and Patronage*, edited by Erin Griffey, 57–72. Aldershot: Ashgate, 2008.
Brody, Jennifer DeVere. *Punctuation: Art, Politics, and Play*. Durham, NC: Duke University Press, 2008.
Brown, Pamela Allen. 'Why Did the English Stage Take Boys for Actresses?' *Shakespeare Survey* 70 (2017): 182–7. Cambridge: Cambridge University Press.

Bullough, Geoffrey. *Narrative and Dramatic Sources of Shakespeare*, vol. 8. New York: Columbia University Press, 1975.

Burrows, I. R. '"The Peryod of My Blisse": Commas, Ends and Utterances in *Soliman and Perseda*'. *Textual Cultures* 8, no. 2 (2013): 95–120.

Butler, Martin. 'Introduction: from *Workes* to Texts'. In *Re-Presenting Ben Jonson: Text, History, Performance*, edited by Martin Butler, 1–19. New York: St. Martin's Press, 1999.

Calderwood, John. *The Properties of Othello*. Amherst, MA: University of Massachusetts Press, 1989.

Caputi, Celia R. 'A Tale of Two Tamings: Reading the Early Modern Shrew Debate from a Feminist Transnationalist Perspective'. In *Shakespeare, Italy, and Transnational Exchange: Early Modern to Present*, edited by Chris Stamatakis and Enza De Francisci, 40–52. London: Routledge, 2017.

Caputi, Celia R. '"A Whore You Are, Madam", or the Binary that Wasn't: Female Dyads and Doubling in John Fletcher's *The Chances* and *Women Pleased*'. *Early Modern Literary Studies* 27 (2017): 1–15.

Carlson, Marvin. 'The Status of Stage Directions'. *Studies in the Literary Imagination* 24, no. 2 (1991): 37–48.

Cave, Richard. 'Script and Performance'. In *Ben Jonson and Theatre: Performance, Practice, and Theory*, edited by Richard Cave, Elizabeth Schafer, and Brian Woolland, 23–32. London: Routledge, 1999.

Cefalu, Paul. 'The Burdens of Mind Reading in Shakespeare's *Othello*: A Cognitive and Psychoanalytic Approach to Iago's Theory of Mind'. *Shakespeare Quarterly* 64, no. 3 (2013): 265–94.

'Chance, n., adj., and adv'. *The Oxford English Dictionary Online*, 2018. www.oed.com/view/Entry/30418. Accessed 7 February 2018.

Chess, Simone. *Male-to-Female Crossdressing in Early Modern English Literature: Gender, Performance, and Queer Relations*. London: Routledge, 2016.

Clark, Sandra. *The Plays of Beaumont and Fletcher: Sexual Themes and Dramatic Representation*. 1994. Reprint, London: Routledge, 2013.

Clubb, Louise George. 'Theatregrams'. In *Comparative Critical Approaches to Renaissance Comedy*, edited by Donald Beecher and Massimo Ciavolella, 15–33. Ottawa: Dovehouse Editions Canada, 1986.

Cook, Margaret McLaren and F. P. Wilson, eds. *Demetrius and Enanthe* by John Fletcher . Oxford: Malone Society, 1951.

Craik, T. W. '"Tell" in *The Tempest*, II.i.15: Speech or Stage Direction?'. *Notes and Queries* 44 (1997): 514.

Daileader, Celia R. *Eroticism on the Renaissance Stage: Transcendence, Desire, and the Limits of the Visible*. Cambridge: Cambridge University Press, 1998.

Daileader, Celia R. and Gary Taylor, eds. *The Tamer Tamed, or, The Woman's Prize* by John Fletcher . Manchester: Manchester University Press, 2006.
Derrida, Jacques, and Pierre-Jean Labarrière. *Altérités: Jacques Derrida et Pierre-Jean Labarrière, avec des études de Francis Guibal et Stanislas Breton*. Paris: Osiris, 1986.
de Somogyi, Nick, ed. *Macbeth* by William Shakespeare. London: Nick Hern Books, 2003.
Dessen, Alan C. and Leslie Thomson. *A Dictionary of Stage Directions in English Drama 1580–1642*. Cambridge: Cambridge University Press, 1999.
Donaldson, Ian. *Jonson's Magic Houses: Essays in Interpretation*. Oxford: Oxford University Press, 1997.
Doran, Madeleine. *Shakespeare's Dramatic Language*. Madison: The University of Wisconsin Press, 1976.
Dowd, Michelle. 'Dramaturgy and the Politics of Space in *The Tragedy of Mariam*'. *Renaissance Drama* 44, no. 1 (2016): 101–22.
Drummond, William. 'Ben Jonson's Conversations with William Drummond of Hawthornden'. In *Ben Jonson*, edited by C. H. Herford and Percy Simpson, vol. I, 128–78. Oxford: Oxford University Press, 1925.
Dusinberre, Juliet. *Shakespeare and the Nature of Women*. New York: Barnes and Noble Books, 1975.
Dustagheer, Sarah and Gillian Woods. Introduction. *Stage Directions and Shakespearean Theatre*, 1–16. London: Bloomsbury, 2018.
Dutton, Richard. *Ben Jonson: To the First Folio*. Cambridge: Cambridge University Press, 1983.
Dutton, Richard. *Licensing, Censorship, and Authorship in Early Modern England*. New York: Palgrave, 2000.
Dutton, Richard. '*Volpone*: Textual Essay'. In *The Cambridge Edition of the Works of Ben Jonson Online*, 1–15. Cambridge: Cambridge University Press. http://universitypublishingonline.org/cambridge/benjonson/k/essays/Volpone_textual_essay/1/
Elam, Keir. '"Wanton Pictures": The Baffling of Christopher Sly and the Visual-Verbal Intercourse of Early Modern Erotic Arts'. In *Shakespeare and the Italian Renaissance: Appropriation, Transformation, Opposition*, edited by Michele Marrapodi, 123–46. Burlington, VT: Ashgate, 2014.
'epicene, adj. and n'. *Oxford English Dictionary Online*, January 2018, www.oed.com/view/Entry/63248. Accessed 22 January 2018.
Evans, Bertrand. *Shakespeare's Comedies*. Oxford: Oxford University Press, 1960.
Ewbank, Inga-Stina. 'From Narrative to Dramatic Language: *The Winter's Tale* and Its Source'. In *Shakespeare and the Sense of Performance:*

Essays in the Tradition of Performance Criticism in Honor of Bernard Beckerman, edited by Marvin and Ruth Thompson, 29–47. Newark, DE: University of Delaware Press, 1989.
Faucit, Helena and Martin Lady. *On Some of Shakespeare's Female Characters*. 7th edn. Edinburgh: Blackwood and Sons, 1904.
Ferguson, George B., ed. *John Fletcher The Woman's Prize or The Tamer Tamed: A Critical Edition*. The Hague: Mouton & Co., 1966.
Findlay, Alison. 'Ceremonies and Time in Shakespeare'. *Shakespeare* 15, no. 3 (2019): 223–32.
Finkelpearl, Philip J. *Court and Country Politics in the Plays of Beaumont and Fletcher*. Princeton: Princeton University Press, 1990.
Fletcher, John. *The Chances*. Edited by George Walton Williams. In *The Dramatic Works in the Beaumont and Fletcher Canon*, edited by Fredson Bowers, vol. IV, 541–645. Cambridge: Cambridge University Press, 1979.
Fletcher, John. *The Faithful Shepherdess by John Fletcher: A Critical Edition*. Edited by Florence Ada Kirk. New York: Garland Publishing, 1980.
Fletcher, John. *The Humorous Lieutenant*. Edited by Cyrus Hoy. In *The Dramatic Works in the Beaumont and Fletcher Canon*, edited by Fredson Bowers, vol. V, 289–440. Cambridge: Cambridge University Press, 1982.
Fletcher, John. *The Loyal Subject*. Edited by Fredson Bowers. In *The Dramatic Works in the Beaumont and Fletcher Canon*, edited by Fredson Bowers, vol. V, 151–288. Cambridge: Cambridge University Press, 1982.
Fletcher, John. *The Mad Lover*. Edited by Robert Kean Turner. In *The Dramatic Works in the Beaumont and Fletcher Canon*, edited by Fredson Bowers, vol. V, 1–149. Cambridge: Cambridge University Press, 1982.
Fletcher, John. *Women Pleas'd*. Edited by Hans Walter Gabler. In *The Dramatic Works in the Beaumont and Fletcher Canon*, edited by Fredson Bowers, vol. V, 441–538. Cambridge: Cambridge University Press, 1982.
Fletcher, John. *The Wild-Goose Chase*. London: Humphrey Mosely, 1652.
Fletcher, John and Philip Massinger. *Beggars' Bush*. Edited by Fredson Bowers. In *The Dramatic Works in the Beaumont and Fletcher Canon*, edited by Fredson Bowers, vol. III, 225–362. Cambridge: Cambridge University Press, 1976.
Foucault, Michel. 'What is an Author?'. In *Textual Strategies: Perspectives in Post-Structuralist Criticism*, edited by Josuè V. Harari, 141–60. Ithaca: Cornell University Press, 1979.

Freeburg, Victor Oscar. *Disguise Plots in Elizabethan Drama: A Study in Stage Tradition*. New York: Columbia University Press, 1915.

Frey, Charles. 'Tragic Structure in *The Winter's Tale*: The Affective Dimension'. In *Shakespeare's Romances Reconsidered*, edited by Carol McGinnis Kay and Henry E. Jacobs, 113–24. Lincoln, NE: University of Nebraska Press, 1978.

Gabler, Hans Walter. 'Textual Introduction'. *Monsieur Thomas* by John Fletcher. In *The Dramatic Works in the Beaumont and Fletcher Canon*, edited by Fredson Bowers, vol. IV, 417–23. Cambridge: Cambridge University Press, 1979.

Galey, Alan and Rebecca Niles. 'Moving Parts: Digital Modeling and the Infrastructures of Shakespearean Editing'. *Shakespeare Quarterly* 68, no. 1 (2017): 21–55.

Gaines, Barry and Margaret Maurer, eds. *Three Shrew Plays*. Indianapolis: Hackett Publishing Company Inc., 2010.

Gants, David. 'The 1616 Folio (F1): Textual Essay'. In *The Cambridge Edition of the Works of Ben Jonson Online*, 1–9. Cambridge: Cambridge University Press. http://universitypublishingonline.org/cambridge/benjonson/k/essays/F1_textual_essay/1/.

Garber, Marjorie. *Quotation Marks*. London: Routledge, 2003.

Garber, Marjorie. 'Third Person Interruption'. In *The Book of Interruptions*, edited by David Hillman and Adam Phillips, 17–25. New York: Peter Lang, 2007.

Garber, Marjorie. *Vested Interests: Cross-dressing & Cultural Anxiety*. Routledge, 1992.

Gesta Grayorum: or, the History of the High and mighty Prince Henry. London: W. Canning, 1688.

Gibbons, Brian. '*The Tempest* and Interruptions'. *Cahiers Elisabéthains* 45 (1994): 47–58.

Glover, Arnold, ed. *The Works of Francis Beaumont and John Fletcher: Cambridge English Classics*, vol. I. Cambridge: Cambridge University Press, 1905.

Greene, Robert. *The Historie of Orlando Furioso: One of the Twelve Pieres of France*. London: John Danter for Cuthbert Burby, 1594.

Gurr, Andrew. *The Shakespearean Stage 1574–1642*, 4th edn. Cambridge: Cambridge University Press, 2013.

Hamlet, Jess. '"Born in a Tempest When My Mother Died": Shakespeare's Motherless Daughters'. In *The Absent Mother in the Cultural Imagination: Missing, Presumed Dead*, edited by Berit Åström, 111–26. London: Palgrave Macmillan, 2017.

Hammond, Anthony. 'Encounters of the Third-Kind in Stage-Directions in Elizabethan and Jacobean Drama'. *Studies in Philology* 89, no. 1 (1992): 71–99.

Hardman, C. B. 'Theory, Form, and Meaning in Shakespeare's *The Winter's Tale*'. *The Review of English Studies* 36, no. 142 (1985): 228–35.

Haughton, Hugh. 'Xanadu and Porlock: Thoughts on Composition and Interruption'. In *The Book of Interruptions*, edited by David Hillman and Adam Phillips, 27–43. New York: Peter Lang, 2007.

Henze, Catherine. '"With the Power of my Enchanting Song": Functions of Music in the Drama of Beaumont and Fletcher'. PhD Dissertation, University of Chicago, 1995.

Henze, Catherine. 'Unraveling Beaumont from Fletcher with Music, Misogyny, and Masque'. *SEL: Studies in English Literature 1500–1900* 44, no. 2 (2004): 379–404.

Heywood, Thomas. *The Four Prentices of London*. Edited by William N. West. *The Routledge Anthology of Early Modern Drama*, edited by Jeremy Lopez, 195–266. London: Routledge, 2020.

Heywood, Thomas. *The Second Part of If You Know Not Me, You Know Nobody*. London: Nathanial Butter, 1606.

Hieatt, Charles W. 'The Function of Structure in *The Winter's Tale*'. *The Yearbook of English Studies* 8 (1978): 238–48.

Higginbotham, Jennifer. *The Girlhood of Shakespeare's Sisters: Gender, Transgression, Adolescence*. Edinburgh: Edinburgh UP, 2013.

Hillman, David and Adam Phillips, ed s. *The Book of Interruptions*. New York: Peter Lang, 2007.

Hirschfeld, Heather. 'Early Modern Collaboration and Theories of Authorship'. *PMLA* 116, no. 3 (2001): 609–22.

Holderness, Graham and Bryan Loughery, eds. *A Pleasant Conceited Historie, Called The Taming of a Shrew*. New York: Harvester Wheatsheaf, 1992.

Holland, Peter and William Sherman. Introduction. *The Alchemist* by Ben Jonson. In *The Cambridge Edition of the Works of Ben Jonson*, edited by David Bevington, Martin Butler, and Ian Donaldson, vol. 3, 543–53. Cambridge: Cambridge University Press, 2012.

Hornback, Robert. '"But I Do It More Naturally.": Falstaff's "Original Clowning Practice" vs. Theatrical Naturalism'. *The Hare* 2, no. 1, March 2014. https://thehareonline.com/article/%E2%80%9C-i-do-it-more-naturally%E2%80%9D-falstaff%E2%80%99s-%E2%80%9Coriginal-clowning-practice%E2%80%9D-vs-theatrical-naturalism.

Hosley, Richard. 'Was There a "Dramatic Epilogue" to *The Taming of the Shrew*?'. *Studies in English Literature, 1500–1900* 1, no. 2 (1961): 17–34.

Howard, Jean E. 'Crossdressing, The Theatre, and Gender Struggle in Early Modern England'. *Shakespeare Quarterly* 39, no. 4 (1988): 418–40.

Howard-Hill, T. H. *Ralph Crane and Some Shakespeare First Folio Comedies*. Charlottesville: University Press of Virginia, 1972.
Hoy, Cyrus. 'Fletcherean Romantic Comedy'. *Research Opportunities in Renaissance Drama* 27 (1984): 3–11.
Hoy, Cyrus. 'The Shares of Fletcher and His Collaborators in the Beaumont and Fletcher Canon (I-VII)'. *Studies in Bibliography* (1956–1962): 8–15.
Hutchings, Mark. 'The Interval and Indoor Playmaking'. *Studies in Theatre and Performance* 33, no. 3 (2013): 263–79.
Hyland, Peter. *Disguise on the Early Modern Stage*. Burlington, VT: Ashgate, 2011.
Ichikawa, Mariko. *Shakespearean Entrances*. London: Palgrave Macmillan, 2002.
Issacharoff, Michael. *Discourse as Performance*. Stanford: Stanford University Press, 1989.
Iser, Wolfgang. 'Interaction between Text and Reade'. In *The Reader in the Text: Essays on Audience and Interpretation*, edited by Susan Rubin Suleiman and Inge Crosman, 106–19. Princeton: Princeton University Press, 1980.
Jolles, André. *Simple Forms*. Translated by Peter J. Schwartz. New York: Verso, 2017.
Jones, Emrys. *Scenic Form in Shakespeare*. Oxford: Oxford University Press, 1971.
Jones, John and John Macklin, eds. *Exemplary Novels IV: Lady Cornelia, The Deceitful Marriage, The Dialogue of the Dogs*, by Miguel de Cervantes Saavedra. Warminster: Aris & Phillips Ltd, 1992.
Jonson, Ben. *The Alchemist*. Edited by F. H. Mares, *The Revels Plays*. London: Methuen & Co Ltd, 1967.
Jonson, Ben. *The Alchemist*. Edited by Peter Holland and William Sherman. In *The Cambridge Edition of the Works of Ben Jonson*, edited by David Bevington, Martin Butler, and Ian Donaldson, vol. 3, 541–710. Cambridge: Cambridge University Press, 2012.
Jonson, Ben. *The Alchemist*. Edited by W. Gifford. In *The Works of Ben Jonson*, vol. IV, 1–192. London: G. and W. Nicol, et al., 1816.
Jonson, Ben. *Cynthia's Revels: Quarto Version*. Edited by Eric Rasmussen and Matthew Steggle. In *The Cambridge Edition of the Works of Ben Jonson*, edited by David Bevington, Martin Butler, and Ian Donaldson, vol. 1, 429–547. Cambridge: Cambridge University Press, 2012.
Jonson, Ben. *The Devil is an Ass*. In *The Devil is an Ass and Other Plays*, edited by Margaret Jane Kidnie, 223–329. Oxford: Oxford University Press, 2000.
Jonson, Ben. *Epicene, or The Silent Woman*. Edited by David Bevington. In *The Cambridge Edition of the Works of Ben Jonson*, edited by

David Bevington, Martin Butler, and Ian Donaldson, vol. 3, 373–516. Cambridge: Cambridge University Press, 2012.
Jonson, Ben. *Every Man Out of His Humour*. Edited by Randall Martin. In *The Cambridge Edition of the Works of Ben Jonson*, edited by David Bevington, Martin Butler, and Ian Donaldson, vol. 1, 249–428. Cambridge: Cambridge University Press, 2012.
Jonson, Ben. *Volpone 1607*. Menston, England: The Scolar Press Limited, 1968.
Jonson, Ben. *Volpone, or the Fox*. London: Thomas Thorpe, 1607.
Jonson, Ben. *Volpone, or The Fox*. Edited by Richard Dutton. In *Cambridge Edition of the Works of Ben Jonson*, edited by David Bevington, Martin Butler, and Ian Donaldson, vol. 3, 1–191. Cambridge: Cambridge University Press, 2012.
Jonson, Ben. *The Workes of Beniamin Jonson*. London: Will Stansby, 1616.
Jowett, John. 'Full Pricks and Great p's: Spelling, Punctuation, Accidentals'. In *Shakespeare and Textual Studies*, edited by Margaret Jane Kidnie and Sonia Massai, 317–31. Cambridge: Cambridge University Press, 2015.
Jowett, John. 'Shakespeare and the Kingdom of Error'. In *The New Oxford Shakespeare: Critical Reference Edition*, edited by Gary Taylor, John Jowett, Terri Bourus, and Gabriel Egan, vol. 1, xlix–lxiv. Oxford: Oxford University Press, 2017.
Jump, John. 'Shakespeare's Ghosts'. *Critical Quarterly* 12 (1970): 339–51.
Karim-Cooper, Farah. 'To Glisten in a Playhouse: Cosmetic Beauty Indoors'. In *Moving Shakespeare Indoors: Performance and Repertoire in the Jacobean Playhouse*, edited by Andrew Gurr and Farah Karim-Cooper, 184–200. Cambridge: Cambridge University Press, 2014.
Kathman, David. 'How Old were Shakespeare's Boy Actors?' *Shakespeare Survey* 58, 220–46. Cambridge: Cambridge University Press, 2005.
Kean, Charles. *Shakespeare's Tragedy of Macbeth*. London: John K. Chapman & Co., 1853.
Knapp, Margaret and Michal Kobialka. 'Shakespeare and the Prince of Purpoole: The 1594 Production of The Comedy of Errors at Gray's Inn Hall'. In *The Comedy of Errors: Critical Essays*, edited by Robert S. Miola, 431–45. New York: Garland Publishing, 1997.
Koerth, Maggie. 'How Many Times Did Trump Interrupt Clinton In the First Debate? Depends On How You Count'. *FiveThirtyEight: Politics*, 9 Oct 2016, FiveThirtyEight. https://fivethirtyeight.com/features/how-many-times-did-trump-interrupt-clinton-in-the-first-debate-depends-on-how-you-count/.
Kott, Jan. *Shakespeare Our Contemporary*. Translated by Boleslaw Taborski. New York: W.W. Norton, 1974.

Levine, Caroline. *Forms: Whole, Rhythm, Hierarchy, Network*. Princeton: Princeton University Press, 2017.
Lopez, Jeremy. 'Fletcher's *Mad Lover* and Late Shakespeare'. In *Shakespeare Up Close: Reading Early Modern Texts*, edited by Russ McDonald, Nicholas D. Nace, and Travis D. Williams, 182–7. London: Arden Shakespeare, 2012.
Lopez, Jeremy. 'Hard Pastoral'. *The Hare* 4, no. 1 (2018). http://thehareonline.com/article/hard-pastoral.
Lopez, Jeremy. *Theatrical Convention and Audience Response in Early Modern Drama*. Cambridge: Cambridge University Press, 2003.
Loughnane, Rory, ed. *The Tempest* by William Shakespeare. In *The New Oxford Shakespeare: Modern Critical Edition*, edited by Gary Taylor, John Jowett, Terri Bourus, and Gabriel Egan, 3069–131. Oxford: Oxford University Press, 2016.
Lupić, Ivan and Brett Greatley-Hirsch. '"What Stuff is Here?" Edmond Malone and the 1778 Edition of Beaumont and Fletcher'. *Papers of the Bibliographical Society of America* 111, no. 3 (2017): 294–5.
McEvoy, Sean. *Ben Jonson: Renaissance Dramatist*. Edinburgh: Edinburgh University Press, 2008.
Mackay, Elizabeth Ann. 'Good Grammar, Possessive Pronouns, and Preposterous Possessions in *The Taming of the Shrew*'. *Journal of Early Modern Cultural Studies* 17, no. 1 (2017): 31–67.
McJannet, Linda. *The Voice of Elizabethan Stage Directions: The Evolution of a Theatrical Code*. Newark, DE: University of Delaware Press, 1999.
McKeithan, Daniel Morley. *The Debt to Shakespeare in the Beaumont and Fletcher Plays*. 1938. Reprint, New York: AMS Press, 1970.
McLoughlin, Kate. 'Interruption Overload: Telephones in Ford Madox Ford's "4692 Padd," *A Call* and *A Man Could Stand Up*—'. *Journal of Modern Literature* 36, no. 3 (2013): 50–68.
McLuskie, Kathleen. *Renaissance Dramatists: Feminist Readings*. New York: Harvester Wheatsheaf, 1989.
McMullan, Gordon. *The Politics of Unease in the Plays of John Fletcher*. Amherst: The University of Massachusetts Press, 1994.
McMullin, B. J. 'T. Johnson, Bookseller in the Hague'. In *An Index of Civilisation: Studies of Printing and Publishing History in Honour of Keith Maslen*, edited by R. Harvey, W. Kirsop and B. J. McMullin, 99–112. Clayton, Victoria: Centre for Bibliographical and Textual Studies, Monash University, 1993.
Magnusson, A. Lynne. 'Interruption in "The Tempest"'. *Shakespeare Quarterly* 37, no. 1 (1986): 52–65.
Maguire, Laurie. 'The Boundaries of Stage Directions'. In *Stage Directions and Shakespearean Theatre*, edited by Sarah Dustagheer and Gillian Woods, 45–67. London: Bloomsbury, 2018.

Maguire, Laurie. *The Rhetoric of the Book*. Oxford: Oxford University Press, 2020.
Mahood, M. M. *Bit Parts in Shakespeare Plays*. Cambridge: Cambridge University Press, 1992.
Mann, Jenny C. 'The "Figure of Exchange": Shakespeare's "Master Mistress," Jonson's *Epicene*, and the English Art of Rhetoric'. *Renaissance Drama* 38 (2010): 173–98.
Marcus, Leah. *Unediting the Renaissance: Shakespeare, Marlowe, Milton*. London: Routledge, 1996.
Marston, John. *The History of Antonio and Mellida, the First Part*. London: Matthew Lownes and Thomas Fisher, 1602.
Martin, Randall. '*Every Man Out of His Humour*: Stage History'. In *The Cambridge Edition of the Works of Ben Jonson Online*, 1. Cambridge: Cambridge University Press. http://universitypublishingonline.org/cambridge/benjonson/k/essays/stage_history_EMO/
Martin, Randall. Introduction. *Every Man Out of His Humour* by Ben Jonson. In *The Cambridge Edition of the Works of Ben Jonson*, edited by David Bevington, Martin Butler, and Ian Donaldson, vol. 1, 235–47. Cambridge: Cambridge University Press, 2012.
Martin, Randall. 'Stepping into Risky Business: Jonson's Canine Ventures in *Every Man Out of His Humour*'. *The Ben Jonson Journal* 12 (2005): 1–21.
Masefield, John, ed. *The Loyal Subject* by John Fletcher. In *The Works of Francis Beaumont & John Fletcher: Variorum Edition*, edited by A. H. Bullen, vol. III, 221–356. London: George Bell and Sons, 1908.
Masten, Jeffrey. *Textual Intercourse: Collaboration, authorship, and sexualities in Renaissance drama*. Cambridge: Cambridge University Press, 1997.
Maus, Katharine Eisaman. Introduction. *Epicene* by Ben Jonson. In *English Renaissance Drama: A Norton Anthology*, edited by David Bevington, 775–81. New York: W.W. Norton & Co., 2002.
Maus, Katharine Eisaman. *Inwardness and Theater in the English Renaissance*. Chicago: University of Chicago Press, 1995.
Mecklenberg, Anne-Charlotte. 'The Sensational Temporality of Spoilers in *The Woman in White* and *Avengers: Endgame*'. *Nineteenth-Century Contexts* 43, no. 1 (2021): 55–67.
Mentz, Steven R. 'Wearing Greene: Autolycus, Robert Greene, and the Structure of Romance in *The Winter's Tale*'. *Renaissance Drama* 30 (1999–2000): 73–92.
Menzer, Paul. 'Dislocating Shakespeare: Scene Locators and the Place of the Page'. *Shakespeare Bulletin* 24, no. 2 (2006): 1–19.
Middleton, Thomas and William Rowley. *The Changeling*. Edited by Douglas Bruster. In *Thomas Middleton: The Collected Works*, edited

by Gary Taylor and John Lavignino, 1632–78. Oxford: Oxford University Press, 2007.

Milhous, Judith and Robert D. Hume. *The Publication of Plays in London 1660–1800: Playwrights, Publishers, and the Market*. London: The British Library, 2015.

Miola, Robert, ed. *Macbeth* by William Shakespeare. New York: W.W. Norton, 2014.

Mirabelli, Philip. 'Silence, Wit, and Wisdom in *The Silent Woman*'. *Studies in English Literature* 29 (1989): 309–36.

Miyashita, Yayoi. 'Authorial Design in *The Winter*'s *Tale*: Evaluation of the Statue Scene from a Narrative Point of View'. *The Annual Report on Cultural Studies: Hokkaido University* 122 (2007): 59–96.

Moorman, F. W. 'Shakespeare's Ghosts'. *The Modern Language Review* 1, no. 3 (1906): 192–201.

Moshenka, Joe. 'Sir Kenelm Digby's Interruptions: Piracy and Lived Romance in the 1620s'. *Studies in Philology* 113, no. 2 (2016): 424–83.

Muir, Kenneth, ed. *Macbeth* by William Shakespeare. London: Arden Shakespeare, 2nd Series, 1951.

Munro, Lucy. '*The Alchemist*: Stage History'. *The Cambridge Edition of the Works of Ben Jonson Online*, 1–45. https://universitypublishin gonline.org/cambridge/benjonson/k/essays/stage_history_Alchemist/1/.

Munro, Lucy. *Children of the Queen's Revels: A Jacobean Theatre Repertory*. Cambridge: Cambridge University Press, 2005.

Munro, Lucy, ed. *The Tamer Tamed*, by John Fletcher. London: Methuen Drama, 2010.

Murphy, Andrew. *Shakespeare in Print: A History and Chronology of Shakespeare Publishing*. Cambridge: Cambridge University Press, 2003.

Neville, Sarah, ed. *The Comedy of Errors* by William Shakespeare. In *The New Oxford Shakespeare: Modern Critical Edition*, edited by Gary Taylor, et al., 723–71. Oxford: Oxford University Press, 2016.

Nietzsche, Friedrich. *The Birth of Tragedy and the Case of Wagner*. Translated by Walter Kaufmann. New York: Vintage Books, 1967.

Nunberg, Geoffrey. *The Linguistics of Punctuation*. Stanford, CA: Center for the Study of Language and Information, 1990.

Outterson-Murphy, Sarah. '"Remember me:" The Ghost and Its Spectators in *Hamlet*.' *Shakespeare Bulletin* 34, no. 2 (2016): 253–75.

Orgel, Stephen. *Impersonations: The Performance of Gender in Shakespeare's England*. Cambridge: Cambridge University Press, 1996.

Ostovich, Helen. Introduction. *Every Man Out of His Humour* by Ben Jonson, 1–95. Manchester: Manchester University Press, 2001.

Ostovich, Helen. '"To Behold the Scene Full": Seeing and Judging in Every Man Out'. In *Re-Presenting Ben Jonson: Text, History, Performance*, edited by Martin Butler, 76–92. New York: St. Martin's Press, 1999.

Palfrey, Simon and Tiffany Stern. *Shakespeare in Parts*. Oxford: Oxford University Press, 2007.
Palmer, Daryl W. *Writing Russia in the Age of Shakespeare*. Burlington, VT: Ashgate, 2004.
Parker, Patricia. 'Shakespeare and Rhetoric: "Dilation" and "Delation" in *Othello*'. In *Shakespeare and the Question of Theory*, edited by Patricia Parker and Geoffrey Hartman, 55–74. London: Metheun, 1985.
Parkes, M. B. *Pause and Effect: An Introduction to the History of Punctuation in the West*. Berkeley: University of California Press, 1993.
Pasupathi, Vimala C. 'The King's Privates: Sex and the soldier's place in *The Humorous Lieutenant* (ca. 1618)'. *Research Opportunities in Medieval and Renaissance Drama* 47 (2008): 25–50.
Partridge, E. B. *The Broken Compass: A Study of the Major Comedies of Ben Jonson*. New York: Columbia University Press, 1958.
Patterson, Annabel. *Censorship and Interpretation: The Conditions of Writing and Reading in Early Modern England*. Madison: University of Wisconsin Press, 1984.
Pearse, Nancy Cotton. *John Fletcher's Chastity Plays: Mirrors of Modesty*. Lewisburg, PA: Bucknell University Press, 1973.
Pechter, Edward. '"Iago's Theory of Mind": A Response to Paul Cefalu'. *Shakespeare Quarterly* 64, no. 3 (2013): 295–300.
Pérez Díez, José A. Introduction. *Love's Cure, or the Martial Maid* by John Fletcher and Philip Massinger, 1–61. Manchester: Manchester University Press, 2021.
Pérez Díez, José A. 'The Wide Gap of Sixteen Years: The Performance of Time in The Winter's Tale in Britain, 2001–2017'. *Shakespeare Bulletin* 36, no. 2 (2018): 299–317.
Pirnie, Karen. 'In Changèd Shapes: The Two Jonsons' Volpones and Textual Editing'. *Comitatus* 27, no. 1 (1996): 42–54.
Priess, Richard. *Clowning and Authorship in Early Modern Theatre*. Cambridge: Cambridge University Press, 2014.
Puttenham, George. *The Arte of English Poesie*. London: Richard Field, 1589.
Pyle, Fitzroy. *The Winter's Tale: A Commentary on the Structure*. London: Routledge & Kegan Paul, 1969.
Rackin, Phyllis. 'Androgyny, Mimesis, and the Marriage of the Boy Heroine on the English Renaissance Stage'. *PMLA* 102, no. 1 (1987): 29–41.
Radel, Nicholas F. 'Fletcherian Tragicomedy, Cross-dressing, and the Construction of Homoerotic Desire in Early Modern England'. *Renaissance Drama* 26 (1995): 53–82.

Sanchez, Reuben. '"Things like Truths, Well Feigned": Mimesis and Secrecy in Jonson's *Epicoene*'. *Comparative Drama* 40, no. 3 (2006): 313–36.

Salisbury, Laura. 'Beside Oneself: Beckett, Comic Tremor and Solicitude'. *parallax* 11, no. 4 (2005): 81–92.

Schafer, Elizabeth and Emma Cox. '*The Alchemist* on the Stage: Performance, Collaboration and Deviation'. In *The Alchemist: A Critical Reader*, edited by Erin Julian and Helen Ostovich, 43–74. London: Bloomsbury, 2013.

Schechner, Richard. 'Drama, Script, Theatre and Performance'. *The Drama Review: TDR* 17, no. 3 (1973): 5–36.

Scheible, Jeff. *Digital Shift: The Cultural Logic of Punctuation*. Minneapolis: University of Minnesota Press, 2015.

Schneider, Rebecca. *Performing Remains: Art and War in Times of Theatrical Reenactment*. London: Routledge, 2011.

Senelick, Laurence. *The Changing Room: Sex, Drag, and Theatre*. Routledge, 2000.

Shakespeare, William. *Macbeth*. In *The Plays of William Shakespeare*, edited by Thomas Keightley, vol. 6, 1–77. London: Bell and Daldy, 1864.

Shakespeare, William. *Mr. William Shakespeare, His Comedies, Histories, and Tragedies*. Edited by Edward Capell, vol. IV. London: J. and R. Tonson, 1768.

Shakespeare, William. *The New Oxford Shakespeare: Critical Reference Edition*. Edited by Gary Taylor, John Jowett, Terri Bourus, and Gabriel Egan, 1–2. Oxford: Oxford University Press, 2017.

Shakespeare, William. *The New Oxford Shakespeare: Modern Critical Edition*, edited by Gary Taylor, John Jowett, Terri Bourus, and Gabriel Egan. Oxford: Oxford University Press, 2016.

Shakespeare, William. *The Norton Facsimile: The First Folio of Shakespeare*, prepared by Charlton Hinman, 2nd ed., New York: W.W. Norton & Co., 1996.

Shakespeare, William. *The Plays and Poems of William Shakespere*. Edited by Edmund Malone, vol. III. London: J. Rivington and Sons, et al., 1790.

Shakespeare, William. *The Tragedy of Macbeth*. London [the Hague], [T. Johnson], 1711.

Shapiro, Michael. 'Audience v. Dramatist in Jonson's *Epicoene* And Other Plays of the Children's Troupes'. *English Literary Renaissance* 3 (1973): 400–17.

Shapiro, Michael. 'Framing the Taming: Metatheatrical Awareness of Female Impersonation in "The Taming of the Shrew"'. *The Yearbook of English Studies* 23 (1993): 143–66.

Shapiro, Michael. *Gender in Play on the Shakespearean Stage: Boy Heroines and Female Pages*. Ann Arbor: University of Michigan Press, 1994.
Sherman, William. '*The Alchemist*: Textual Essay'. *The Cambridge Edition of the Works of Ben Jonson Online*, 1–6. Cambridge: Cambridge University Press. https://universitypublishingonline.org/cambridge/benjonson/k/essays/Alchemist_textual_essay/1/.
Sidney, Philip. 'A Defence of Poetry (1595)'. In *English Renaissance Literary Criticism*, edited by Brian Vickers, 336–91. Oxford: Oxford University Press, 1999.
Sillars, Stuart. *Shakespeare and the Visual Imagination*. Cambridge: Cambridge University Press, 2015.
Slights, William W. E. *Ben Jonson and the Art of Secrecy*. Toronto: University of Toronto Press, 1994.
Smith, Bruce R. 'Scene'. In *Early Modern Theatricality*, edited by Henry S. Turner, 93–112. Oxford: Oxford University Press, 2013.
Snell, Megan. 'Shakespeare's Babies: "Things to Come at Large"'. In *Shakespeare's Things: Shakespearean Theatre and the Non-Human World in History, Theory, and Performance*, edited by Brett Gamboa and Lawrence Switzky, 79–90. New York: Routledge, 2019.
Sofer, Andrew. *The Stage Life of Props*. Ann Arbor: University of Michigan Press, 2003.
Sofer, Andrew. '"Take up the Bodies": Shakespeare's Body Parts, Babies, and Corpses'. *Theatre Symposium* 18 (2010): 135–48.
Sprague, Arthur Colby. *Beaumont and Fletcher on the Restoration Stage*. Cambridge, MA: Harvard University Press, 1926.
Squier, Charles L. *John Fletcher*. Boston: Twayne Publishers, 1986.
Stallybrass, Peter. 'Naming, Renaming and Unnaming in the Shakespearean Quartos and Folios'. In *The Renaissance Text: Theory, Editing, Textuality*, edited by Andrew Murphy, 108–34. Manchester: Manchester University Press, 2000.
Stanislavski, Constantin. *Building a Character*. Translated by Elizabeth Reynolds Hapgood. New York: Theatre Arts Books/Routledge, 1989.
States, Bert O. *Great Reckonings in Little Rooms: On the Phenomenology of Theater*. Berkeley: University of California Press, 1985.
Steevens, George, ed. *The Plays of William Shakespeare*. In fifteen volumes. London: T. Longman, et al., 1793. Eighteenth Century Collections Online.
Stern, Tiffany. 'Before the Beginning; After The End: When Did Plays Start and Stop?'. In *Shakespeare and Textual Studies*, edited by Margaret Jane Kidnie and Sonia Massai, 358–74. Cambridge: Cambridge University Press, 2015.
Stern, Tiffany. *Documents of Performance in Early Modern England*. Cambridge: Cambridge University Press, 2009.

Stern, Tiffany. 'Inventing Stage Directions; Demoting Dumb Shows'. In *Stage Directions and Shakespearean Theatre*, edited by Sarah Dustagheer and Gillian Woods, 19–43. London: Bloomsbury, 2018.

Sweeney, John Gordon. *Jonson and the Psychology of Public Theater: To Coin the Spirit, Spend the Soul*. Princeton: Princeton University Press, 1985.

Taylor, Gary. 'Artiginality: Authorship after Postmodernism'. In *The New Oxford Shakespeare: Authorship Companion*, edited by Gary Taylor and Gabriel Egan, 3–26. Oxford: Oxford University Press.

Taylor, Gary, ed. *The History of Cardenio adapted as 'Double Falsehood'* by John Fletcher and William Shakespeare. In *The New Oxford Shakespeare: Modern Critical Edition*, edited by Gary Taylor, et al., 3133–77. Oxford: Oxford University Press, 2016.

Taylor, Gary. 'A History of *The History of Cardenio*'. In *The Quest for Cardenio: Shakespeare, Fletcher, Cervantes, and the Lost Play*, edited by David Carnegie and Gary Taylor, 11–61. Oxford: Oxford University Press, 2012.

Taylor, Gary. *Moment by Moment by Shakespeare*. London: Macmillan, 1985.

Taylor, Gary. 'Shakespeare's Early Gothic *Hamlet*'. *Critical Survey* 31, no ½ (2019): 4–25.

Taylor, Gary. 'The Structure of Performance: Act Intervals in the London Theatres, 1576–1642'. In *Shakespeare Reshaped, 1606–1623*, edited by Gary Taylor and John Jowett, 3–50. Oxford: Clarendon Press, 1993.

Taylor, Gary. 'The Tamer Tamed: Dating Fletcher's Interactions with Shakespeare'. *Memoria di Shakespeare* no. 5 (2018): 118–48.

Taylor, Gary and Rory Loughnane. 'The Canon and Chronology of Shakespeare's Works'. In *The New Oxford Shakespeare: Authorship Companion*, edited by Gary Taylor and Gabriel Egan, 417–602. Oxford: Oxford University Press, 2017.

Tifft, Stephen. 'Catharsis Interrupta'. In *The Book of Interruptions*, edited by David Hillman and Adam Phillips, 107–26. New York: Peter Lang, 2007.

Theile, Verena and Linda Tredennick, ed s. *New Formalisms and Literary Theory*. New York: Palgrave Macmillan, 2013.

Turner, Robert Kean and Virginia Westling Haas, ed s. *A New Variorum Edition of Shakespeare's The Winter's Tale*. New York: The Modern Language Association of America, 2005.

Urkowitz, Steven. 'Interrupted Exits in *King Lear*'. *Educational Theatre Journal* 30 (1978): 203–10.

Varty, Anne. 'The Rise and Fall of the Victorian Stage Baby'. *New Theatre Quarterly* 21, no. 3 (2005): 218–29.

Vince, Ronald W. 'didascalia'. *The Oxford Encyclopedia of Theatre and Performance*. Oxford: Oxford University Press, 2005. *Oxford Reference*.

Vinh, Garziella. 'Athens in Euripides' *Suppliants*: Ritual, Politics, and Theatre'. In *Why Athens?: A Reappraisal of Tragic Politics*, edited by D. M. Carther, 325–44. Oxford: Oxford University Press, 2011.
Waith, Eugene. *The Pattern of Tragicomedy in Beaumont and Fletcher*. New Haven: Yale University Press, 1952.
Wagoner, Michael M. 'The Dramaturgical Space of Solo Scenes, or a Study of the Jailer's Daughter'. *Shakespeare Bulletin* 35, no. 1 (2017): 97–118.
Wagoner, Michael M. 'Imaginative Bodies and Bodies Imagined: Extreme Casting in Shakespeare's *The Tempest* and Fletcher and Massinger's *The Sea Voyage*'. In *The Bear Stage: Shaping Shakespeare for Performance*, edited by Sid Ray and Catherine Loomis, 103–11. Madison: Farleigh Dickinson University Press, 2016.
Wagoner, Michael M. 'Ofelia's Interruption of Ophelia in *Hamlet*'. *Critical Survey* 31, no. 1/2 (2019): 43–57.
Watson, Robert N. *Ben Jonson's Parodic Strategy: Literary Imperialism in the Comedies*. Cambridge, MA: Harvard University Press, 1987.
Watson, Robert N. 'The Fox and his Pause: Punctuating Consciousness in Jonson's *Volpone*'. In *Shakespeare Up Close: Reading Early Modern Texts*, edited by Russ McDonald, Nicholas D. Nace, and Travis D. Williams, 199–207. London: Arden Shakespeare, 2012.
Webster, John. *The Induction to the Malcontent*. In *The Malcontent* by John Marston, sig. A3r–A4v. London: William Aspley, 1604.
Wells, Stanley. 'Introduction to *The Taming of the Shrew*'. In *William Shakespeare: A Textual Companion*, by Stanley Wells and Gary Taylor with John Jowett and William Montgomery, 169–71. New York: Norton & Co., 1997.
Wells, Stanley. 'Staging Shakespeare's Ghosts'. In *The Arts of Performance in Elizabethan and Early Stuart Drama: Essays for G.K. Hunter*, edited by Murray Biggs, Philip Edwards, Inga-Stina Ewbank, and Eugene M. Waith, 50–69. Edinburgh: Edinburgh University Press, 1991.
Welsh, Robert F., ed. '*May Day* by George Chapman'. In *The Plays of George Chapman: The Comedies, A Critical Edition*, edited by Allan Holady, 311–90. Urbana: University of Illinois Press, 1970.
Werner, Hans. 'The Date of "Byrsa Basilica" and "The Swedish Intelligencer"(s) of 1635'. *Notes and Queries* 41, no. 4 (1994): 522.
Wiggins, Martin with Catherine Richardson. *British Drama 1533–1642: A Catalogue*, vols. II–VII. Oxford: Oxford University Press, 2012–2016.
Wilson, Diana de Armas. 'Of Piracy and Plackets: Cervantes' *La señora Cornelia* and Fletcher's *The Chances*'. In *Cervantes for the 21st Century/Cervantes para el siglo XXI: Studies in Honor of Edward Dudley*, edited by Francisco La Rubia Prado, 49–60. Newark, DE: Juan de la Cuesta Hispanic Monographs, 2000.

Wilson, F. P. *Introduction. Every Man Out of His Humour, 1600*, by Ben Jonson, v–viii. London: Malone Society Reprints, 1920.

Woodbridge, Linda. *Women and the English Renaissance: Literature and the Nature of Womankind, 1540–1620*. Urbana-Chicago: University of Illinois Press, 1984.

Woudhuysen, H. R. '"Dead, for My Life": Stopping, Starting and Interrupting in *Love's Labour's Lost*'. *Actes des congrès de la Société française Shakespeare* 32 (2015): paras 1–37. DOI : 10.4000/shakespeare.2892.

Woudhuysen, H. R. 'The Foundations of Shakespeare's Text'. *Proceedings of the British Academy: 2003 Lectures* 125 (2004): 69–100. Oxford: Oxford University Press.

INDEX

Act divisions   96–9
Aebischer, Pascale   224–5 n.1
The Alchemist   19, 92–9,
    216 n.25, 228 n.30,
    234 n.76
All is True (Henry VIII)   154,
    247 n.103
American Shakespeare
    Center   210–11 n.31,
    212–13 n.43
Antonio and Mellida   124, 163,
    203, 238 n.23, 257 n.3
aposiopesis   10, 11, 59, 78, 140
Aristophanes   128
arguments   204
Aristotle   5
As You Like It   145, 159, 189,
    194, 197
audience   8, 12, 13, 18, 20, 60,
    80–2, 86, 121, 123, 126–7,
    134–5, 143, 157–60, 172,
    177, 186, 239–40 n.33,
    246 n.92, 254–5 n.64,
    256 n.85
authorship   14–15, 213 n.48

baby   148, 151–2, 154–5,
    247 n.97
backchanneling   208 n.11
Barbour, Richmond   182
Barton, Anne   204, 240 n.35
bear   242 n.63
Beaumont, Francis   201, 227–8
    n.24, 239 n.32

Beaumont and Fletcher   164,
    197, 240 n.42, 241 n.53,
    254 n.58
Beaumont and Fletcher First
    Folio   26, 35–6, 109–12,
    151, 211–12 n.37,
    212 n.41, 214 n.55,
    217 n.29, 245 n.84
Beckett, Samuel   14, 246 n.90
Beggars' Bush   212 n.39
Berek, Peter   190, 256 n.93
Bevington, David   43–4, 66–8,
    175, 220 n.13
Bilmes, Jack   208 n.11
Bjork, Mary   144, 148, 244 n.78
Blackfriars Playhouse   96,
    243 n.70, 245 n.85
Blisset, William   128, 242 n.63
Booth, Stephen   202
Boro, Joyce   153, 244 n.78
Bourne, Claire M. L.   25,
    211 n.37, 214 n.4, 226 n.9,
    245 n.85, 258 n.5
Bourus, Terri   242 n.57
Bowers, Fredson   14, 115,
    235 n.82
boy actor   159, 171–2, 176, 178,
    180, 188, 252 n.36
Boyer, Arlynda   8
Bradshaw, Graham   223 n.39
breaches   63, 203, 205,
    221 n.14, 258 n.5,
    258 n.14, 258 n.5
Bringing Up Baby   224 n.49

Capell, Edward   103–4, 232 n.56
Caputi, Celia (Daileader)   202,
     244 n.78, 248 n.112,
     251 n.34
Cardenio   6–7, 233–4 n.67
Catiline His Conspiracy   62–8,
     216 n.25
Cave, Richard   226 n.12
Cefalu, Paul   78, 223 n.37
Censorship   6–7
Cervantes   20, 144–5, 148, 151,
     244 n.78
The Chances   20, 108–9, 143–
     57, 233–4 n.67, 245 n.84
The Changeling   232–3 n.65
Chapman, George   164, 172,
     178, 252 n.37
character   18, 57–60, 68, 88,
     137–8, 167, 176, 178,
     182–3, 186, 197, 199–200,
     238 n.23, 241 n.50,
     249 n.7, 256 n.86
Chess, Simone   160, 182–3,
     185, 249 n.7, 250 n.12,
     250 n.14, 257 n.101
Children of the Queen's
     Revels   164, 173
chorus, *see* Grex
Churchill, Caryl   14, 216 n.20
Clark, Sandra   187, 189,
     257 n.97
clowns   8, 162, 210 n.30
cognitive studies   76–8
Coleridge, Samuel Taylor   43,
     209 n.17
collaboration   14
Colman, George, the Elder
     114–15
comedy   62, 82–3, 132–3,
     248 n.110
The Comedy of Errors   7–8, 12,
     61–2
conjunctions   74–5, 79–80

convention   12, 13, 20–1, 158,
     160–2, 167, 170–2
Coriolanus   145
The Coxcomb   240 n.42
Craik, T. W.   45
Crane, Ralph   35–6, 217 n.28
cross-dressing
   female-to-male   159, 197,
       249–50 n.9
   male-to-female   20–1, 159–61,
       172–3, 184–6, 197, 199–
       200, 249–50 n.9, 252 n.36,
       252 n.37
cues   10, 93, 115, 154, 155, 181,
     248 n.111
Cupid's Revenge   240 n.42
Cymbeline   100, 141, 241 n.53,
     245 n.85, 246 n.93
Cynthia's Revels   21, 45, 203–6,
     238 n.22, 257 n.3

Daileader, Celia, *see* Caputi
dash   8–10, 17, 25–6, 28, 30,
     40–1, 65–70, 111, 205,
     211 n.37, 212 n.41,
     215 n.9, 218 n.35, 221 n.16
Derrida, Jacques   10, 206,
     212 n.39
Dessen, Alan   124, 198
The Devil is an Ass   165,
     227 n.16, 228 n.30,
     228 n.32
didascalia   89, 99, 225 n.1
disguise   20–1, 159–60, 162,
     170–1, 173, 252 n.36,
     254 n.58, 256 n.85
dogs   133, 155, 248 n.110
Donaldson, Ian   214 n.54
Doran, Madeline   77, 223 n.40
Double Falsehood   7, 233–4 n.67
dramatic irony   62, 78–9, 81–2,
     100, 107, 141, 166, 173,
     179, 254 n.57

Dramatis Personae   176, 196
dramaturgy   12, 20, 121–3,
    127, 129, 135–6, 143–6,
    227 n.14, 228–9 n.32,
    232 n.59, 243 n.75
Drummond, William   174,
    253 n.53
Dryden, John   33, 214 n.56
Dutton, Richard   65, 173, 184,
    204

editors   9, 19–20, 25, 90, 92,
    101, 103–4, 108, 114–18,
    196, 252 n.35
Elizabeth I   6, 123, 154
English Grammar (Ben
    Jonson)   175
entrances   90–1, 93–5, 225 n.5,
    225–6 n.8
Epicene   21, 117, 133, 161,
    172–84, 190, 192, 199,
    254–5 n.64
Evans, Bertrand   140–1, 242 n.65
*Every Man In His
    Humour*   216 n.25
*Every Man Out of His
    Humour*   6, 20, 123–35,
    137, 155, 157, 158, 203
Ewbank, Inga-Stina   137
exposition   145–6, 150, 166,
    246 n.87

The Faithful Shepherdess   13,
    209 n.16, 233 n.66,
    240 n.36, 240 n.42, 247 n.96
Faucit, Helena   142
feminism, proto   114, 156,
    248 n.112
Ferguson, George   115
Field, Nathan   14, 164, 165,
    247 n.103
Fifty Comedies and Tragedies
    (Beaumont and Fletcher
    Second Folio)   112–14

Findlay, Allison   135
Finkelpearl, Philip   185, 190
First Folio (Shakespeare)   28–9,
    42–3, 100–3, 108, 171,
    217 n.28, 218 n.37,
    218 n.39, 220 n.11, 223 n.38,
    223 n.39, 224 n.42, 224 n.45,
    224 n.50, 242 n.57, 243 n.71,
    250 n.20, 252 n.35
Fletcher, John   5, 14, 16, 26,
    122, 135–6, 157, 165, 185,
    198, 200–2, 206, 209 n.16,
    212 n.41, 240 n.36
formalism   3, 82
Forman, Simon   106, 230 n.41
Four Plays in One   247 n.103
The Four Prentices of London
    125, 129, 257 n.3

Galey, Alan   104
Garber, Marjorie   21
genre   13, 56, 62, 132–3,
    246 n.89
George a Greene   162, 163, 169,
    251 n.32
ghosts   9, 19, 99–108,
    229 n.38, 230 n.43,
    231 n.48, 232 n.59
Gibbons, Brian   26
Greene, Robert   136–9, 163
Grex   20, 124, 127–8, 130,
    133–4, 239 n.30, 239 n.32
Gurr, Andrew   237 n.17

Hamlet   8, 9, 28–33, 58–9, 73,
    89, 99–100, 152, 212–13
    n.43, 216 n.17, 222 n.30,
    223 n.34, 229–30 n.40
Hamlet, Jess   243 n.74
1 Henry VI   245 n.85
3 Henry VI   154, 247 n.103
Henze, Catherine   233 n.66
Heywood, Thomas   124, 129,
    165, 198, 257 n.3

Hieatt, Charles 141
Hirsh, James 153
The History of Cardenio
   6–7
Holland, Peter 92, 94, 97
homosexuality 49, 170, 182,
   189, 190, 196–7, 199,
   219 n.51
Howard, Jean 182
Hoy, Cyrus 15, 143,
   213 n.52, 217 n.29,
   219 n.49, 244 n.76
The Humorous Lieutenant 18,
   27, 35–6, 48–56, 215–16
   n.16, 244 n.76
Hutchings, Mark 228 n.30
Hyland, Peter 256 n.85

Ichikawa, Mariko 225–6 n.8
*If You Know Not Me, You Know
   Nobody, Part Two* 198
inductions 124–6, 203–4,
   238 n.22
interiority 57–9, 61–2, 86–7
interpellation 26–7
interruptions
   action 11–12, 18–19
   creational 6–7
   dialogue 10, 17–18, 25–8,
      139–40, 219–20 n.1
   external 6–8
   form of 3–5, 57
   internal 8–13, 17
   macrointerruption 12–13,
      20–1, 121–2, 158–9, 172,
      184, 186, 204–6
   microinterruption 9–12,
      25–8, 121, 179–81, 192,
      204–6
   self-interruption 11, 18,
      57–60, 139–40, 195, 205,
      208 n.7, 219–20 n.1
Iser, Wolfgang 58
The Island Princess 202

Johnson, Thomas 231 n.50
Jonson, Ben 15–16, 26, 164,
   165, 200, 203–6, 252 n.37,
   253 n.53
Jowett, John 31, 216 n.18,
   225 n.6
Julius Caesar 99–100

Keightley, Thomas 104
Kidnie, M. J. 228–9 n.32
A King and No King 240 n.42,
   241 n.53
King Lear 1, 4–5, 241 n.53
The Knight of Malta 247 n.103
Knight of the Burning Pestle
   201, 227–8 n.24, 239 n.32
Kott, Jan 236 n.3

Lambarde Manuscript 109–11
Levine, Caroline 3
Lopez, Jeremy 158, 166
Loughnane, Rory 42, 44,
   218 n.35, 218 n.47
Love's Cure 165, 185
Love's Labours Lost 1–2, 4–5,
   243 n.75
The Loyal Subject 21, 161, 165,
   185–200, 244 n.76

Macbeth 19, 100–8, 245 n.85
McDonald, Russ 128
McKeithan, Daniel 190, 191
McLuskie, Kathleen 14
McMullan, Gordon 189–90,
   202, 213 n.50
The Mad Lover 71–6, 89–90,
   202, 221–2 n.24, 244 n.76,
   246 n.86
A Mad World, My Masters
   250 n.14
The Magnetic Lady 154,
   228 n.30, 237 n.12,
   245 n.85
Magnusson, Lynne 41

Maguire, Laurie 220 n.5
The Maid's Tragedy 197,
  240 n.42, 241 n.53
The Malcontent 238 n.23
Malone, Edmund 104
Marcus, Leah 90, 107
Mares, F. H. 94, 228 n.28
Marlowe, Christopher 201
marriage 192–4
Marston, John 124, 163, 164,
  203, 238 n.23, 257 n.3
Martin, Randall 123, 238 n.24
Masefield, John 196
Massinger, Philip 14, 165, 185,
  212 n.39
Maus, Katherine 57, 173
May Day 164, 172, 178
The Merry Wives of Windsor
  82–7, 161, 162, 164,
  250 n.12
Middleton, Thomas 108, 136,
  164, 201, 232–3 n.65,
  250 n.14
misogyny 83, 116, 117, 176,
  233 n.66, 250 n.12
Miyashita, Yayoi 140, 241 n.46
Morgan, Oliver 209 n.1
Much Ado About Nothing 145,
  156
Muir, Kenneth 105–7
Munro, Lucy 115, 116,
  173
music 108, 233 n.66

names 146–8, 167, 169–70,
  219 n.48, 246 n.92,
  247 n.96, 251 n.26
Nashe, Thomas 245 n.85
neoformalism 3, 208 n.6
Neptune's Triumph 175
Neville, Sarah 7
The New Inn 92, 165, 204,
  228 n.30, 254 n.58

The New Oxford Shakespeare
  6–7, 31, 42, 44–5,
  240 n.42, 242 n.57,
  243 n.71, 250 n.13, 251 n.24
The Night Walker 245 n.84
Niles, Rebecca 104

Orgel, Stephen 159
Orlando Furioso 162, 163
Ostovich, Helen 123, 226 n.13,
  239 n.30
Othello 76–82

Palmer, Daryl 186
Pandosto 136–8, 242 n.63
parenthesis 11, 63, 70, 80,
  137–8, 221 n.21,
  224 n.45
Parks, Suzan-Lori 14, 201
Pechter, Edward 76
Percy, William 238 n.21
Pericles 141, 154, 247 n.103
Philaster 197, 240 n.42,
  241 n.53, 254 n.58
Pinter, Harold 14, 74, 201
Pirnie, Karen 65
Plautus 124, 128, 132
Poetaster 238 n.22, 253 n.53
Preiss, Richard 8
prologue 124–5, 128–9, 177–8,
  203–4, 238 n.22, 254–5
  n.64
punctuation 10, 17, 25, 28–33,
  63–8, 211 n.37, 216 n.17,
  220 n.8
Puttenham, George 5, 11, 60–1,
  208–9 n.15
Pyle, Fitzroy 243 n.68

Rackin, Phyllis 182, 184
Radel, Nicholas 185–6, 189
readers 8, 19, 91, 94, 98, 103–4,
  111, 137–8, 228–9 n.32

Richard III 99
Richardson, Catherine 15
Romeo and Juliet 1, 4–5, 138, 204
Rowe, Nicholas 29–30, 211 n.34

Salisbury, Laura 82
Sanchez, Reuben 175, 254 n.57
scene 19, 91–9, 145, 226 n.9
 French scene 92, 95, 216–17 n.26, 226 n.11, 227 n.15, 239 n.30, 245 n.85
 solo scene 152–5, 245 n.84
Schechner, Richard 210 n.9
The Scornful Lady 164, 240 n.42
Sejanus 92
Shakespeare, William 5, 12–13, 15, 163, 164, 190–1, 200, 206, 209 n.16, 243 n.75, 245 n.85
Shapiro, Michael 160, 166, 254–5 n.64
Sherman, Peter 92, 94, 97
Sherman, William 99
Sidney, Philip 5, 209 n.15
Slights, William 173, 175
Smith, Bruce R. 91–2
Snell, Megan 247 n.97
Sofer, Andrew 154
song 19, 108–17, 233 n.66
spoilers 122, 236 n.2
stage directions 9, 19, 63–4, 89, 93, 102, 124–5, 151, 198, 204–5, 225 n.3
Stallybrass, Peter 170, 251 n.26
The Staple of News 228 n.30, 237 n.12
States, Bert 158
Stationer's Register 174
Steevens, George 103, 107, 231 n.48

Stern, Tiffany 111, 173–4, 204, 218 n.45, 224 n.1, 234 n.76, 237 n.17
Sweeney, John 172–3, 204

Tamburlaine 201
The Tamer Tamed, see The Woman's Prize
The Taming of a Shrew 163, 167, 169–71, 202, 251 n.30, 252 n.36
The Taming of the Shrew 20–1, 160–73, 178, 185, 199, 250 n.13
Taylor, Gary 7, 220 n.6, 233–4 n.67
The Tempest 17, 26, 27, 35, 41–8, 246 n.87
Terry, Ellen 248 n.110
Theory of Mind 78, 81
Thomsen, Leslie 124, 198
time 106, 107, 121, 128–9, 140–2, 161, 209 n.16, 228 n.28
titles 145, 173–6, 246 n.89, 253 n.50, 253 n.53
Titus Andronicus 154, 247 n.103, 248 n.108
tragicomedy 132–3, 195, 209 n.16, 240 n.36
Twelfth Night 189–91, 194, 197, 198, 202, 246 n.89
The Two Gentlemen of Verona 155, 248 n.110
The Two Noble Kinsmen 153, 247 n.101

Valentinian 233 n.66
Varty, Anne 248 n.110
Vaughn, Virginia Mason and Alden T. 44
Vinh, Grazielle 207 n.2
Vogel, Paula 216 n.20

Volpone 17, 27, 33–41, 65–71, 253 n.53, 255 n.66

Waith, Eugene 56, 202–3
The Wars of Cyrus 162, 163, 169, 250 n.16, 251 n.32
Watson, Robert N. 240 n.35
Webster, John 164, 238 n.23
Whitman, Walt 74
The Widow 201
Wiggins, Martin 15, 174–5, 240 n.42, 250 n.13, 257 n.3
Williams, George Walton 151, 245 n.84, 248 n.111
Wilson, Diana de Armas 244 n.78

The Winter's Tale 20, 121, 135–43, 146, 154, 240 n.42, 243 n.75, 246 n.93
The Woman Hater 240 n.42
The Woman's Prize, or the Tamer Tamed 19, 109–17, 202, 233–4 n.67, 234 n.70, 235 n.85, 248 n.112
Women Pleas'd 108, 233–4 n.67, 248 n.112
Woodbridge, Linda 249–50 n.9
The Works of Benjamin Jonson (1616 Folio) 176, 216 n.25, 226 n.12, 237 n.15, 238 n.22, 238 n.24